Essentials of
Medical Astroogy

Dr. K S Charak
M.S. (SURGERY)
F.R.C.S. (U.K.)

**UMA
Publications**

Essentials of
Medical Astrology

First Edition : June 1994
Second Edition : October 1996
Third Edition : August 1999
Reprinted : June 2002
Fourth Edition : February 2005
Reprinted : June 2007
Reprinted : February 2010
Reprinted : August 2012
Reprinted : August 2015
Reprinted : August 2017

ISBN 81-901008-3-1

Price :
Rs. 250/- US$ 21 £ 15

Cover Design:
Rajeev Jhanji

Published by:
UMA Publications
72 Gagan Vihar, Delhi - 110 051, India
Phone: 91-11-22632831

Design & Printed by:
PRINTFORCE
(M) 9958392130 • rawatys2011@gmail.com

PREFACE TO THE FOURTH EDITION

Medical astrology is a highly specialised branch of Vedic astrology. Over the past few years, this subject has undergone great evolution, and this process continues. No longer are the age- old inhibitions of the medical fraternity in evidence, and more and more medical personnel are taking up the study of this exalted discipline. Astrologers in general too are concentrating more on this branch of astrology which, if sufficiently developed, can immensely help the suffering patient as well as his treating physician.

The revision and upgradation of the fourth edition of the *Essentials of Medical Astrology* is a result of our continued endeavour to make medical astrology eminently useful for the suffering humanity. New material has been added and some of the older concepts modified in view of our continuous research in this area. The highly scientific approach to the study of this subject has been maintained throughout the book. We hope this new and upgraded edition of the *Essentials of Medical Astrology* better serves the medical as well as the astrological fraternity.

February 10, 2005 — Dr. K S Charak

72 Gagan Vihar,
Delhi - 110051 (India)
Ph: 91-11-22045955
E-mail: kscharak@gmail.com

PREFACE TO THE FIRST EDITION

I have been constantly persuaded, nay pressurised, over the past few years by Mr. K.N. Rao to produce a standard book on medical astrology. The need for this has arisen from the fact that we must have a suitable textbook for teaching our students at the Bharatiya Vidya Bhawan, New Delhi. The existing books on medical astrology fell far short of our requirements. Most of these books have been written by non-medical people who know little about disease and its genesis. Then they mention only some very generalised combinations on bare horoscopes, without even referring to the divisional charts or vargas, and this lapse makes such principles inapplicable to actual horoscopes. Furthermore, there is hardly any hint about the timing of an illness. The mere presence in a horoscope of a combination for an ailment carries little meaning unless the relevant dasha or operational period comes into play. There is little fun looking, for example, for a combination for death in a horoscope, which in any case is present. What is important is the actual time when the event is going to take place. So, the promise of an event is one aspect; its timing is another, and more important also.

There can thus be no book worth any use if it does not advocate the use of the vargas as well as the dashas.

Mr. Rao has been particular in stressing that a book on medical astrology must be written by a qualified doctor. His own forays into medical astrology involve the timing of the period of illness, and the severity or outcome of it. But he carefully stops short of the area of astro-medical diagnosis which he labels as his area of ignorance. He feels that the diagnosis is best left to the medical doctor. His suggestion in fact has been that I should produce a *triology* on medical astrology, viz.,

(a) Elements of medical astrology with major stress on the timing of an illness as presented in this book.

(b) The actual disease and its diagnosis, which has been hinted at in the present book but which requires a lot of further research since it involves a very vast and intricate area.

(c) The final outcome strictly according to the principles of astrology. This area has been hinted at in the present work, but greater details demand methods of calculation of longevity which has not been the aim of this book.

It is the first of these three areas which this book deals with extensively. The other areas have been adequately hinted at. It is hoped that at a subsequent time, not too far removed in future, the other two areas will also be suitably dealt with. In this connection, I must put on record my deep indebtedness to some of my American friends, especially Rakesh Sharma, Ingrid Naiman, James Kelleher, Deborah Ress and others who contributed valuable astro-medical data to me for my research work. Their data, particularly on cancer, AIDS, homosexuals, etc., will be utilised in covering further areas of research in medical astrology. I find it pertinent to point out here that in order to conduct astrological researches, an Indo-US sharing of astro-medical data is of vital importance. However, whereas the Indian data is rich as far as the chronology of events is concerned, it is sometimes unreliable because of incorrect birth time recording. On the other hand, while the American horoscopes available to us appear to be fairly correct and accurate, the chronological aspect is sadly lacking there. We will have to be particularly careful in collecting highly accurate data both in respect of birth time as well as the chronology of events.

The best and the most popular method of timing the events consists of using the Vimshottari dasha on the birth chart as well as the divisional charts. In some areas of India, particularly the northern states, some astrologers use another dasha system known as the Yogini dasha; they do not employ the Vimshottari dasha at all and still make wonderful predictions. In fact, when I started getting acquainted with astrology during my early years, the first dasha that I was introduced to was the Yogini dasha. My father, not an astrologer, had told me then that the Yogini dasha was said to be applicable to the state of Jammu and Kashmir, as also to some other hilly regions. Now I understand that this dasha can be applied anywhere though it was primarily used in the regions mentioned above. The Yogini dasha has been applied in this book along with the Vimshottari dasha in order, primarily, to confirm the indications available from the Vimshottari dasha and, secondarily, to stress the fact that the Yogini is capable of independent application.

Vedic astrology has an extremely rich methodology which can be employed to decipher the occurrence of events, as well as their timing, very accurately. Besides the two dashas, the Vimshottari and the Yogini, employed in this book, there are a host of other dashas in the Parashari system. Similarly, there are as many as forty-four different dashas in the Jaimini system which is relatively less well known. A composite approach involving the application of two or more dashas to the rashi and the divisional charts is essential in order to obtain foolproof predictions.

My book on the Vedic techniques of annual horoscopy, *A Textbook of Varshaphala*, was prompted by the need to produce a standard book on the subject for the students whom I was teaching annual horoscopy. Varshaphala has been the most effective tool in the hands of astrologers in northern India to forewarn people about impending ill health. If the principles of Varshaphala are employed along with the methods given in this book on an accurate horoscope, it leads to virtually infallible results. Several methods of determining illness and relief have been mentioned in my book on Varshaphala. Those methods, while recommended for use, are not included here lest that should increase the bulk of this book.

The present work, *Essentials of Medical Astrology*, contains detailed account of finding out good and adverse planets and planetary combinations indicative of health and disease. General rules for the houses, the signs and the planets indicating the nature of disease and the body part affected have been discussed thoroughly. Combinations for ill health to the newborn, and varying afflictions and their cancellation, are described. A very detailed and illustrated chapter on the onset and outcome of disease has been included. Towards the end of the book, planetary combinations for several diseases and the astrological principles underlying them, have been described. Our own researches have been included in these chapters.

The book also opens up several areas for research. We have mentioned combinations which indicate surgical or medical treatment, as also the removal or non-removal of a body part or organ. Combinations as well as underlying principles for several diseases are not yet known and have to be found out. Mr. K.N. Rao has suggested that we should bring out some additional points including some Ayurvedic principles for a special American edition of this book. In the meantime, what has been produced is a textbook of medical astrology. I assure the reader that each new and revised edition of this book will contain our newer and newer researches in this field. It may become possible some day to unify through astrology the apparently varied concepts of allopathy, homeopathy and Ayurveda.

I fervently hope that this book fulfils the longstanding need of astrologers desirous of getting initiated into medical astrology, while also serving as a stepping-stone for further astro-medical research.

May 29, 1994 Dr. K S CHARAK
72 Gagan Vihar
Delhi - 110 051 (India)

CONTENTS

CHAPTER ONE

INTRODUCTION TO MEDICAL ASTROLOGY

पश्येम शरदश्शतं जीवेम शरदश्शतं
श्रृणुयाम शरदश्शतम्।
प्रब्रवाम शरदश्शतमदीनाः स्याम
शरदश्शतम्।।

May I see for a hundred years, live for a hundred years, hear for a hundred years.
May I speak for a hundred years, live in comfort and freedom for a hundred years.

—YAJURVEDA 26/24

Since times immemorial, both medicine and astrology have constituted a way of life in India. The ancient Indian scriptures which have come down to us through the ages contain profuse references to the system of medicine of those days, known as the Ayurveda, as well as to that highly evolved system of astrology known as the Vedic Astrology. In addition, the ancient Indians, true to their wont, transmitted a lot of their knowledge by word of mouth, down the generations, so that highly advanced knowledge was preserved in the families. It is not for nothing that our classical system of learning lays greater stress on personal instruction than on book learning. This holds true for, not only medicine and astrology but, all branches and disciplines of learning.

A Way of Life

Both astrology and medicine were developed as a part of religion in ancient India. Principles of hygiene and prevention of diseases were as much a part of the day-to-day rituals as were those of astrology applicable to a person's mundane affairs.

Physical cleanliness was necessary before performing any religious rituals, including the daily prayers. The 'Shaucham' of the *Gita* stressed on both the physical and the mental cleansing as a part of the day-to-day spiritual discipline. Astrological guidance was sought for, virtually, all day-to-day work, including the taking of medicines for the remedies of ailments. Medicines were administered only at astrologically suitable times of the day. Even the medicinal herbs were collected and treated at appropriate times only. Following the medical and astrological principles, separately and together, was thus a way of life which even a layman could afford to follow. The intellectual accepted these principles through logic, the layman through faith and devotion. The result was the same: a physically and mentally healthy society!

Both are Ancient

Astrology and medicine are both ancient forms of knowledge in India. Besides the several astrological texts available today, we have in the Puranas the stories of Lord Shiva and his divine consort Parvati discussing astrology or making astrological references.

Stories about Ayurveda are legion too. Very early accounts take us to Lord Shiva transplanting the head of a baby elephant on his own child who came to be known as Lord Ganesha. Lord Shiva also transplanted the head of a goat on the beheaded Daksha Prajapati, the father of his wife who committed suicide in a fit of anger against her father. The Ashwini Kumaras are well-known as the physicians of the gods.

The fascinating story of the churning of the ocean by the gods and the demons brought forth the divine physician Dhanwantari from whom the knowledge of healing spread. Principles of medicine were well-known to the Pandavas, especially to Nakula and Sahadeva, the youngest twins who were the offsprings of the Ashwini Kumaras. They knew the principles of veterinary medicine too, which they employed to full advantage in the kingdom of king Virata where they spent a year incognito. Charaka and Sushruta, respectively the fathers of ancient Indian medicine and surgery, came later. Even today their principles remain useful. The method of reconstruction of the nose as employed by the plastic surgeons of today all over the world is the same as the one employed by Sushruta thousands of years ago, and is known as the Indian method of Rhinoplasty.

Astrology and Medicine are Inseparable

Texts on ancient Indian medicine contain certain references to planetary combinations causing specific diseases. True, these combinations are too general to be of any great help in medical diagnosis, but they reveal certain principles which can be of use.

Similarly, astrological texts are replete with planetary combinations indicating specific ailments. These combinations are also fairly generalised and not easily applicable to individual charts. They can be of some utility only if the essence of their underlying principles is understood. Vedic astrology is unique in another respect. It advocates remedial measures in the form of propitiation of planets in the event of an untoward planetary combination.

There are three main systems of medicine today. The most prevalent is the Allopathy, which means treating an illness by producing results opposite to those produced by disease. It is based on sound scientific principles and has the greatest acceptance. Its practitioners have an open mind to all new ideas, as is expected of scientists, and that is the reason for the progress of this system. Homeopathy is the other system which is based on the principle of treating an illness by a medicine which would normally produce the same results as the disease itself. Surgery, of course, is not a constituent of Homeopathy. The ancient Indian system of medicine is known as Ayurveda, literally, 'the science of life'. While many consider it as a separate system, it actually encompasses both Allopathy and Homeopathy.

After having written the Mahabharata, the great Indian epic, sage Vyasa still did not enjoy divine bliss. It was in that disturbed state of his that sage Narada came to him and sought the reason for his disappointment. When Vyasa told Narada about his dismay, the latter gave him some piece of advice. Vyasa had no doubt written a divine work, monumental and intellectually unparalleled, but it did not reflect sufficient devotion to Lord Krishna. "Any knowledge," said Narada, "which could normally lead to 'moksha', if bereft of devotion to the Lord, tends to lose its grace. Write, therefore, in praise of the Lord."

He further continued,

आयमो यश्च भूतानां जायते येन सुव्रत।
तदेव ह्यामयं द्रव्यं न पुनाति चिकित्सितम्।।

meaning thereby:

"When a substance in its gross form produces an ailment, doesn't its refined form produce relief of the same ailment?"

— SHRIMAD BHAGAVATA MAHAPURANA, CANTO I, CH V, S 33.

Vyasa understood, and produced the *Bhagavata Purana*.

Narada was thus referring to a principle of Ayurveda, which today is labelled as Homeopathy. Ayurveda in its original form also advocates surgery as a means of cure. It may be pointed out that all systems of healing can be labelled as Ayurveda, the science of life. Astrology, Allopathy, Homeopathy, and the present version of Ayurveda have all their role as well as their limitations. The wisest recourse lies in realising the limitations of each and using them not as antagonistic but as complementary to each other. Only thus can they be used to benefit humankind!

An Astro-Medical Narration

A Classical Example from Vamana Purana.

A typical example of how in the classical Indian literature great truths are revealed in the form of stories is being given. The astromedical implications of this narration are obvious. Very often the principles are revealed in a more subtle form and need a lot of meditative thinking, but the results are always profound.

The description that follows is from the Vamana Purana. Lord Shiva, the Destroyer, danced the dance of death in order to destroy the yajna (sacrificial ritual, which took an animated form in the wake of lord Shiva's attack and fled!) of Daksha Prajapati (the father of lord Shiva's divine consort, who had managed to earn the wrath of the said Lord!). In that death-inflicting form of His, the Lord occupied the whole of the zodiac. Various divisions of the zodiac were represented in various parts of His body. The narration goes thus:

Sage Pulastya said (to sage Narada), "Best of sages, I shall now describe to you that form of the formidable lord Shiva, the destroyer of Tripura, who for the good of the world spread over the whole of the universe.

"The whole of the constellations Ashvini and Bharani, and the first quarter of Krittika, constituting the sign Mesha (Aries) owned by Mars, represent the head of the redoubtable Mahadeva (Lord Shiva).

"O Brahmin! Three quarters of Krittika, complete Rohini and the first two parts of Mrigashira, constituting Vrisha (Taurus) owned by Venus, are His mouth.

"The remaining two quarters of Mrigashira, complete Ardra and three quarters of Punarvasu, constituting Mithuna (Gemini), the zone of Mercury, represent the two upper limbs of the all-encompassing Lord.

"One quarter of Punarvasu, and complete Pushya and Ashlesha, the Moon's region called Karka (Cancer), represent the two sides of Lord Shankara (another name for lord Shiva), the destroyer of the yajna.

"Brahmin! The Sun's region of Simha (Leo), constituted by the whole of Magha and Poorva Phalguni, and a quarter of Uttara Phalguni, is considered the heart of lord Shankara.

"Mercury's second region called Kanya (Virgo), constituted by three quarters of Uttara Phalguni, complete Hasta and two quarters of Chitra, represents the digestive system (stomach and intestines) of Shankara.

"The remaining two parts of Chitra, complete Swati and three quarters of Vishakha, constituting the second region of Venus called Tula (Libra), represent the umbilical region of Mahadeva (Shiva).

"Vrishchika (Scorpio), the second region of Mars, constituted by a quarter of Vishakha and complete Anuradha and Jyeshtha, represent His generative organ.

"The whole of Moola as well as Poorva Ashadha and a quarter of Uttara Ashadha, forming Jupiter's region of Dhanu (Sagittarius), are the two thighs of the Maheshwara (Shiva).

"O Sage! Saturn's region of Makara (Capricorn) formed by the remaining three quarters of Uttara Ashadha, complete

Signs of the zodiac and parts of the body

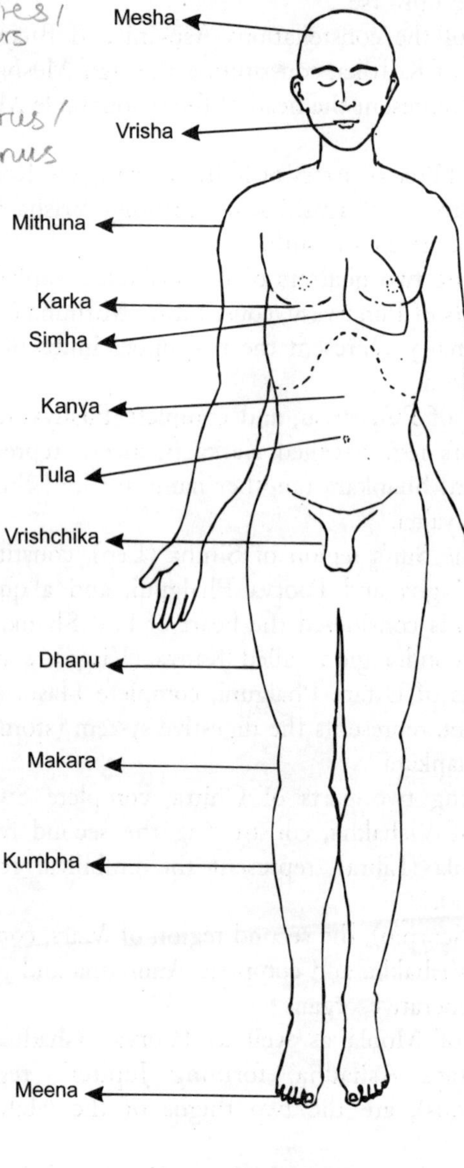

Figure I-1

Shravana, and the first two quarters of Dhanishtha, represent his two knees.

"The second half of Dhanishtha, complete Shatabhisha and three quarters of Poorva Bhadrapada constitute Kumbha (Aquarius), the second house of Saturn, which represents His two legs.

"Meena (Pisces), the second house of Jupiter, consisting of a quarter of Poorva Bhadrapada, and complete Uttara Bhadrapada and Revati, represents His two feet."

The various parts of the body represented by the various zodiacal signs are depicted in fig. I-1.

Having heard the above narration from sage Pulastya, the sage Narada further requests him to reveal the nature and characteristics of these signs.

Pulastya readily agrees, saying, "Sage Narada! Now I narrate to you how these various signs look like, as also the areas they reside in or haunt."

"The sign Mesha resembles a ram. It circulates among the goats, the sheep and the regions holding wealth and precious stones. It wanders on grassy lands, and around lakes surrounded by vegetation.

"The sign Vrisha resembles a bull. Cowhouses and farmlands are its places of residence.

"A man and a woman bearing a trumpet and a harp represent the sign Mithuna whose places of residence are the couch and the lounge. It circulates amongst the singers, the dancers and the sculptors. This dual sign haunts the sports lovers and the pleasure houses.

"Karkata has the appearance of a crab and lives in water. Its places of residence include water-filled garden beds, river banks and un-inhabited lands.

"Simha (resembling a lion) resides in the mountains, forests, caves, inaccessible places, deep ditches and the living places of hunters.

"Kanya (consists of a woman) standing in a boat and holding corn and a lamp in her hand, inhabits women's pleasure rooms.

"Narada! Tula is represented by a man holding a balance in his hand, and its residences include lanes, bazaars, towns, routes and buildings.

"Vrishchika resembles the scorpion in appearance. It moves in crevices and pits. Its areas of residence include poisons, animal excreta, stones and insects.

"Of Dhanu, the legs are like those of a horse. It is radiant and holds a bow and arrow. Well versed in horse riding, in handling of arms and in doing daring and brave deeds, it resides in elephants, chariots, etc.

"O Brahmin! The mouth of Makara is like that of a deer, shoulders like those of a bull and eyes like those of an elephant. It moves in the rivers and resides in the ocean.

"Kumbha resembles a man wearing wet clothes and holding on his shoulders an empty pitcher. It moves in gambling houses and resides in drinking dens.

"The sign Meena consists of two fishes lying side by side, the head of one being beside the tail of the other. It circulates in the places of pilgrimage and in the oceans. It haunts pious places, temples of gods and houses of Brahmins."

Relevance of Medical Astrology Today

The term Medical Astrology at once brings to one's mind two points:

1. The occurrence of "DISEASE" or the disturbance of one's "EASE".
2. The role of Astrology as applied to disease.

According to the *Charaka Samhita,* that classic of ancient Indian system of medicine, the mind and the body are the abodes of disease. Health as defined by the World Health Organisation is a state of complete physical, mental and social well-being and not merely an absence of illness; not being satisfied with the vagueness of the term 'social well-being', someone has suggested that spiritual well-being (whatever that means!) should also be included in the definition of health. For our purpose the definition of the *Charaka Samhita* should suffice. As a consequence, our consideration of disease would include physical and mental disease only. The physical disease will also include the accidents which mean an application of sudden, excessive, generally external, force causing a disruption of some body mechanism.

Ancient Literature on Medical Astrology

There is a lot of ancient literature available, separately, on astrology as also on medicine. On medical astrology, however, the literature is scanty. Whatever references to medical astrology we get in our classical works are often too generalised and not applicable to individual horoscopes. The present day works on medical astrology too are deficient in many ways. The main reason for this deficiency is that, generally, astrologers are not trained in medicine and the best of them may not have enough understanding of the functioning of the human body. Another problem is that medical men are not astrologers. Until recently, men from the medical fraternity had not shown much inclination toward astrology, though the times are fast changing. In order that there is sound research in medical astrology and that astrology finds any utility in the present day medical sciences, it is essential that medial men of today take up the study of astrology seriously. Medical astrology cannot be left in the hands of non-medical people.

There is another problem for the present day medical man. The understanding of disease according to the modern allopathic system is very different from what it is according to the classical Indian system known as the Ayurveda. The classical texts only use the standard Ayurvedic terminology. Those terms are difficult to translate into the modern allopathic system. It is thus going to be no easy job doing appropriate research in medical astrology in order to render astrology of any utility to modern medicine. No fantastic claims can be made about astro-medical diagnosis in our present state of knowledge of medical astrology. Any tall claims made by non-medical astrologers in this connection are liable to subject the divine science of astrology to ridicule.

Important Aspects of Disease

A medical astrologer may consider the following factors while studying a chart with respect to disease:

1. Timing of disease
2. Diagnosis
3. Severity
4. Treatment

The above factors are equally important to the medical astrologer as well as to the consultor or the patient. Each may be briefly discussed, and the role of the astrologer versus that of the medical man outlined as follows:

1. *Timing (Onset) of disease*: This is the strong area of an astrologer. A sound astrologer, on examining a horoscope, should be able to indicate the time when a person is liable to fall ill. This may help in taking some preventive steps, especially the astrological remedial measures, to forestall the malady.

For a medical man, it is not possible to predict a future illness. There are certain diseases which run in families and may be expected to occur in some of the blood relations of the native. Which particular relative of the native will suffer, and when, cannot be predicted with any degree of accuracy on the basis of the existing medical knowledge.

2. *Diagnosis (or the nature) of disease* : This is a weak area for the astrologer. To be sound in this will require a lot of research by medical men proficient in astrology.

Diagnosis of a disease is the strongest area of the medical man, with all the sophisticated investigations at his disposal to help him in this regard.

3. *Severity (and Outcome) of disease*: A patient or a consultor is naturally concerned about the severity of an ailment and its outcome. Generally, a medical practitioner of today, with his sound knowledge, will be able to accurately decipher the possible course that an ailment may take in a given patient. An astute astrologer, too, should be able to indicate the severity and outcome of an illness with a fair amount of accuracy, sometimes perhaps better than the medical practitioner.

4. *Treatment* : There is no doubt that medical remedies of today are far superior to, and more reliable than, any astrological remedies. Astrology can, however, help in two ways. Firstly, when adverse planetary influences indicate the occurrence of an ailment at a future date, and medical science understandably has no clue about it, resorting to propitiation of planets as a remedial astrological measure may be undertaken. Secondly, astrology can sometimes indicate whether or not surgical intervention is going

to help, and when. In addition it is also possible that a sound astrologer may be able to point to a diseased organ or region when the medical man is finding it difficult to locate the site of illness; without doubt, this happens only infrequently.

In conclusion, medical astrology of today is a relatively new subject. There are many challenging opportunities for research. The known basic principles of classical astrology have to be extended into the unknown areas of medical science. In the pages that follow, an attempt will be made to approach the subject in a highly scientific manner, taking help from the classical texts and applying their principles to disease as it is understood in the modern terms. Following this approach, it is hoped that medical astrology would someday be of great help to the medical profession.

CHAPTER TWO

GENERAL CONSIDERATION

युक्ताहारविहारस्य युक्तचेष्टस्य कर्मसु।
युक्तस्वप्नावबोधस्य योगो भवति दुःखहा।।

For the one balanced in food and recreation, who is restrained in his actions, whose sleep and waking are regulated, there ensues a discipline which destroys all ailment.

—GITA VI-17

A horoscope is a chart of planetary positions at a specific time. When cast, it consists of three main parts:

(a) The Houses;
(b) The Signs; and
(c) The Planets.

The Houses

There are twelve houses in a horoscope. These houses rule over all the conceivable aspects of life, including also the tendencies of the past lives and prospects for any future ones. The first house is known as the lagna or the ascendant, and is by far the most important house of the horoscope. The remaining houses are studied only as they are related to the first house. The various houses of a horoscope can be classed into certain groups as indicated below:

(a) *The Kendras (or Quadrants)* : Houses 1, 4, 7, and 10. Benefic and malefic influences on these houses are crucial for health and disease.

(b) *The Panapharas (or Successant House)* : Houses 2, 5, 8 and 11.

(c) *The Apoklimas (or Cadent House)* : House 3, 6, 9 and 12.

(d) *The Trikonas (or Trines)* : Houses 1, 5 and 9. These are the most auspicious houses of the horoscope. They too are important in relation to health and disease.

(e) *The Ayu-sthanas (or Houses of Longevity)* : Houses 8 and 3 (8th from the 8th). Being indicative of longevity, they indirectly also indicate death.

(f) *The Maraka-Sthanas (or Houses of Death)* : Houses 2 and 7.

(g) *The Upachayas* : Houses 3, 6, 10 and 11. These houses, excluding the 10th, are sometimes considered adverse.

(h) *The Trika House*s : Houses 6, 8 and 12. They are particularly adverse for health.

The twelve houses of the horoscope rule over various parts of the body. This has been partly indicated in the previous, i.e., the introductory, chapter and shall be discussed in greater details later.

The Signs (or Rashis)

The zodiac is divided into twelve parts called the rashis or signs, each having an extent of 30 degrees. Their names, extent and symbols are shown in table II-1.

The sign rising in the horizon at a given moment is called the lagna or the ascendant, and constitutes the first house of the horoscope. The subsequent signs fall in regular order in the remaining houses of the horoscopic chart.

Table - II-1

	Rashis	*English Names*	*Extent (degrees)*	*Symbols*
1.	Mesha	Aries	0 - 30	♈
2.	Vrisha	Taurus	30 - 60	♉
3.	Mithuna	Gemini	60 - 90	♊
4.	Karka	Cancer	90 - 120	♋
5.	Simha	Leo	120 - 150	♌
6.	Kanya	Virgo	150 - 180	♍
7.	Tula	Libra	180 - 210	♎
8.	Vrishchika	Scorpio	210 - 240	♏
9.	Dhanu	Sagittarius	240 - 270	♐
10.	Makara	Capricorn	270 - 300	♑
11.	Kumbha	Aquarius	300 - 330	♒
12.	Meena	Pisces	330 - 360	♓

Some Characteristics of the signs:

1. *Malefic/Masculine*: The odd signs, viz., 1, 3, 5, 7, 9 and 11.
2. *Benefic/Feminine*: The even signs, viz., 2, 4, 6, 8, 10 and 12.
3. *Movable Signs*: Signs 1, 4, 7 and 10. They are changeable. Ailments that occur involving these signs are of short duration and soon change for the better or the worse.
4. *Fixed Signs*: Signs 2, 5, 8 and 11. They don't change easily. Ailments involving these signs last longer and tend to become chronic.
5. *Mixed Signs*: Signs 3, 6, 9 and 12. They have the qualities of both the movable and the fixed signs.
6. *Dominant Nature* :
   (a) Fiery - Signs 1, 5 and 9. They are the best for recovery from illness. They are, however, more accident prone.
   (b) Earthy - Signs 2, 6 and 10. They are the next best.
   (c) Airy - Signs 3, 7 and 11.
   (d) Watery - Signs 4, 8 and 12. They generally tend to have poor resistance against disease.

The twelve signs of the zodiac, not unlike the twelve houses of a horoscope, also rule over various parts of the body which have been indicated elsewhere.

The Anatomy of the Chart

In India, a horoscopic chart is drawn in one of the following manners.

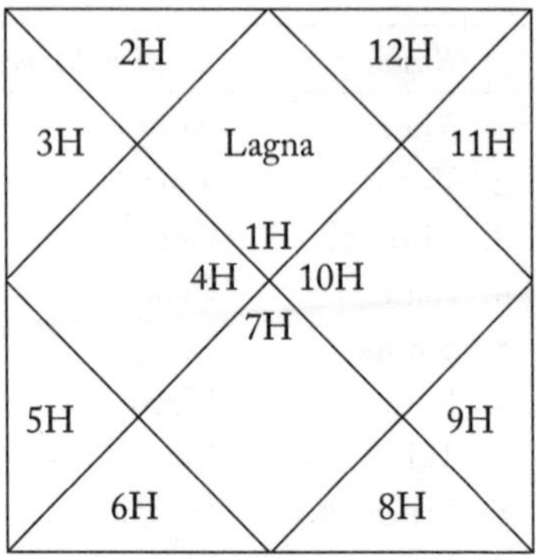

(a) *The North Indian Chart*: Here the houses are fixed. The four quadrants (corresponding to houses 1, 4, 7 and 10) are rhomboid in shape while the remaining houses are triangular. The lagna or ascendant is marked in the upper central rhomboid. The remaining signs are marked in the regular order in an anticlockwise direction. The planets are then located in the houses bearing the appropriate signs.

(b) *The South Indian Chart* : In this chart, the signs are fixed. The first house or lagna is marked in the sign which rises at the moment of birth; and the remaining house are counted (in a clockwise manner) from this first house.

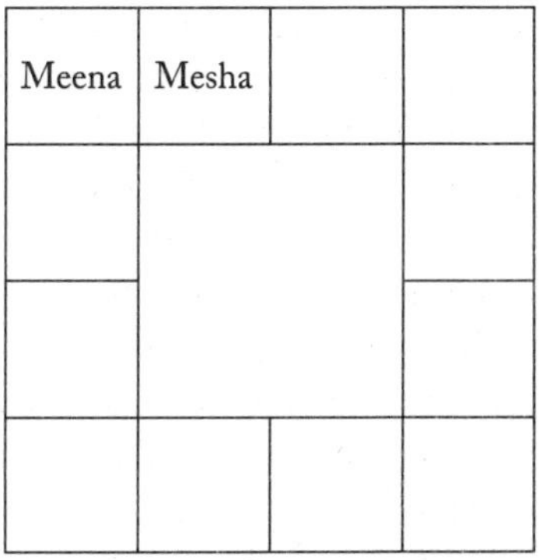

(c) *The East Indian (Bengali, Oriya) Chart*. Here too the signs are fixed, and the lagna has to be marked in the sign rising at the moment of birth. The signs and houses are counted in an anticlockwise direction.

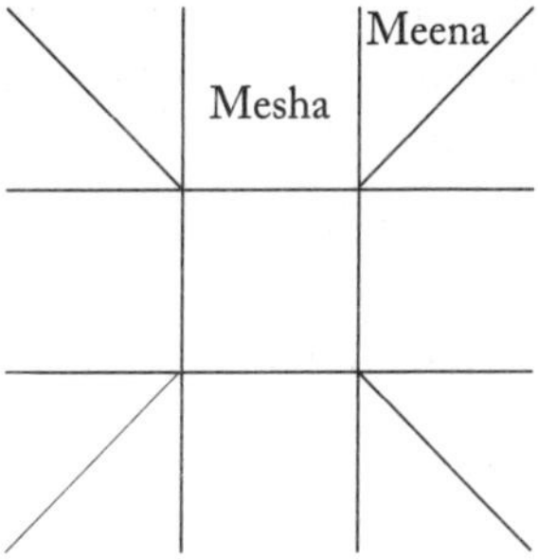

The Planets

Nine main planets are used in the Vedic astrology.

Table II-2 gives their English and Vedic names and their symbols.

Table II-2

Planets	*Vedic Name*	*Symbol*
Sun	Ravi (Surya)	☉
Moon	Chandra	☽
Mars	Mangala	♂
Mercury	Budha	☿
Jupiter	Guru (Brihaspati)	♃
Venus	Shukra	♀
Saturn	Shani	♄
Rahu (Dragon's head)	Rahu	☊
Ketu (Dragon's tail)	Ketu	☋

The Sun and the Moon are the luminaries and not planets in the astronomical sense. Rahu and Ketu are considered shadowy planets, having no material existence. Besides these, there are several sub-planets, again without any material existence, described in the Vedic astrology. These sub-planets have particular use in medical astrology. Two of these, the Gulika and the Mandi, have been discussed elsewhere. A lot of research is necessary in order to clarify the specific role of these sub-planets.

It may be pointed out here that medical astrology, as in fact any other branch of astrology, is an intricate play of forces represented by the houses, the signs and the planets. An understanding of these along with that of the operational periods or the dasha scheme is all that is required for successful prediction. In practice, however, too many variables have to be considered. That is where the skill and judgement of an astrologer come into play.

(a) *Planetary Lordship* : The seven planets, excluding Rahu and Ketu, own the twelve signs of the zodiac. The Sun and the Moon own a single sign each while the remaining planets own two signs each. This is being indicated below.

The Sun owns Simha.

The Moon owns Karka.

Mars owns Mesha and Vrishchika.

Mercury owns Mithuna and Kanya.

Jupiter owns Dhanu and Meena.

Venus owns Vrisha and Tula.

Saturn owns Makara and Kumbha.

(b) *Benefics and Malefics*: Jupiter, Mercury, Venus and the Moon are the natural benefics.

The Sun, Mars, Saturn, Rahu and Ketu are natural malefics. The waning Moon and afflicted Mercury also acquire maleficence. The natural malefics have an important role in causing disease while the natural benefics protect against disease as well as cause recovery from disease.

Besides being natural benefics or malefics, planets could also acquire benevolence or malevolence depending upon the houses they own. There would thus be different benefics and malefics for different lagnas. This has been dealt with elsewhere.

(c) *Exaltation, Debilitation and Moola Trikona signs*: Planets are strong and favourable when placed in their exaltation signs or in Moola Trikona signs. Six signs or 180 degrees away from its exaltation point lies the debilitation point of a planet. See Table II-3 for clarity.

Table II-3

Exaltation, Debilitation and Moola Trikona of Planets

Planet	*Exaltation*		*Debilitation*		*Moola Trikona*	
Sun	Mesha	10	Tula	10	Simha	0-20
Moon	Vrisha	3	Vrishchika	3	Vrisha	4-20
Mars	Makara	28	Karka	28	Mesha	0-12
Mercury	Kanya	15	Meena	15	Kanya	16-20
Jupiter	Karka	5	Makara	5	Dhanu	0-10
Venus	Meena	27	Kanya	27	Tula	0-15
Saturn	Tula	20	Mesha	20	Kumbha	0-20

(d) *Mutual Relationship of Planets*: Planets according to their nature, are disposed as friends or enemies or neutrals towards other planets. The great Varahamihira sponsors the view of Satyacharya in determining the natural mutual relationship of planets. According to this view, a planet's friends are the lord of its exaltation sign as also the planets owning houses 2, 12, 5, 9, 4 and 8 from its Moola Trikona sign. Table II-4 shows the natural mutual relationship of planets according to the above view.

Table II-4

Natural mutual relationship

Planet	*Friends*	*Enemies*	*Neutrals*
Sun	Mon, Mar, Jup	Ven, Sat	Mer
Moon	Sun, Mer	–	Mar, Jup, Ven, Sat
Mars	Sun, Mon, Jup	Mer	Ven, Sat
Mercury	Sun, Ven	Mon	Mar, Jup, Sat
Jupiter	Sun, Mon, Mar	Mer, Ven	Sat
Venus	Mer, Sat	Sun, Mon	Mar, Jup
Saturn	Mer, Ven	Sun, Mon, Mar	Jup

(e) *Aspects* : Planets exert their influence on the houses and planets that they aspect. All planets fully aspect the seventh house, or planets located therein, from their own position. In addition, the outer planets (Mars, Jupiter and Saturn) have been granted special aspects. Thus Mars also fully aspects houses 4 and 8, Jupiter houses 5 and 9, and Saturn houses 3 and 10. The remaining planets cast a quarter glance on houses 3 and 10, half an aspect on houses 5 and 9, and three-quarter aspect on houses 4 and 8.

(f) *Combustion and Retrogression of Planets* : Planets when close to the Sun tend to lose their strength and vitality, and are considered to be combust. A combust planet loses its capacity to do good and produces adverse results. Planets also become retrograde when, during their motion, they appear to be moving in a reverse direction. The Sun and the Moon do not become retrograde while Rahu and Ketu (almost) always move in a retrograde direction. A retrograde planet produces unexpected results and generally is adverse for health.

The various body parts and diseases signified by the planets have been dealt with elsewhere.

The Nakshatras

The zodiac is divided into twenty-seven equal parts, each of 13°20' extent. Each such part is called a constellation or a Nakshatra. The Nakshatras form three group of nine each. Their lords are Ketu, Venus, Sun, Moon, Mars, Rahu, Jupiter, Saturn and Mercury in this order. This concept forms the basis of the Vimshottari dasha which is the most excellent and the most widely used system for timing of events.

Table II-5 lists the various nakshatras as well as their lords, and shows their relationship with the zodiacal signs.

Table II-5

Rashis, Nakshatras and Nakshatra Lords

Rashis	*Nakshatra*	*Extent* *s*	*d*	*m*	*Pada*	*Lord*
1. Mesha (Aries)	1. Ashvini	0	13	20	4	Ketu
	2. Bharani	0	26	40	4	Venus
	3. Krittika	1	0	0	1	Sun
2. Vrisha (Taurus)	3. Krittika	1	10	0	3	Sun
	4. Rohini	1	23	20	4	Moon
	5. Mrigashira	2	0	0	2	Mars
3. Mithuna (Gemini)	5. Mrigashira	2	6	40	2	Mars
	6. Ardra	2	20	0	4	Rahu
	7. Punarvasu	3	0	0	3	Jupiter
4. Karka (Cancer)	7. Punarvasu	3	3	20	1	Jupiter
	8. Pushya	3	16	40	4	Saturn
	9. Ashlesha	4	0	0	4	Mercury
5. Simha (Leo)	10. Magha	4	13	20	4	Ketu
	11. P Phalguni	4	26	40	4	Venus
	12. U Phalguni	5	0	0	1	Sun
6. Kanya (Virgo)	12. U Phalguni	5	10	0	3	Sun
	13. Hasta	5	23	20	4	Moon
	14. Chitra	6	0	0	2	Mars
7. Tula (Libra)	14. Chitra	6	6	40	2	Mars
	15. Swati	6	20	0	4	Rahu
	16. Vishakha	7	0	0	2	Jupiter
8. Vrishchika (Scorpio)	16. Vishakha	7	3	20	1	Jupiter
	17. Anuradha	7	16	40	4	Saturn
	18. Jyeshtha	8	0	0	4	Mercury
9. Dhanu (Sagittarius)	19. Moola	8	13	20	4	Ketu
	20. P Ashadha	8	26	40	4	Venus
	21. U Ashadha	9	0	0	1	Sun
10. Makara (Capricorn)	21. U Ashadha	9	10	0	3	Sun
	22. Shravana	9	23	20	4	Moon
	23. Dhanishtha	10	0	0	2	Mars
11. Kumbha (Aquarius)	23. Dhanishtha	10	6	40	2	Mars
	24. Shata Bhishaj	10	20	0	4	Rahu
	25. P Bhadrapada	11	0	0	3	Jupiter
12. Meena (Pisces)	25. P Bhadrapada	11	3	20	1	Jupiter
	26. U Bhadrapada	11	16	40	4	Saturn
	27. Revati	12	0	0	4	Mercury

The Vargas

The sage Parashara advocates the use of sixteen vargas or divisional horoscopes for astrological analysis. For the purposes of medical astrology, we would particularly need five of them. They are:

1. *The Rashi Chart* : This is the basic horoscope or the birth chart. All the vargas are the finer sub-divisions of the rashi chart only.

2. *The Navamsha Chart* : This is the most important sub-division. Each sign is divided into nine equal parts of 3°20'. In movable signs (signs 1, 4, 7 and 10), the first Navamsha belongs to the same sign while the remaining ones follow in regular order. In case of the fixed signs (signs 2, 5, 8 and 11), the first Navamsha falls in the sign ninth from itself. In the case of mixed signs (signs 3, 6, 9 and 12), the first Navamsha falls in the fifth sign from itself. It is said, and for good reason, that when there is a conflict between the results indicated by the rashi chart and those indicated by the Navamsha chart, it is the planetary indications of the Navamsha chart that hold sway. Table II-6 indicates the Navamshas for various signs.

Table II-6

The Navamsha Chart

Signs → **Navamsha**	**1**	**2**	**3**	**4**	**5**	**6**	**7**	**8**	**9**	**10**	**11**	**12**
1. 3°20'	1	10	7	4	1	10	7	4	1	10	7	4
2. 6°40'	2	11	8	5	2	11	8	5	2	11	8	5
3. 10°00'	3	12	9	6	3	12	9	6	3	12	9	6
4. 13°20'	4	1	10	7	4	1	10	7	4	1	10	7
5. 16°40'	5	2	11	8	5	2	11	8	5	2	11	8
6. 20°00'	6	3	12	9	6	3	12	9	6	3	12	9
7. 23°20'	7	4	1	10	7	4	1	10	7	4	1	10
8. 26°40'	8	5	2	11	8	5	2	11	8	5	2	11
9. 30°00'	9	6	3	12	9	6	3	12	9	6	3	12

3. *The Drekkana Chart* : The Drekkana has a special significance in medical astrology. Each sign is divided into three parts of 10 degrees. The first part belongs to the sign itself, the second to the sign falling in the fifth house from it, and the third to the sign ninth from it. See Table II-7 for Drekkana.

Table II-7

The Drekkana Chart

Signs → **Drekkana**	**1**	**2**	**3**	**4**	**5**	**6**	**7**	**8**	**9**	**10**	**11**	**12**
1st 0°-10°	1	2	3	4	5	6	7	8	9	10	11	12
2nd 10°-20°	5	6	7	8	9	10	11	12	1	2	3	4
3rd 20°-30°	9	10	11	12	1	2	3	4	5	6	7	8

4. *The Dwadashamsha Chart* : The Dwadashamsha is normally analysed in order to know about one's parents. It, however, also has a special significance in medical astrology. Each sign is divided into twelve equal parts of 2°30' extent. The first Dwadashamsha belongs to the same sign while the remaining ones to the signs that follow in order. Table II-8 shows the Dwadashamshas for the various signs.

Table II-8

The Dwadashamsha Chart

Signs → **Dwadashamsha**	**1**	**2**	**3**	**4**	**5**	**6**	**7**	**8**	**9**	**10**	**11**	**12**
1. 0°00' - 2°30'	1	2	3	4	5	6	7	8	9	10	11	12
2. 2°30' - 5°00'	2	3	4	5	6	7	8	9	10	11	12	1
3. 5°00' - 7°30'	3	4	5	6	7	8	9	10	11	12	1	2
4. 7°30' - 10°00'	4	5	6	7	8	9	10	11	12	1	2	3
5. 10°00' - 12°30'	5	6	7	8	9	10	11	12	1	2	3	4
6. 12°30' - 15°00'	6	7	8	9	10	11	12	1	2	3	4	5
7. 15°00' - 17°30'	7	8	9	10	11	12	1	2	3	4	5	6
8. 17°30' - 20°00'	8	9	10	11	12	1	2	3	4	5	6	7
9. 20°00' - 22°30'	9	10	11	12	1	2	3	4	5	6	7	8
10. 22°30' - 25°00'	10	11	12	1	2	3	4	5	6	7	8	9
11. 25°00' - 27°30'	11	12	1	2	3	4	5	6	7	8	9	10
12. 27°30' - 30°00'	12	1	2	3	4	5	6	7	8	9	10	11

5. *The Trimshamsha Chart*:This division is sometimes employed to determine particularly adverse indications in a horoscope. In the case of a Trimshamsha, in an odd sign, the first five degrees belong to Mars, the next five 5° to Saturn, the next 8° to Jupiter, the next 7° to Mercury, and the last 5° to Venus. The order gets reversed in the case of an even sign. Here, the first five degrees belong to Venus, the next 7° to Mercury, the next 8° to Jupiter, the next 5° to Saturn and the last 5° to Mars. The Sun and the Moon do not own any Trimshamsha. See Table II-9 for clarification.

Table II-9

The Trimshamsha Chart

	ODD Signs (1,3,5,7,9,11)		**EVEN Signs (2,4,6,8,10,12)**	
Trimshamsha	*Degrees*	*Lord*	*Degrees*	*Lord*
1.	0 - 5	Mars	0 - 5	Venus
2.	5 - 10	Saturn	5 - 12	Mercury
3.	10 - 18	Jupiter	12 - 20	Jupiter
4.	18 - 25	mercury	20 - 25	Saturn
5.	25 - 30	Venus	25 - 30	Mars

Other divisional charts or vargas may need to be used in medical astrology sometimes. For example, a Saptamsha may be used to know about one's children, a Drekkana to know about one's siblings, and a Dwadashamsha to know about the well being of one's parents. In such situations, the specific *Karakas* (e.g., Jupiter for children, Mars for siblings, the Sun for father, the Moon for mother, etc.) also play an important role in the analysis of these divisional charts.

The Dashas

The dashas or operational periods are a unique system of Vedic astrology which are employed for the timing of events. There are scores of dasha systems both in the Parashari as well as the Jaimini systems of astrology. For our purpose, we are suggesting in this work to use two of the Parashari dashas. Both these dashas are Nakshatra-based.

(1) *The Vimshottari dasha,* which involves a cycle of 120 years and is the most widely used by astrologers all over the world with excellent results.

(2) *The Yogini dasha,* involving a cycle of 36 years. This is to be used to confirm the indications of the Vimshottari system. Yogini dasha is the second most commonly used dasha system in India.

1. *The Vimshottari Dasha* : The nine planets run this dasha in a specific order and for specific periods. These are, the Sun for 6 years, the Moon for 10 years, Mars for 7 years, Rahu for 18 years, Jupiter for 16 years, Saturn for 19 years, Mercury for 17 years, Ketu for 7 years and Venus for 20 years in this order. The dasha operating at the time of birth is indicated by the lord of the nakshatra of the Moon at the time of birth. The lords of various nakshatras have been given already in Table II-5. The balance of dasha is calculated from the extent of nakshatra that remains uncovered by the Moon at the time of birth. In the case of medical astrology, the major period (Mahadasha; MD), the sub-period (Antardasha; AD), and the sub-sub-period (Pratyantardasha; PD) for the time of illness or any specific related event should be calculated.
2. *The Yogini Dasha* : There are eight Yoginis with a specific lord of each as also the specific duration, as indicated in Table II-10.

Table II-10

The Yogini Dasha

S.No.	*Yogini Dasha*	*Lord*	*Duration*
1.	Mangala	Moon	1 year
2.	Pingala	Sun	2 years
3.	Dhanya	Jupiter	3 years
4.	Bhramari	Mars	4 years
5.	Bhadrika	Mercury	5 years
6.	Ulka	Saturn	6 years
7.	Siddha	Venus	7 years
8.	Sankata	Rahu/Ketu	8 years
		Total	36 years

The Yogini dasha is also based on the nakshatra of the Moon in the birth chart. Add 3 to the nakshatra of the Moon at birth and divide by 8. The remainder gives the number of the Yogini dasha operating at the time of birth according to the order given above. The balance of the particular Yogini at birth is calculated from the remaining part of the Moon's nakshatra, as in case of the Vimshottari dasha. In case of the Yogini dasha the MD and AD are to be calculated. The following table (Table II-11) gives the various Yogini dashas and the nakshatras associated with them.

Table II-11

Nakshatras and the Yogini Dasha

S.No.	*Yogini Dasha*	*Nakshatras*
1.	Mangala	Ardra, Chitra, Shravana
2.	Pingala	Punarvasu, Swati, Dhanishtha
3.	Dhanya	Pushya, Vishakha, Shatabhishaj
4.	Bhramari	Ashlesha, Anuradha, P. Bhadrapada, Ashvini
5.	Bhadrika	Magha, Jyeshtha, U. Bhadrapada, Bharani
6.	Ulka	P. Phalguni, Moola, Revati, Krittika
7.	Siddha	U. Phalguni, P. Ashadha, Rohini
8.	Sankata	Hasta, U. Asadha, Mrigashira

Table II-12 gives the Yogini dasha operative at the time of birth from the longitude of the Moon.

Table II-12

Yogini Dasha by longitude of the Moon

Long of Moon	*Rashi*	*Dasha*	*Rashi*	*Dasha*	*Rashi*	*Dasha*
0°00' - 13°20'	Mesha	Bhramari	Simha	Bhadrika	Dhanu	Ulka
13°20' - 26°40'		Bhadrika		Ulka		Siddha
26°40' - 30°00'		Ulka		Siddha		Sankata
0°00' - 10°00'	Vrisha	Ulka	Kanya	Siddha	Makara	Sankata
10°00' - 23°20'		Siddha		Sankata		Mangala
23°20' - 30°00'		Sankata		Mangala		Pingala
0°00' - 6°40'	Mithuna	Sankata	Tula	Mangala	Kumbha	Pingala
6°40' - 20°00'		Mangala		Pingala		Dhanya
20°00' - 30°00'		Pingala		Dhanya		Bhramari
0°00' - 3°20'	Karka	Pingala	Vrish-	Dhanya	Meena	Bhramari
3°20'-16°40'	Dhanya	chika	Bhramari			Bhadrika
16°40' - 30°00'		Bhramari		Bhadrika		Ulka

Table II-13 gives at a glance the nature of antardashas operating under various Yogini mahadashas (based on *Shri Ranbir Jyotirmahanibandha*).

Table II-13

Nature of various antardashas under the Yogini Mahadashas

Mahadasha (MD)	Antardasha (AD)		
	Benefic	*Malefic*	*Neutral*
1. Mangala	Mangala, Dhanya Bhadrika, Siddha	Pingala, Bhramari, Ulka, Sankata	—
2. Pingala	Mangala, Pingala, Dhanya, Bhadrika	Bhramari, Ulka, Sankata	Siddha
3. Dhanya	Mangala, Dhanya, Bhadrika, Siddha	Pingala, Bhramari, Ulka, Sankata	—
4. Bhramari	Mangala, Dhanya, Siddha	Pingala, Bhramari, Ulka, Sankata	Bhadrika
5. Bhadrika	Mangala, Pingala Dhanya, Bhadrika, Siddha	Ulka, Sankata	Bhramari
6. Ulka	—	Pingala, Dhanya, Bhramari, Bhadrika, Ulka, Siddha, Sankata	Mangala
7. Siddha	Mangala, Dhanya, Bhadrika, Siddha	Pingala, Bhramari, Ulka, Sankata	—
8. Sankata	Siddha	Mangala, Pingala, Dhanya, Bhramari, Ulka, Sankata	Bhadrika

For a detailed discussion of the Yogini dasha, the reader is referred to the *Applications of Yogini Dasha* by Jhanji and Sharma.

The Tri-Doshas of Ayurveda

According to the Ayurveda, there are three basic humours a balance of which is required for the maintenance of health.

Any imbalance in these three humours, or Tri-doshas, leads to illness. They are technically termed as the Vaata, the Pitta and the Kapha, and are inadequately translated respectively as the wind, the bile and the phlegm. The Ayurvedic understanding of disease and the various remedies advocated take into account these three humours. The Vaata element produces 'windy' complaints, neurological disorders, joint pains, etc. The Pitta element is concerned with 'heat', inflammations, fever, liver and gall bladder problems, etc. The Kapha element concerns with most of the respiratory ailments, colds, asthma, etc. Astrologically the various planets and their related humours are being indicated as follows.

1. Sun : Pitta
2. Moon : Kapha (and Vaata)
3. Mars : Pitta
4. Mercury : All three (Vaata, Pitta and Kapha)
5. Jupiter : Kapha
6. Venus : Excess of Vaata and Kapha
7. Saturn : Vaata

CHAPTER THREE

BENEFIC AND MALEFIC PLANETS

असाधुः साधुतामेति साधुर्भवति दारुणः ।
अरिश्च मित्रं भवति मित्रं चापि प्रदुष्यति ।

The wicked turns benign, and the benign assumes wretchedness; The foe turns into a friend, while even a friend becomes an enemy.

—SHANTIPARVA (RAJADHARMA) CH.80,SL8

Disease is caused by the influence of malefic planets while health is restored and preserved by the benefic planets. Whereas this statement sounds too simple, it is not always easy to be able to decide whether a given planet will behave as a malefic or as a benefic. Several principles have been laid down to determine the nature of planets in a given horoscope. These principles will be outlined in the description that follows. It is appropriate, however, to caution the reader at the outset that a lot of flexibility is needed in the application of these principles. Any rigidity in the attitude is liable to lead to failure in predictions.

Benefic and malefic planets produce their results when their appropriate dashas operate. Dashas thus help us in the timing of events.

Malefics and Benefics by nature

Planets may be malefic or benefic depending upon their inherent nature. Thus, Jupiter, Venus, waxing Moon and well-associated Mercury are natural benefics. Similarly, the Sun, Mars, Saturn, Rahu and Ketu, waning Moon and afflicted Mercury are natural malefics. The Moon and Mercury are naturally weak. The Moon though a mild and benevolent planet, behaves as a malefic when too close to the Sun. Mercury gets influenced too easily; it thus behaves as a benefic under benefic influence and as a malefic under malefic influence. Rahu and Ketu too can behave as benefics especially when placed in the signs of Jupiter and Mercury.

Benefics and Malefics for different Lagnas

Parashara's Principles

Planets behave as benefics and malefics depending on the houses they own. The ownership would naturally vary from one lagna to the other. In other words, for a given lagna, certain planets will behave as benefics while others will behave as malefics or neutrals. This will be independant of their inherent nature as already described above. The lagna signifies the body of the individual as well as his health. Naturally any planet ill-disposed to the lagna will also affect the health adversely while the benefics would do the reverse. The standard principles in this regard, as laid down by the sage Parashara in his celebrated *Brihat Parashara Hora Shastra* are being given below.

Principles – Part I

(a) Natural benefics as lords of quadrants (house 1,4,7 and 10) shed their beneficence.

(b) Natural malefics as lords of quadrants shed their malefic nature.

Note:

(i) Natural benefics are the Moon, Mercury, Jupiter and Venus; Natural malefics are the Sun, Mars, Saturn, Rahu and Ketu.

(ii) Lordship of quadrants has a neutralising influence on the nature of planets. The natural benefics thus lose the capacity to give benefic results, while the natural malefics lose their capacity to do harm.

(iii) Only the ownership of quadrants does not convert benefics into malefics, and vice versa.

(c) Lords of trines (house 1, 5 and 9) give benefic results no matter whether by their inherent nature they are benefics or malefics.

Note :

Lord of the lagna is both the lord of a quadrant and a trine. It is thus supposed to give benefic results irrespective of its inherent nature.

(d) Lords of the third, the sixth and the eleventh houses are always malefic.

(e) Lords of the second, the eighth and the twelfth houses behave as neutrals. They give results according to their location as well as association.

Note :

Lords of the 2nd, 8th and 12th houses are impressionable neutrals.

Principles – Part II

The twelve houses in a horoscope have been divided into four groups above: (a) the quadrants; (b) the trines; (c) the 3, 6, 11 group; and (d) the 2, 8, 12 group. In each group the relative strength of the various house lords is described thus.

(a) Of the lords of the quadrants, the 4th lord is more powerful than the lagna lord; the 7th lord is more powerful than the 4th lord; and the 10th lord is more powerful than the 7th lord.

(b) Of the trine lords, the 5th lord is more powerful than the lagna lord, while the 9th lord is more powerful than the 5th lord.

(c) Of the 3, 6, 11 group, the sixth lord is more powerful than the 3rd lord while the 11th lord is more so than the 6th lord.

(d) Of the 2, 8, 12 group, the *12th lord* is more powerful than the 2nd, while the 8th lord is more so than the 12th.

Principles – Part III

The lord of the 8th house, though considered a neutral above, has a special propensity to do evil. The eighth house represents obstruction, obstacles, failures, intrigues, ailments, death and the like. The following points must be remembered while considering the 8th house.

(a) Eighth house is the 12th from the 9th (indicating loss of Bhagya); hence its lord is ever malefic.

Note:

(i) Twelfth house from lagna indicates loss. Twelfth house from any house indicates loss of that house. Since the ninth house stands for Bhagya (luck), virtues, pious deeds, religious inclinations, father, etc., the twelfth from it (i.e., the 8th) indicates the loss of all these. Loss of fortune or luck is considered the biggest loss.

(ii) When the 8th lord is also the lagna lord, the benefic nature of the lagna lordship prevails, and the 8th lord tends to behave as a benefic unless it is particularly afflicted or ill-placed.

(b) The eighth lord is still more malefic when it also lords over the 3rd or the 11th house.

Note:

(i) For Meena lagna, Venus is the lord of the third and the 8th houses and is bad.

(ii) For Kanya lagna, Mars is the lord of the third and the eighth houses and, therefore, adverse.

(iii) For Vrisha lagna, Jupiter is the lord of the 8th and the 11th houses, and is adverse.

(iv) For Vrishchika lagna, Mercury as the lord of the 8th and the 11th houses is bad.

(c) The eighth lord becomes a benefic when it also owns a trine.

Note:

(i) Jupiter and Mercury for Simha and Kumbha lagnas respectively own the 5th and 8th houses, and behave as benefics.

(ii) For Mithuna lagna, Saturn as the lord of the 8th house as well as the 9th house (a trine) does not become an outright benefic and, according to the *Bhavartha Ratnakara*, gives mixed results only.

(d) The evil effects of the eighth house lordship do not apply to the Sun or the Moon.

Note:

The Moon is the 8th lord for Dhanu lagna, and the Sun for Makara lagna. According to the sage Parashara, the Sun and the Moon remain un-afflicted by the eighth house lordship. This, however, may not hold true in actual practice, at least in medical astrology.

Principles – Part IV

(a) When a planet owns both a quadrant and a trine, it becomes particularly useful and is called a Raja-yoga-karaka (doer of great benefit). It gives additional benefit if it is also located in a quadrant or a trine.

Note :

(i) Mars for Karka and Simha lagnas, Venus for Makara and Kumbha lagnas, and Saturn for Vrisha and Tula lagnas, become Yoga-karakas because of the ownership of a trine and a quadrant.

(ii) Some people doubt the efficacy of Saturn as a benefic for Vrisha lagna despite its ownership of the 9th and the 10th houses (a trine and a quadrant respectively). This is because the 9th lord is considered a Badhaka (an obstructing agent) for a fixed lagna like Vrisha. This, however, is not the view of Parashara which, in our opinion, must be considered more authentic.

(b) Only the ownership of a quadrant does not convert a malefic into a benefic. The malefic must also own a trine to completely shed its malevolence.

Note :

Saturn, as the lord of the 10th and the 11th houses for Mesha lagna, as lord of the 3rd and the 4th houses for Vrishchika lagna, and as the lord of the 6th and the 7th houses for Simha lagna, remains a malefic despite owning a quadrant in each cases.

(c) The blemish of kendra lordship (ownership of quadrants), as applicable to benefics, increases progressively from the Moon, to Mercury, to Jupiter, to Venus.

(d) Full Moon, Mercury, Jupiter and Venus, in this order, are progressively more powerful as benefics.

(e) Waning Moon, the Sun, Saturn and Mars, in this order, are progressively more powerful as malefics.

Principles – Part V (Raja Yogas)

When the lord of a quadrant is in some way related to the lord of a trine, a Raja Yoga (or a highly benefic combination) is formed. Benefic combinations in a horoscope neutralise affliction and are good for remaining free from disease. Relationship between any two house lords can be in one of the following ways:

(a) By location in the same house (conjunction).

(b) By mutual aspect.

(c) By an exchange of houses (Parivartana Yoga).

(d) When one of them is placed in the other's house and this latter aspects the former.

Note :

When the lords of quadrants and trines are related in one of the ways indicated above, they still do not produce a Raja yoga if they also own the Papasthanas (adverse houses), i.e., houses 3, 6 and 11.

Principles – Part VI (Rahu and Ketu)

(a) Rahu and Ketu give results according to the house where they are located; and according to the planet (i.e., the lord of a house) whom they join.

(b) Rahu and Ketu become Yogakarakas (productive of Raja Yoga) in the following situations:

- (i) When they are placed in a quadrant, and join a trine lord; or
- (ii) When they are placed in a trine, and join a quadrant lord.

(c) Rahu also behaves as Saturn and Ketu also as Mars.

Trika Houses and their Lords

Houses 6, 8 and 12 are known as Trika houses. While these houses, their lords, as well as the planets that associate with these houses and their lords are productive of adverse results, they are particularly adverse in relation to health. The sixth house and the sixth lord, among other things, indicate disease and accidents. The eighth house and the eighth lord indicate chronic disease, incurable disease, or death. The twelfth house and its lord indicate suffering and also hospitalisation. The dasha periods of the planets associated with these houses and their lords must be carefully watched for determining illness.

The Marakas (Death Inflictors)

It has already been stated that the twelfth house from any house indicates loss of that house. Now, the eighth house governs longevity. The eighth from the 8th (i.e., the third house) is the alternate house of longevity. Twelfth from the eighth house is the 7th house; twelfth from the third house is the 2nd. The lords of the 2nd and the 7th houses thus indicate loss of longevity, in other words death. These death inflictors, or *marakas* as they are called, do not cause death each time their major or sub-periods operate. But they do disturb health. Their dashas should be watched for health.

The classical Sanskrit texts tend to use very strong terms. The word maraka means a 'killer'. While the periods of marakas are important in determining the time of death, they should not always be taken to mean death. It is the rigid application of the stated principles of astrology that is fraught with failures.

Relationship of Planets to Various Lagnas

It is appropriate now to tabulate the relationship of planets to the various lagnas on the basis of the aforesaid principles.

S. No.	*Lagna*	*Benefics*	*Malefics*	*Marakas*	*Yogakarakas*
1.	Mesha (Aries)	Sun, Jup	Mer, Ven, Sat	Ven	–
	(i) Mere conjunction of Jupiter and Saturn (9th and 10th lords) does not produce a Raja Yoga. (ii) Jupiter becomes malevolent if ill-associated. (iii) Mars tends to behave as a benefic on account of the lagna lordship.				
2.	Vrisha (Taurus)	Sun, Sat	Mon, Jup Venus	Mars (Mon, Jup, Ven)	Sat
	(i) Mercury is partly beneficial. (ii) Even Venus is not too good for Vrisha lagna.				
3.	Mithuna (Gemini)	Venus	Sun, Mars Jupiter	Moon	–

<table>
<tr><th>S. No.</th><th>Lagna</th><th>Benefics</th><th>Malefics</th><th>Marakas</th><th>Yogakarakas</th></tr>
<tr><td colspan="6">(i) Combination of Saturn (9th lord) and Jupiter (7th and 10th lord) does not produce a Rajayoga.
(ii) Jupiter as a benefic is the lord of two quadrants (excluding the lagna). It is, therefore, particularly liable to the blemish of kendra lordship. Such blemish is applicable to Mercury and Jupiter only.
(iii) Mercury is neutral. Saturn may give mixed results.</td></tr>
<tr><td>4.</td><td>Karka (Cancer)</td><td>Mon, Mars Jup</td><td>Mer, Ven</td><td>Sat</td><td>Mars</td></tr>
<tr><td colspan="6">(i) Sun acts as a benefic or malefic depending upon its association.</td></tr>
<tr><td>5.</td><td>Simha (Leo)</td><td>Sun, Mars Jup</td><td>Mer, Ven Sat</td><td>Sat</td><td>Mars</td></tr>
<tr><td colspan="6">(i) Combination of Jupiter (5th lord) and Venus (10th lord) does not produce a Rajayoga.
(ii) The Moon (12th lord) gives results depending upon its association.</td></tr>
<tr><td>6.</td><td>Kanya (Virgo)</td><td>Mer, Ven</td><td>Mon, Mars Jup</td><td>Ven</td><td>–</td></tr>
<tr><td colspan="6">(i) Association of Venus (9th lord) and Mercury (10th lord and lagna lord) produces a Rajayoga.
(ii) The Sun (12th lord) gives results based on its association.
(iii) Mercury as lagna lord and lord of the 10th house (the most powerful quadrant) becomes a benefic while Jupiter (4th and 7th lord) suffers from the blemish of lordship of two kendras.</td></tr>
<tr><td>7.</td><td>Tula (Libra)</td><td>Mer, Sat</td><td>Sun, Mars Jup</td><td>Mars</td><td>Sat</td></tr>
<tr><td colspan="6">(i) Venus is neutral.
(ii) Combination of the Moon (10th lord) with Mercury (9th lord) produces a Rajayoga.</td></tr>
<tr><td>8.</td><td>Vrishchika (Scorpio)</td><td>Mon, Jup</td><td>Merc, Ven Sat</td><td>Ven</td><td>–</td></tr>
<tr><td colspan="6">(i) Mars is neutral (cf. Venus for Vrisha lagna).
(ii) Sun - Moon (10th lord and 9th lord respectively) association produces a Rajayoga.</td></tr>
</table>

S. No.	Lagna	Benefics	Malefics	Marakas	Yogakarakas
9.	Dhanu (Sagittarius)	Sun, Mars	Ven	Ven, Sat	–
	(i) Jupiter is neutral as is the Moon.				
	(ii) Sun-Mercury (9th and 10th lords) association produces a Rajayoga.				
10.	Makara (Capricorn)	Merc, Ven	Mon, Mars Jup	Mars (and other malefics)	Ven
	(i) The Sun is a neutral.				
	(ii) Saturn (2nd lord) itself is not a maraka as it is the lord of the lagna also.				
11.	Kumbha (Aquarius)	Ven, Sat	Mon, Mars Jup	Sun, Mars Jup	Ven
	(i) Mercury is mediocre, perhaps more beneficial than harmful.				
12.	Meena (Pisces)	Mon, Mars Jup	Sun, Merc Ven, Sat	Mer, Sat	–
	(i) Mars is not a maraka despite being the second lord (cf. Venus for Kanya lagna).				
	(ii) Association of Mars (9th lord) and Jupiter (10th lord as well as lagna lord) produces a Rajayoga.				
	(iii) Compare this with the role of Jupiter and Mercury in the case of Kanya lagna.				

On the basis of the above information it is generally possible to determine the benefics and malefics in a given horoscope, and to determine therefrom the periods of sound health, illness and recovery from illness.

Gulika and Mandi

There are two subplanets which are the representatives of Saturn. They have no physical existence although they behave as extremely malefic planets. Several authorities on astrology, including Parashara, hold that the two are not separate but one and the same thing, and their malefic results because of their occupation of a house or association with other planets are the same. However, according to some, they are to be calculated in different ways and we shall describe here the methods of their calculation.

Before the actual calculation of their position, however, it is important to realise that according to classic Vedic astrology a day of twenty four hours extends from one sunrise to the next sunrise (not from midnight to midnight). Thus a day birth would be a birth taking place between sunrise and sunset, and a night birth between sunset and sunrise. Another concept is of importance; that is, that instead of considering 24 hours as the duration of the day and night, the ancient system considers it as 60 Ghatis. Thus, each one hour is equivalent to 2.5 Ghatis, or a Ghati equivalent to 24 minutes. A Ghati is further divided into 60 Palas (Vighatis), each Pala being equivalent to 24 seconds. A Pala is further divided into 60 Vipalas (each being 0.4 seconds).

Thus,

One Ghati	:	24 minutes
One Pala	:	24 seconds
One Vipala	:	0.4 seconds

The hours can be easily converted into Ghatis by multiplying them by 2.5; and Ghatis can be converted into hours by dividing them by 2.5.

The Gulika **:** The following steps are to be gone through.

(a) Divide the duration of day (in case of daytime birth) or night (in case of night-time birth) in eight parts.

(b) Each part belongs to a planet, starting from the lord of the day (e.g., Sun for Sunday, Moon for Monday, Mars for Tuesday, and so on) in case of day time birth, or from the 5th from it (e.g., Jupiter for Sunday, Venus for Monday, Saturn for Tuesday, and so on) in case of night time birth. The eighth part is without a lord.

(c) Saturn's part is known as the Gulika. A lagna or ascendant is cast for the time when Gulika (i.e., Saturn's part) begins. This represents the longitude of the Gulika.

The Mandi **:** When day and night are of equal duration (12 hours or 30 Ghatis each), the Mandi rises at 26 Ghatis on Sunday, at 22 Ghatis on Monday, at 18 Ghatis on Tuesday, at 14 Ghatis on Wednesday, at 10 Ghatis on Thursday, at 6 Ghatis on Friday, and at 2 Ghatis on Saturday, in case the birth occurs during daytime. In case of night time birth on any given day, consider the values given for the day falling 5th from itself, i.e., 10 Ghatis for Sunday, 6 for Monday, 2 Ghatis for Tuesday, 26 Ghatis for Wednesday, and so on. When the duration of the day or of the night is not exact 30 Ghatis as is usually the case, the time for Mandi should be appropriately altered. An 'ascendant' calculated for the time of rise of Mandi gives the position of Mandi.

The formula for the calculation of Mandi:

(a) *Day time birth :*

$$\frac{\text{Duration of day in Ghati-Palas}}{30} \times 26, 22, 18, 14, 10, 6 \text{ or } 2$$

depending upon the day of birth from Sunday onwards.

(b) *Night time birth :*

$$\frac{\text{Duration of night in Ghati-Palas}}{30} \times 10, 6, 2, 26, 22, 18 \text{ or } 14$$

depending upon the day of birth from Sunday onwards.

Results of Gulika in several houses as appropriate to medical astrology:

Just as malefics produce good results and promote health when placed in houses 3, 6, 10 and 11, so also Gulika is favourable in these houses according to the sage Parashara. In the remaining houses, however, it only yields adverse results as given below.

First house	:	Ailing and miserable
Second House	:	Disabled
Fourth House	:	Diseased body with excess of 'Vaata' (wind) and 'Pitta' (bile)
Fifth House	:	Short-lived and impotent
Seventh House	:	Weak bodied
Eighth House	:	Easily provoked to anger
Ninth house	:	Weak of body and mind
Twelfth House	:	Disabled and ugly in looks

Mandi in several houses of the horoscope:

Mantreshwara, in the Phaladeepika, describes the results of Mandi in different houses. Those results as are relevant to medical astrology are given below.

First House	:	Thin, built, diseased eyes
Second House	:	Harsh speech, poor intellect
Third House	:	Conceited, good for health
Fourth House	:	Bereft of home comforts
Fifth House	:	Pervert thinking, unstable mind, short life
Sixth House	:	Good for health
Seventh House	:	Poor intellect
Eighth House	:	Short stature, diseased face and eyes
Ninth House	:	Suffers deprivations of various sorts
Tenth House	:	Indulges in unscrupulous deeds, not bad for health
Eleventh House	:	Good for health
Twelfth House	:	Miserable

As can be seen, there is a lot of overlap in the results of Gulika and Mandi as described in the classical texts. Either or both may be considered in a horoscope for purposes of medical astrology. Conforming with the view of Parashara, we feel that the two are in fact identical and must be calculated according to the method for Gulika calculation as mentioned above.

Miscellaneous Adverse Factors

While a fair judgement can be made on the basis of what has been mentioned already, some lesser known factors must also bc taken into account while examining a chart for illness. These must not be ignored since their major and sub-periods can also produce illness (and even death if other factors so indicate).

1. *The twenty-second Drekkana* : The twenty-second Drekkana is the Drekkana that falls exactly seven houses away from the lagna. It thus falls in the 8th house on the same degrees as those of the lagna. Place the degrees of the lagna in the sign occupying the 8th house of the birth chart and determine its Drekkana. The lord of that sign and the planets falling in that sign in the

Drekkana chart are evil and capable of causing death and disease. When a Drekkana chart is cast, the 8th house of this chart indicates the 22nd Drekkana. The lord of this house as well as the planets falling in that house prove malefic.

2. ***The sixty-fourth Navamsha*** **:** Whereas the 22nd Drekkana is calculated from the lagna, the 64th Navamsha is calculated from the Moon. It falls exactly seven houses away from the Moon. Place the degrees of the Moon in the sign 8th from it, and determine the Navamsha of that sign. The lord of that Navamsha is the lord of the 64th Navamsha, and, along with planets falling therein in the Navamsha chart, behaves as a malefic. In the usual Navamsha chart, the sign falling in the 4th house from the Moon happens to be the lord of the 64th Navamsha; this lord as also its associates, and the planets falling in that house in the Navamsha chart behave as evil planets.

3. ***Sarpa Drekkana*** **:** The second and third Drekkanas of the sign Karka, the first and the second of the sign Vrishchika, and the last Drekkana of the sign Meena are termed the Sarpa (serpent) Drekkanas. Planets falling in these Drekkanas tend to produce ill health during their periods and sub-periods if other factors also indicate thus.

CHAPTER FOUR

HOUSES, SIGNS AND BODY PARTS

तदेवाग्निस्तदादित्यस्तद्वायुस्तदु चन्द्रमाः।
तदेव शुक्रं तद् ब्रह्म ता आपः स प्रजापति।।

He alone is Fire, He is the Sun, He is Wind, He is the Moon, He is the shining star, He is Brahma, He is Water, He is Prajapati.

—YAJURVEDA, 32:1

In order to be able to locate the site of disease, it is important to understand how various parts of the body are represented in a horoscope. Unfortunately, the classical texts provide us only brief information in this direction; far too many details are generally required in actual practice. Even that information, however, when properly used could serve as a stepping stone for further research. This chapter deals with certain basic principles which will help in ascertaining the site of disease and, when read with the succeeding one, also the nature of disease.

The Concept of Kalapurusha

The term 'Kalapurusha' is often used in astrology. The concept of Kalapurusha involves imagining a supernatural human form, which is spread over the whole zodiac. The various signs and dividions of the zodiac thus fall in the various parts of the body of the 'Kalapurusha', and, therefore, represent those parts. Right at the outset, in chapter I, we have given an indication of how the various signs of the zodiac represented various parts of the body of lord Shiva, as narrated in the *Vamana Purana*. Lord Shiva here represented the Kalapurusha. Most of the astrological texts, in principle, agree with the description of the Vamana Purana, with slight variation here and there. Varahamihira, for example, would distribute the body parts of the Kalapurusha amongst the various signs of the zodiac as shown in table IV-1.

Table IV-1

Body Parts of Kalapurusha

S.No	*Rashi (Sign)*	*Body Part*
1.	Mesha	Head
2.	Vrisha	Face
3.	Mithuna	Shoulders, neck and upper chest (between the two breasts)
4.	Karka	Heart
5.	Simha	Stomach (upper abdomen)
6.	Kanya	Umbilical region (waist and intestines)
7.	Tula	Lower abdomen
8.	Vrishchika	External genitalia (private parts)
9.	Dhanu	Thighs
10.	Makara	Knees
11.	Kumbha	Legs
12.	Meena	Feet

As can be seen, there is some slight disagreement in these main divisions. The most glaring difference is that according to the celebrated Varahamihira the heart falls in the 4th house of Kalapurusha, i.e., Karka, while according to the author of the Vamana Purana it falls in the 5th house of Kalapurusha, i.e., Simha. Varahamihira's distribution is simple in that the first four signs of the zodiac extend from the head to the diaphragm of the Kalapurusha, the next four signs from the diaphragm to the perineum (i.e., representing abdomen, pelvis, and private part) while the last four signs represent the lower limbs from the level of the hip joints. However, in our present understanding of the ailments of the heart, when we consider the individual houses (as different from signs) in a horoscope, we will be inclined to consider the 5th house for heart ailments.

Significations of Houses

It is appropriate now to consider the significations of the various houses of the horoscope as relevant to medical astrology. It may be noted that the right half of the body is represented by houses 1 to 7 and the left half by houses 7 to 1 of the horoscope.

First House : Head, brain, body in general, hair, appearance, skin, sleep, freedom from ill-health, longevity and old age, ability to perform work.

Second House: Face, eyes (right eye), teeth, tongue, mouth, oral cavity, nose, speech, nails, steadiness of the mind.

Third House: Ears (right ear), throat, neck, shoulders, upper limbs, trachea (windpipe), upper part of oesophagus (food pipe), clavicles (collar bone), the 1st web space of the hand (part of the hand between the thumb and index finger), dream, mental instability, physical fitness and physical growth.

Fourth House : Chest (thorax), lungs, heart (according to some), blood vessels of the thorax, diaphragm, potent and effective medicine, breast.

Fifth House : Heart, upper abdomen and its viscera, viz., stomach, liver, gall bladder, spleen, pancreas, duodenum (i.e., derivatives of the foregut), mind, thinking, pregnancy, umbilicus.

Sixth House : Small intestine, mesentery, appendix, part of the large intestine (i.e., derivatives of the midgut), kidney, upper ureter, diseases in general, ill health, wounds, injury, operation, mental agony, madness, phlegmatic illnesses, tuberculosis, tumours, eruptive diseases (small pox!), diseases of the eye, poison, peptic ulcers.

Seventh House : Large intestine and rectum (derivatives of the hindgut), lower urinary tract (lower ureters and urinary bladder), uterus, ovaries and testes, broad ligaments, prostate gland, seminal vesicles, urethra, anal canal, groins, semen, sexual union.

Eighth House : External genitalia, perineum, anal orifice, secondary sex characters, loss of a limb, affliction to face, chronic or incurable disease, longevity, severe mental anguish.

Ninth House : Hips, thighs, femoral arteries, nourishment.

Tenth House : Knee joints, patella (knee-cap), popliteal fossa (the hollow behind the knee joint).

Eleventh House : Legs, left ear, alternate house for disease (sixth from the sixth house) and recovery from disease.

Twelfth House : Feet, left eye, disturbed sleep, mental imbalance, physical ailment, hospitalisation, crippled limbs, death.

Drekkanas and parts of the Body

The Drekkanas are supposed to play an important role in disease. Not all is well understood about them. However, virtually all classical texts stress their role in medical astrology, especially in locating the site of disease in the body.

The three Drekkanas represent three divisions of the body: the first one extends from the head to the mouth; the second from neck to the navel; and the third from the pelvis to the feet. It is said that when the first Drekkana rises in the lagna, the various houses in the horoscope represent the various parts of the body falling between the head and the mouth (the first division). When the second Drekkana rises in the lagna, the parts of the body falling between the neck and the navel (the second division) find representation. Similarly, in the wake of the third Drekkana rising in the lagna, the parts of the body from pelvis onwards upto the feet (the third division) find representation in the twelve houses of the horoscope. The parts of the body on the right side are represented in houses 2 to 6; those on the left side in houses 8 to 12.

Table IV-2 indicates the parts of the body represented by the various houses of the horoscope, when the first Drekkana, the second Drekkana and the third Drekkana rise in the lagna, as given by Varahamihira and others.

Table IV-2 : Drekkanas and Body Parts

Based on the Drekkana rising in the lagna

House	*Ist Drekkana*	*2nd Drekkana*	*3rd Drekkana*
1st	Head	Neck	Pelvis
2nd	Right eye	Right shoulder	Organ of generation
3rd	Right ear	Right arm	Right testicle
4th	Right nostril	Right side of body	Right thigh
5th	Right cheek	Right side (artium & ventricle) of the heart.	Right knee
6th	Right jaw	Right lung & breast	Right calf
7th	Mouth	Navel	Legs & feet
8th	Left jaw	Left lung & breast	Left calf
9th	Left cheek	Left side of the heart	Left knee
10th	Left nostril	Left side of the body	Left thigh
11th	Left ear	Left arm	Left testicle
12th	Left eye	Left shoulder	Anus

When malefic planets occupy a particular Drekkana, they cause wounds or ulcers there. When benefics too occupy such a Drekkana, only a spot or a mark or a mole on the skin results. Varahamihira in his *Brihat Jataka* states thus: "When a planet capable of causing a wound or an ulcer or a mark is in its own house or in association with Saturn, such wound or ulcer or mark is present since birth; else it results later on. If the Moon is the planet causing the affliction, the wound or ulcer will result from a horned animal or by (an irritating) liquid; if Mars be the offending planet, the injury would result from fire, weapon, poison or snake bite; if Mercury be the culprit, the hurt may be caused by fall from a height; the Sun will cause injury from a piece of wood or by a quadruped; and if Saturn be the cause of it, the trouble will arise from injury by a stone or some wind disease. When benefics like the waxing Moon, un-afflicted Mercury, Jupiter or Venus inhabit a Drekkana, they cause no moles or marks or wounds on the part of the body indicated by the Drekkana".

Nakshatras and the Parts of the Body

Just as the various parts of the body are represented by the twelve signs of the zodiac, so also they are represented by the twenty seven nakshatras or constellations. The order of the ruling nakshatras, however, is not as regular as is the case with zodiacal signs. The best description of this subject is again available as a dialogue in the *Vamana Purana,* this time involving the body of lord Vishnu.

According to the *Vamana Purana*, the sage Narada requested the sage Pulastya to describe to him the 'Nakshatra Shareera' (the constellatory form) of the 'Lakshmipati Vasudeva' (lord Vishnu, the Preserver!). Pulastya obliged Narada thus:

"The Constellation Moola represents both the feet of lord Vishnu, Rohini His two legs and Ashwini His two knees.

"Poorva Ashadha and Uttara Ashada represent the two thighs of lord Vishnu, Poorva Phalguni and Uttara Phalguni represent His private parts, and Krittika represents His waist.

"Poorva Bhadrapada and Uttara Bhadrapada are located in the two sides of the Lord, Revati in both His armpits, Anuradha in the heart, and Dhanishtha in His back.

The Nakshatra Shareera of Lord Vishnu

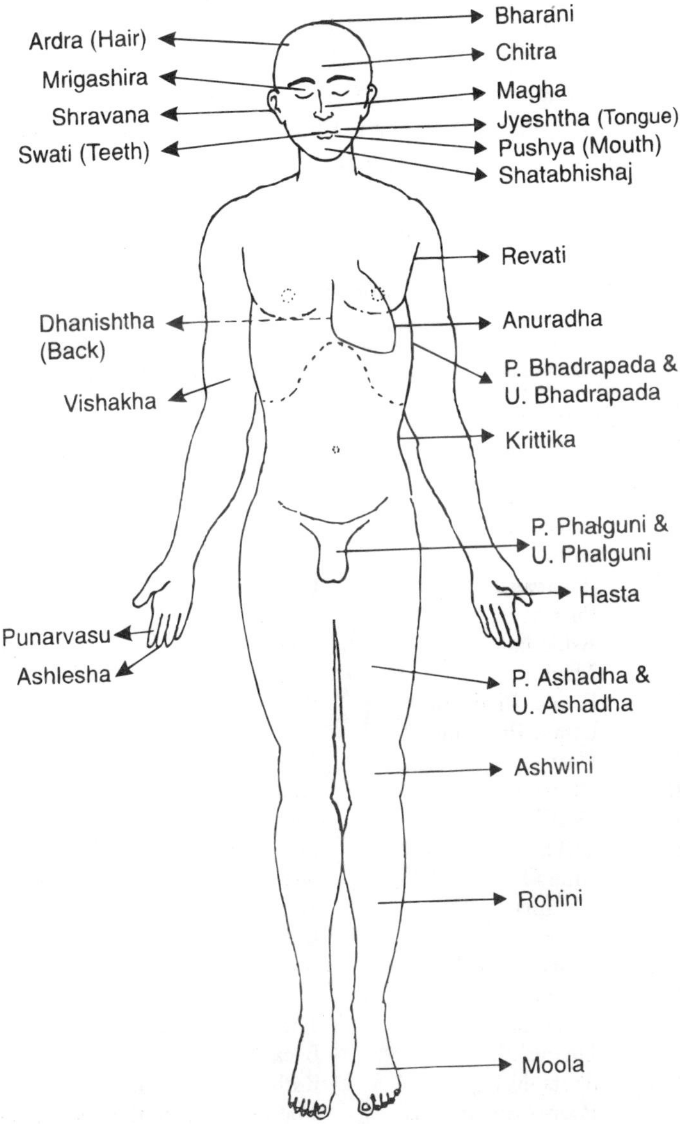

Figure IV - 1

"Vishakha is posited in both His upper limbs. Hasta lies in His two hands. Punarvasu represents His fingers and Ashlesha His nails.

"Jyeshtha is said to be located in His tongue, Shravana in His two ears, Pushya in His mouth and Swati in His teeth.

"Shatabhishaj lies in both sides of his chin, Magha in His nose, and Mrigashira in His two eyes.

"Chitra lies in His forehead, Bharani in His head and Ardra in His hair. This is the Nakshatra-Shareera of lord Vishnu".

The above description may be tabulated as in Table IV-3, and represented diagrammatically as in Fig. IV-1.

Table IV-3

The Nakshatras and body parts

S No.	*Nakshatra*	*Body part represented*
1.	Ashvini	Both knees
2.	Bharani	Head
3.	Krittika	Waist
4.	Rohini	Both legs
5.	Mrigashira	The two eyes
6.	Ardra	Hair
7.	Punarvasu	Fingers
8.	Pushya	Mouth
9.	Ashlesha	Nails
10.	Magha	Nose
11.	Poorva Phalguni }	Private parts
12.	Uttara Phalguni }	
13.	Hasta	The two hands
14.	Chitra	Forehead
15.	Swati	Teeth
16.	Vishakha	Both upper limbs
17.	Anuradha	Heart
18.	Jyeshtha	Tongue
19.	Moola	Both feet
20.	Poorva Ashadha }	Both the thighs
21.	Uttara Ashadha }	
22.	Shravana	The two ears
23.	Dhanishtha	Back
24.	Shatabhishaj	Both sides of chin
25.	Poorva Bhadrapada }	The two sides of the body, ankles.
26.	Uttara Bhadrapada }	
27.	Revati	Both armpits

CHAPTER FIVE

SIGNIFICATIONS OF PLANETS

विसर्गादानविक्षेपैः सोमसूर्यानिला यथा।
धारयन्ति जगद्देहं कफपित्तानिलास्तथा।।

As the Universe is sustained by the Moon, the Sun and the Wind through their processes of rejection, attraction and circulation, so do the Kapha, Pitta and Vaata sustain the body.

—DHANVANTARI

Just as different signs of the zodiac and different Nakshatras rule over various parts of the body, the various planets are also related to different body parts. Besides, they indicate certain illnesses in conformity with their inherent nature. Thus it is only after a thorough consideration of the houses, signs, nakshatras and planets involved, along with the dashas operating at a particular time, that it becomes possible to diagnose the nature and location of disease in the body, as also its time of onset and final outcome.

The significations of various planets as appropriate to medical astrology are being briefly outlined below. The list of significations is in no way complete and there are areas where our knowledge is absolutely negligible. As it is, a beginning has to be made somewhere, and that is precisely what is being done here. The planetary significations mentioned hereunder are primarily based on two classical works: (i) The *Phaladeepika*, a classic on predictive astrology written by Mantreshwara; and (ii) The *Prashna Marga*, a celebrated work of Kerala which is primarily meant for horary astrology but its principles find abundant utility in natal astrology.

The Sun

It has a bilious ('Pitta') temperament. Its strength or weakness reflects the state of general health of an indiviaual. It rules over heart, stomach, bones and right eye. The medical conditions that the Sun rules over include headache, baldness, hyper-irritability, fevers and pains, burns, diseases arising from the inflammation of bile (like certain diseases of the liver and gall bladder), heart troubles, eye disease, stomach ailments, bone disorders, certain skin problems, injuries from falls, weapons and poisoning, disturbances of the blood circulation, epilepsy, leprosy, and fear from quadrupeds, thieves and serpents.

The Moon

It has a phlegmatic ('Kapha') temperament with an element of wind ('Vaata'). Its strength or weakness reflects the stability and soundness of the mind of the individual. It rules over fluids in the body, besides also representing the mind, the blood and the left eye. It stands for psychiatric problems, mental aberrations, nervousness, emotional disturbances, increase of sleep and general inertia.

Phlegmatic disorders, tuberculosis, pleurisy, dropsy, dyspepsias, diarrhoeas, anaemias, serous effusions in the body, septicaemias (blood-poisoning), fever associated with chills and rigors, certain skin problems, jaundice, fear from water and watery animals, and the wounds caused by the horns of animals get representation through the Moon. The Moon in collaboration with Mars controls the menstrual cycle of women. It causes menstrul disorders and diseases of the female reproductive system. Diseases of the breast and the flow of milk are also to be ascertained from the Moon.

Mars

Mars has a bilious ('Pitta') temperament. It is aggressive and energetic. The state of Mars in a chart reflects the soundness of health of a native as also his vigour and vitality. It rules over the head, bone-marrow, bile, haemoglobin (the red pigment in the blood), musculature and the endometrium (the inner lining of the uterus, i.e., the soil, where a 'seed' on implantation produces an offspring). Mars signifies accidents, injuries, surgical operations, burns (especially under the influence of the Sun), blood disorders, tissue disruptions, high blood pressure, biliary inflammations and fever resulting from them, gall stones, injury by weapons, poisoning, diseases caused by heat, excessive thirst, eruptive fevers, mental aberrations (especially of the aggressive type), eye and splenic disorders, epilepsy, itching of the skin, fractures, haemorrhoids, diseases of the uterus, miscarriages and abortions. Mars also indicates head injuries, injuries sustained in fights, and diseases above the neck.

Mercury

Mercury has in its nature all the three humours, viz., wind, bile and phlegm ('Vaata, Pitta and Kapha'). Mercury is concerned with the intelligence of a native. Its disposition in a chart indicates the capacity for discrimination and reasoning. An adverse Mercury, in collaboration with a malefic Moon, can derange one's thinking and be a cause of certain mental aberrations. It rules over skin, throat, nose, lungs and forebrain (concerned with higher functions of the body). It signifies mental aberration, nervous break down, mental instability, mental complexes, abusive language, defective speech, high strung temperament, vertigo, skin diseases, leucoderma, impotence, certain diseases of the eyes, diseases of the nose and throat, ear disease and deafness, sudden falls and bad dreams.

Jupiter

It is phlegmatic ('Kapha') in temperament. Being the best benefic, a strong Jupiter protects the native against a host of diseases and neutralises numerous afflictions in the chart. It rules over liver, gall bladder, spleen, part of the pancreas, ear, and fat in the body. Jupiter signifies liver disorders, gall bladder disease, splenic diseases, obesity, anaemias, fever, fainting, ear troubles, diabetes, etc. It being a slow moving planet, the diseases caused by Jupiter are chronic in nature. Jupiter also causes laziness.

Venus

Venus suffers from excess of wind and phlegm ('Vaata and Kapha'). It governs the sexual drive of an individual. If grossly afflicted and ill placed, it leads to sexual perversions and venereal diseases. It rules over face, eyesight, seminal fluid, reproductive organs, urinary system, lacrimal (tear) glands, etc. It is also the significator for the parts of the body derived from the midgut, viz., intestine, appendix and part of the pancreas. It is a watery planet and is concerned with the endocrine (or hormonal) system of the body. Venus signifies sexual disorders, diseases of the generative organs as well as the urinary system, diseases of the face, eye diseases, cataract, diseases of tear glands, leucoderma, venereal disease, diabetes, carbuncle, urethral stricture, stones in the kidney and urinary bladder, laziness, tiredness and exhaustion; it also indicates diseases like typhoid, appendicitis and endocrine (hormonal) disorders.

Saturn

Saturn has primarily wind ('Vaata') and some phlegm ('Kapha') in its disposition. It is the slowest moving planet and the diseases caused by it are either incurable or very chronic. Saturn rules over legs and feet, nerves, lymphatics, and distal part of the colon and rectum. It signifies chronicity, incurability, insanity, paralysis, idiocy, glandular diseases, elephantiasis, tumours and cancers, unforseen dangers, exhaustion and fatigue, diseases and injuries of the legs and feet, mental disorders characterised by depression and melancholy, stomach troubles, injuries sustained from the fall of trees and stones.

Rahu

It signifies slowness of action, clumsiness, hiccup, insanity, unfounded fears, leprosy, debility, haemorrhoids, chronic boils and ulcers, incurable ailments, poisoning, snake bite, and diseases in the feet. In collaboration with the Moon, Rahu gives rise to various phobias. Being equivalent to Saturn, it indicates chronicity and incurability.

Ketu

Ketu produces all the ailments signified by Rahu. In addition it leads to diseases with uncertain cause, epidemics, eruptive fevers, viral and infective diseases, helminthiasis (intestinal parasites), deafness, defects of speech, as also diagnostic confusion. Ketu being equivalent to Mars also indicates surgical intervention.

CHAPTER SIX

COMBINATIONS FOR BALARISHTA

मनोदेहसमुत्थाभ्यां दुःखाभ्यामर्दितं जगत्।

All beings are subject to mental and physical ailments.

—MAHABHARATA, ARANYAPARVA, CH.2, SL.21

'Arishta' literally means misery or misfortune of any sort. Balarishta yogas in astrology imply those planetary combinations which indicate misfortune to the newborn child. Since the sufferings of the newborn, as understood by those around him, can generally be in physical terms only, the Balarishta yogas indicate ill health (or death) in early childhood.

Balarishta not necessarily death

Almost all classical texts on astrology contain combinations for childhood affliction. There are thus scores of combinations described for this purpose. The language of the classical texts is quite rigid and virtually all of them tend to convey that a Balarishta yoga means the death of the newborn child. It will be seen, however, that although the meaning conveyed to us is *death*, it is generally *ill-health* that actually happens. Death befalls in the presence of a Balarishta yoga only if there is excessive affliction by malefics. A literal meaning, therefore, must not be applied to the various principles as mentioned in the classics.

Untimely death in childhood

The existence of Vedic astrology is absolutely dependant on the concept of transmigration of the soul, and cycles of birth and rebirth. Nothing, according to Vedic astrology, must happen by a mere *chance* and everything must have a cause behind it. The theory of Karma, i.e., a person's physical and mental doings manufacturing a destiny for him, thus comes into play. A child's horoscope is nothing but the result of his past Karmas which he has to suffer and enjoy in this birth. Balarishta or affliction to the child, therefore, has its roots in the past births of the child and his karma in those births.

There is also a concept of interrelated destinies in Vedic astrology. One has no choice in the selection of one's parents or siblings or of one's social or financial ambience at the time of birth. Whatever one gets is whatever one deserves from one's own actions. There is no reason to blame the Almighty God or the poor Nature for one's misfortunes. It is as if those with related destinies come closer to each other, even like suspended particles of similar densities attaining similar zones on centrifugation. It has been said that when the three sons of a father are simultaneously running the Rahu dasha, it is a bad time (or even the time of death) for the father. This has been said to convey that the destinies of a person and his near and dear ones are interrelated.

Adverse results accrue from our bad Karmas, also known as *Papakarmas*, of the present or the past life. It has been suggested that *the newborn child can die or suffer for no apparent reason in his horoscopic chart*. During the first twelve years of his life the child may suffer as follows:

(a) During the first four years, due to its mother's Papakarma;

(b) From four to eight years, from its father's Papakarma; and

(c) From eight to twelve years of life, from its own Papakarma of previous life.

The sages thus advocate that one should not analyse a child's horoscope until it is twelve years old. They, however, do advocate that the child's chart should be seen with a view to determining the presence of a Balarishta combination so that a suitable astrological remedy, like the propitiation of adverse planets, can be undertaken well in time.

ASTROLOGICAL PRINCIPLES

1. *The role of the Moon*: All astrological texts agree that the strength or weakness of the Moon, and its affliction or

absence of affliction have a bearing on the health of the newborn. Most of the classical combinations for Balarishta in fact stress on the various afflictions of the Moon as the cause of death in early childhood.

2. *The lagna and the lagna lord*: It must be emphasised that a weak lagna lord, and the influence of malefics on the lagna and the lagna lord, tend to produce various afflictions in the chart. Even minor afflictions attain significant importance in the wake of an afflicted and weak lagna and lagna lord.
3. *The eighth house and the eighth lord*: The eighth house of the horoscope indicates longevity. The eighth house and the eighth lord under the influence of benefics tend to protect the newborn child. Malefics in the eighth house are bad although Saturn is an exception. The presence of Saturn in the eighth house generally ensures good longevity.
4. *Malefics in the quadrants*: The four quadrants (houses 1, 4, 7 and 10) of the horoscope are like the four pillars of a house. The influence of malefics on these houses is a negative influence for good health. The influence of benefics on these houses generally protects the native against affliction. However, as will be seen later, *the benefics when retrograde* do not render any protection to the native and tend to bring ill health and disease.
5. *The dasha pattern*: Classical combinations of Balarishta are too categorical in stressing on the actual time of fructification of afflictions. It will be seen, however, that often it is an adverse dasha which brings on ill health or death.
6. *Bad transit*: The fructification of afflictions tends to coincide with a bad transit ('Gochara') on sensitive points of the horoscope, like the lagna, the lagna lord, the Moon, etc.

CLASSICAL COMBINATIONS OF BALARISHTA

As has been pointed out earlier, there are numerous combinations for Arishta as described in the astrological classics. Below are mentioned some of these, particularly taken from Parashara and Varahamihira, and a few from the generally not available *Sri Ranbir Jyotirmahanibandha*. The strong language of the combinations is retained, with a repeated warning to the reader that *'death'* in these combinations must be taken to mean *affliction* or *illness*.

1. The location of the Moon in houses 6, 8 or 12, aspected by malefics, causes death soon after birth.

   Note: (a) When only benefics aspect such a Moon, death occurs in eight years.

   (b) Combined aspect of malefics and benefics causes death within four years.

   (c) No affliction ensues if the Moon in the said houses is unaspected.

2. Retrograde benefics in houses 6, 8 or 12, aspected by malefics, cause death within one month of birth.

   Note: (a) Benefics in houses 6 or 8 aspected by a retrograde malefic, unaspected by any benefics, are said to cause death *within one month of birth.*

   (b) Lagna unaspected by any benefics also leads to death *within one month of birth*. This is a very generalised combination.

3. Birth at the time of sunrise or sunset in the Moon's Hora or in Gandanta (i.e., the end of the signs Karka (Cancer), Vrishchika (Scorpio) or Meena (Pisces), or the beginning of the signs Mesha (Aries), Simha (Leo) or Dhanu (Sagittarius)), with the Moon and malefics in quadrants indicates death of the newborn.

   Note: Death ensues soon after birth in case of a birth in the evening, in the Moon's Hora, with malefics in Rashyanta (at the end — i.e., 29 degrees and more — of a sign) associated with the Moon in one of the kendras.

4. Lagna lord defeated in planetary warfare by a malefic, and posited in the 7th house, leads to death within a month of birth. Two planets, other than the luminaries, are said to be at war when they are located within one degree of each other; the one that is the farther advanced of the two is considered subjugated.

5. Placement of the Moon and all malefics in quadrants leads to death of the newborn.

Note: (a) A weak Moon in lagna and malefics in quadrants and the 8th house cause death soon after birth.

(b) The Moon associated with malefics, unaspected by benefics, in the lagna or in the houses 7, 8 or 12 leads to early death.

(c) Death also ensues soon after birth in the case of a weak Moon, in signs other than Mesha (Aries), Vrisha (Taurus) and Karka (Cancer), posited in the ascendant and aspected by malefics.

6. One is bereft of any longevity in the case of Karka or Vrishchika rising, with all malefics placed in the eastern half (houses 10 to 4) and all benefics in the western half (houses 4 to 10) of the zodiac.

   Note: This may be called as the *Vajra-Mushti Yoga*. According to one reading, this yoga arises in case of Vrishchika (Scorpio) lagna, when all malefics are located in houses 1 to 7, and all benefics in houses 7 to 1.

7. The Moon in houses 4, 7 or 8, or in the lagna, hemmed between malefics, unaspected by strong benefics, leads to early death.

   Note: (a) Lagna hemmed between two malefics, and malefics placed in houses 12, 6, 8 or 2, lead to certain death. That is to say that malefics around the lagna and the seventh house - the ascendant and the descendant - are bad for longevity.

   (b) Malefics in houses 2 and 12 from the lagna, or in 6 and 8 from the lagna, unaspected by benefics, cause death in the 6th or 8th month of life.

8. The Moon in the lagna, with malefics in the 7th house, causes early death.

9. Retrograde Saturn in Mesha or Vrishchika in the 6th or the 8th house or in a quadrant, aspected by a strong Mars, leads to death within two years.

10. The Moon in the lagna, Saturn in the 12th house, the Sun in the 9th house and Mars in the 8th house, with Jupiter bereft of power, lead to death soon after birth.

11. Mars, Saturn and the Sun together in the 6th or the 8th house lead to certain death within one month, even though Yama (the god of death) may attempt to protect the native.
12. A malefic in the sixth or the eighth house, aspected by another malefic, causes death within one year despite *'Amrita Paana'* (i.e., consumption of the Elixir of life).

    Note : This combination, as well as the preceding one, despite very strong assertion in the texts, should not be taken literally.
13. Venus in Karka or Simha, in the 6th or the 12th house, aspected by malefics, causes death by the age of 6 years.
14. Mercury in Karka in the 6th or 8th house, aspected by the Moon leads to death by 4 years of age.
15. Rahu in a quadrant, aspected by malefics, causes death by 10 years or 16 years of age.
16. Any of the malefic Drekkanas rising in the lagna, associated with or aspected by malefics, unaspected by its own lord, leads to death within 7 years.

    Note : Malefic Drekkanas are :

    (a) *Sarpa Drekkanas*: The 2nd and 3rd of Karka, the 1st and 2nd of Vrishchika, and the last of Meena.

    (b) *Paasha Drekkanas*: The 1st of Vrisha, Simha as well as Kumbha, the 2nd and 3rd of Tula, and the 1st and last of Makara.
17. One born in extremely ordinary circumstances, with very potent Raja yogas (benefic planetary combinations) in his chart, is said to suffer from affliction.
18. Birth at the time of solar or lunar eclipse (i.e., the Rahu-Ketu axis on the Sun and the Moon), and the lagna aspected by Saturn and Mars, causes death of the native within a fortnight.
19. All planets weak, in Apoklima houses, lead to death by 6 months or by 2 months.

20. A waning Moon in the twelfth house from the lagna, and all malefics in the lagna and the 8th house, with no benefics in kendras, lead to death soon after birth.
21. The Sun, Mars and Saturn in the lagna and a weak Moon in the 6th or the 7th house under Jupiter's aspect: Death in 7 years.
22. Malefic lagna lord in the Navamsha of the Moon, in the 12th house from the Moon, aspected by malefics: Death in 9 years.
23. Benefics in the visible half of the chart and malefics in the invisible half, with Rahu in the lagna: Death in 5 years.

    Note: See the Vajra-Mushti yoga under combination '6' mentioned above.
24. Rahu in the 7th house, aspected by the Sun and the Moon, unaspected by benefics: Death in 12 years.

Affliction to Mother

1. Saturn in the 10th house, the Moon in the 6th house and Mars in the 7th house, is a combination for the death of the newborn along with its mother.
2. The Moon hemmed between malefics, in the lagna, with malefics occupying the 7th or the 8th house causes death of the native along with its mother.
3. The Moon aspected by three malefics indicates death of the mother.
4. The Moon in the 7th or the 8th house from a malefic, associated with a malefic, and aspected by a strong malefic: Death of mother.
5. Exalted or debilitated Sun in the 7th house: the child is deprived of its mother's milk and survives on goat milk.
6. Malefics in the lagna, the 2nd house, the 12th house and the 7th house, lead to destruction of the native's family.
7. Malefics in the 5th or the 9th from a weak Moon: Death of mother within 6 months of the birth of the native.
8. Birth at the time of eclipse, the Moon associated with malefics and posited in the lagna, and Mars located in the 8th house: Death of the native along with his mother, due to weapon (? surgical instrument!).

Affliction to Father

1. Saturn in the lagna, Mars in the 7th house and the Moon in the 6th house: Death of father.
2. Jupiter in the lagna, the Sun, Saturn, Mars and Mercury in the second house: Father's death at the time of native's marriage.
3. The Sun associated with, or hemmed between, malefics, and malefic(s) in the 7th house from the Sun: Death of father.
4. Mars in the 10th house in an inimical sign indicates death of father.
5. The Sun in the Navamsha of Mars, aspected by Saturn: The father leaves home or dies before the birth of the native.
6. Rahu and Jupiter in the lagna or the 4th or the 6th house: Death of father in 23rd year of the native.
7. If the Sun is associated with or aspected by malefics, or hemmed between malefics, the father of the native undergoes suffering (and death!).
8. Affliction of the 6th and the 8th houses from the Sun by malefics, without benefic aspect: Affliction to father.

   Note : When the Moon is so affected, the mother of the native is subject to Arishta.

Time of Fructification of Arishta Yogas

In the several combinations causing Arishta to the newborn, the time of death (or suffering) has been indicated. Where such has not been indicated, the time of death may be ascertained from:

(a) Transit of the Moon over the strongest of the planets causing affliction; or
(b) Transit of the Moon over the natal Moon; or
(c) Transit of the Moon over the ascendant.

When the transiting Moon is itself afflicted, the adverse event comes to pass. The sages say that death in these cases may be expected within one year.

BALARISHTA : Some Examples

Chart VI-1 belongs to a female child who died within eight days of her birth. The fourth house has five planets including the Sun, the Moon, and the lagna lord Venus. Being too close to the Sun, they are all (except the Sun, of course) combust. The lagna lord Venus is on the same degree as the Sun and Mars, and is defeated in warfare by Mars. The adverse combination in the fourth house is also aspected by Saturn from the seventh house, and the retrograde eighth lord Jupiter from the 12th house. The lagna lord and the Moon are thus completely destroyed.

Chart VI-2 shows two malefics in the kendras. The lagna lord in the fourth house receives the aspects of retrograde Mars from the 10th house, and retrograde 8th lord Jupiter from the 12th house. The Moon receives no benefic aspect. Mars also aspects the lagna. The quadrants, the lagna and the lagna lord are all unprotected. This child suffered from

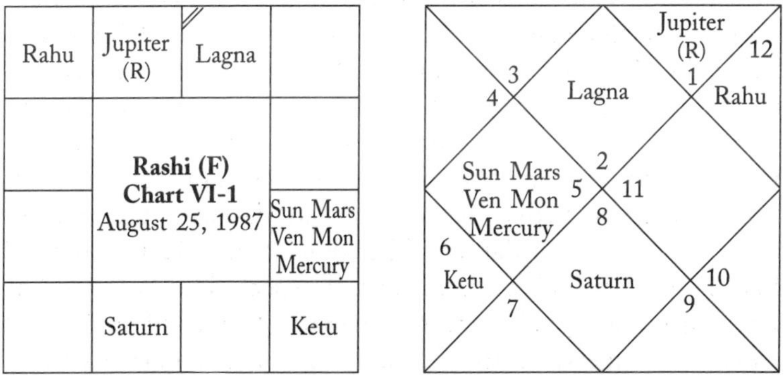

Lagna	19°13'	Mars	07°33'	Venus	07°49'
Sun	07°23'	Mercury	12°20'	Saturn	20°53'
Moon	10°26'	Jupiter (R)	06°00'	Rahu	08°53'

tuberculous meningitis and required an operation for the drainage of her brain fluid (*Ventriculo-peritoneal shunt*) in the Vimshottari dasha of Rahu-Rahu-Sun and the Yogini dasha of Pingala-Bhadrika (corresponding to the Sun-Mer). She died a month after surgery due to meningitis and shunt blockage. The Sun as the lagna lord is afflicted and plays a role both according to the Vimshottari as well as the Yogini dasha.

The native of **chart VI-3**, a female child, was born with a complete cleft palate. The second house which represents the oral cavity is aspected by a retrograde 6th lord Saturn while the

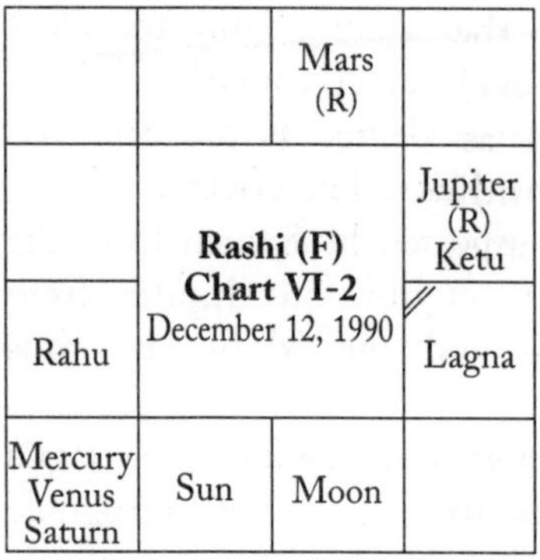

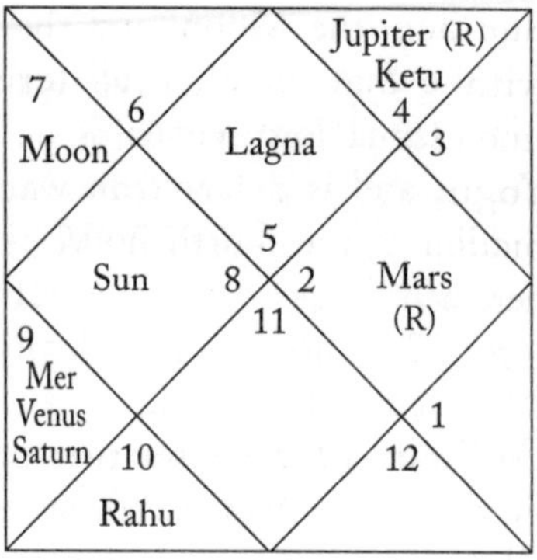

Lagna	00°59'	Mars (R)	06°41'	Venus	06°46'
Sun	26°40'	Mercury	15°52'	Saturn	29°46'
Moon	07°55'	Jupiter (R)	19°36'	Rahu	05°02'

second lord Venus is itself retrograde in the 12th house, in association with the lagna lord Mercury and the 8th lord Mars. The Moon in the 8th house confirms the presence of a Balarishta in the chart. Rahu-Ketu axis on the 4th house, and the 4th lord afflicted by the Sun and retrograde Saturn (the 6th lord) indicate affliction to the mother at the time of birth. It was a cesarean birth. The Vimshottari dasha at the time of birth was Sun-Sun-Saturn. The Sun is the 12th lord and Saturn the 6th lord, both in mutual aspect. The Yogini dasha was Ulka-Ulka (equivalent to Sat-Sat). The child underwent corrective surgery, in the USA, in the Vimshottari dasha of

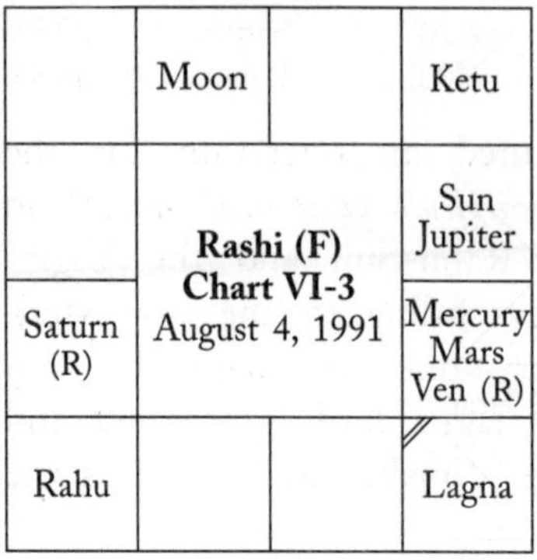

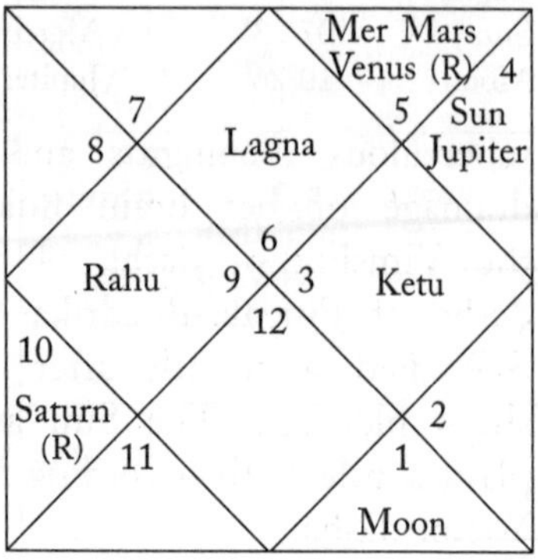

Lagna	21°12'	Mars	18°28'	Venus (R)	13°26'
Sun	17°36'	Mercury	11°34'	Saturn (R)	09°09'
Moon	27°04'	Jupiter	27°46'	Rahu	25°00'

Sun-Mars-Venus. Venus here is the 2nd lord, associated with Mars (indicative of surgery) in the 12th house (indicating hospitalisation as well as a foreign land). The Yogini dasha at the corresponding time was Ulka-Siddha (Saturn-Venus); Venus assumes a role of significance here too.

Chart VI-4

We have mentioned earlier that Rahu in a quadrant, aspected by malefics, causes death by 10 years or 16 years of age. Chart VI-4 belongs to a boy who has Rahu in the 10th house. The malefics Saturn and Mars do not aspect it. But the Sun aspects it from the 4th house from the same degree as the Rahu itself (the Sun and Ketu are conjunct at 19 degrees). The Sun happens to be the lord of the 8th house also. The boy died just at the age of 16 years. The Moon in the 6th house with Mars indicates Balarishta.

A principle of the *Bhavartha Ratnakara* states that when the 12th lord is aspected by or associated with the second lord, he becomes a powerful maraka in his dasha. The native died in the Vimshottari dasha of Jup-Jup-Ven. Jupiter is the 12th lord in the 4th house aspected by the second lord Saturn; Venus too is aspected by Saturn. In the Yogini dasha, it was Ulka-Ulka (Sat-Sat). Saturn is the lord of the 2nd house placed in a maraka house, the seventh.

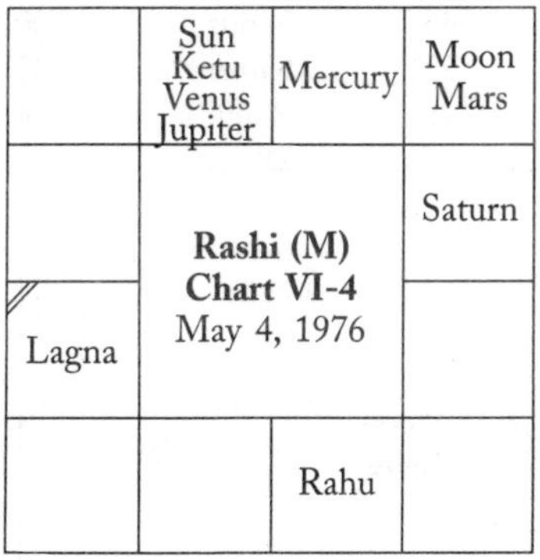

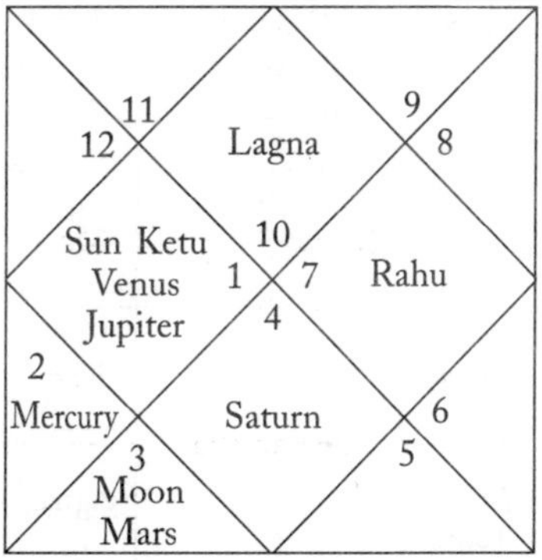

Lagna	21°20'	Mars	29°31'	Venus	07°48'
Sun	19°58'	Mercury	08°57'	Saturn	03°43'
Moon	09°04'	Jupiter	15°34'	Rahu	19°04'

Chart VI-5

A typical example of Balarishta is shown in chart VI-5. The Moon is located in the 6th house in association with Mars and Rahu and aspected by a malefic Saturn. There is no benefic aspect on it. The lagna is aspected by two malefics (Saturn and the Sun) and two benefics (Jupiter and Mercury). Within about three years of birth, the native gets the Vimshottari dasha of the 8th lord, the Moon, which is grossly afflicted in the 6th house.

In Mon-Jup, the child had developed an incurable malignant lesion (retinoblastoma) of the left eye *(see the placement of malefics along the 6/12 axis; refer to the section dealing with eye disease).* The Moon is afflicted in all the relevant divisional charts (the Navamsha, the Drekkana as well as the Dwadashamsha); so also

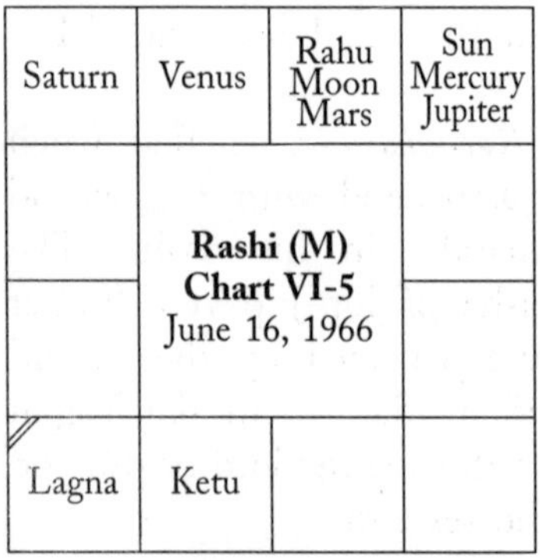

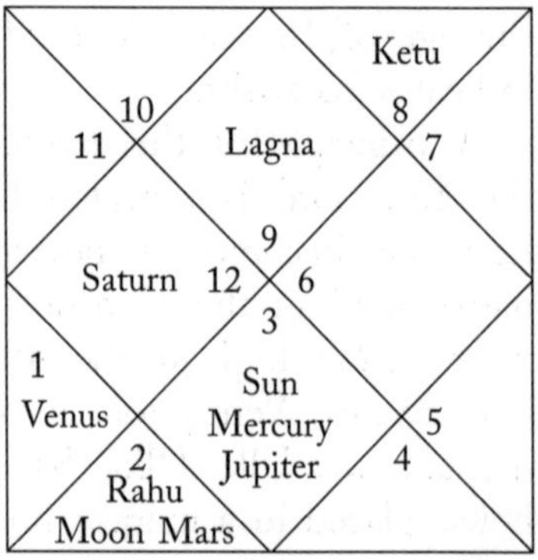

Lagna	22°36'	Mars	19°46'	Venus	24°00'
Sun	01°36'	Mercury	22°25'	Saturn	05°47'
Moon	03°14'	Jupiter	15°26'	Rahu	01°46'

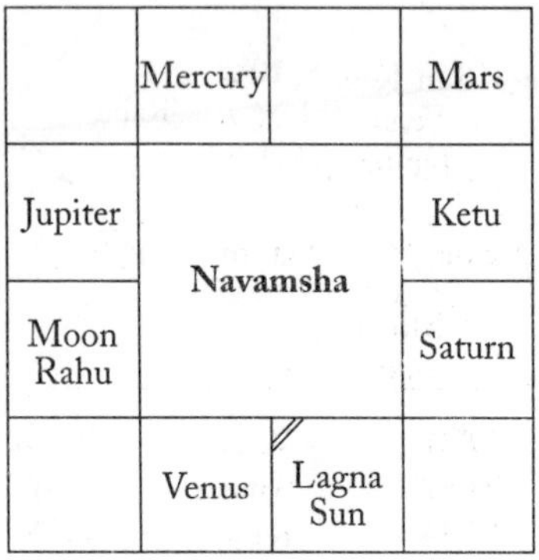

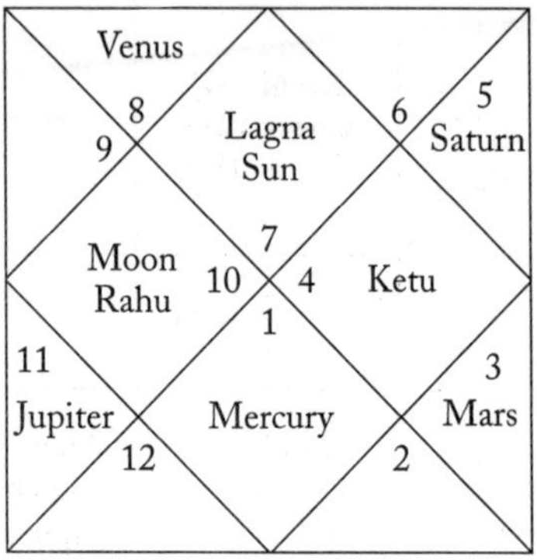

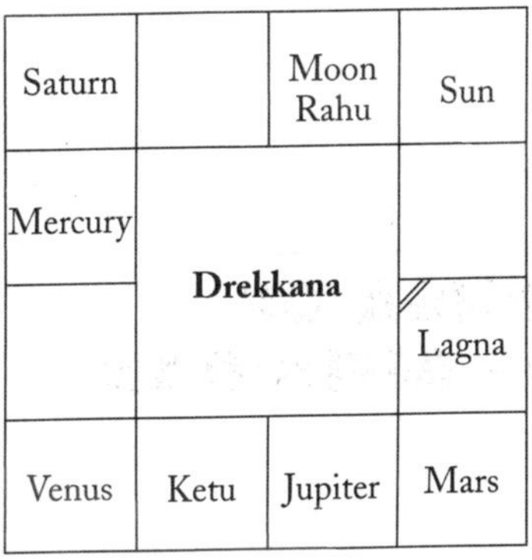

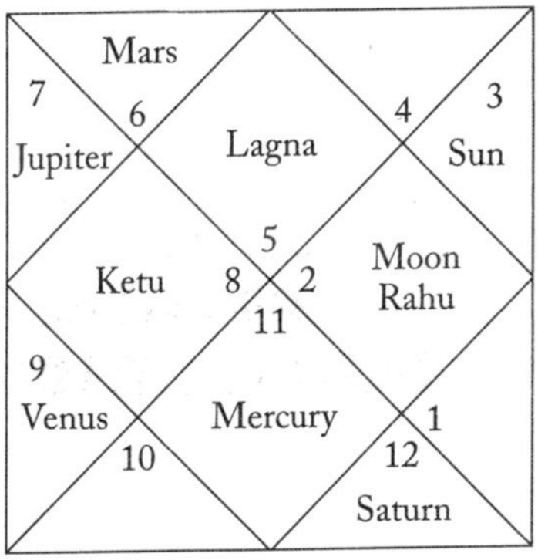

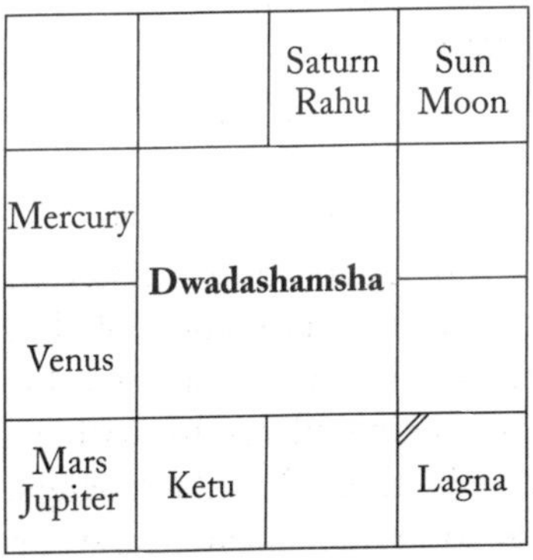

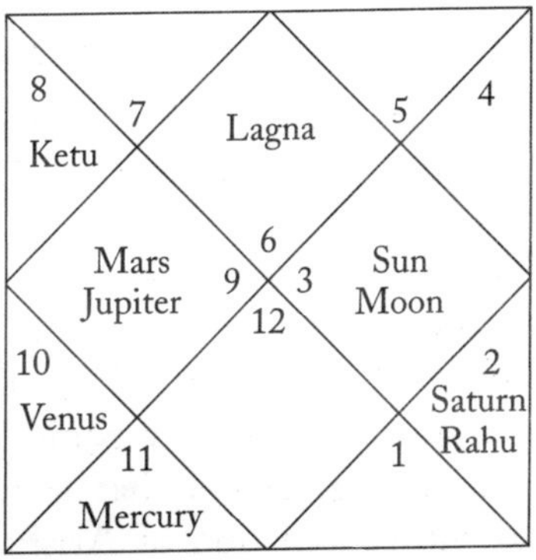

is Jupiter. The sequence of dashas is important in determining whether the native will get any relief or not. After Jupiter sub-period, the subsequent sub-period is that of Saturn, which is a malefic afflicting both the Moon as well as the lagna. Next in the natural order is Mercury, the 7th lord (a maraka) in a maraka house, also placed in the second (another maraka house) from the Moon. This would be followed by Ketu (in the 12th house) and Venus (the 6th lord). Thus the sequence of dashas promises no relief. He died in Mon-Mer-Rahu, equivalent to Sankata-Sankata (Rahu-Rahu) in the Yogini system.

It will thus be seen that the principles of Balarishta must be applied judiciously. Their integration with the dasha scheme is of paramount importance in order to get accurate results.

CHAPTER SEVEN

ARISHTA BHANGA OR CANCELLATION OF AFFLICTION

उत वाप पिताऽसि न उत भ्रातोत नः सखा
सनो जीवात वे कृधि।

Almighty Lord! You are our father, brother and comrade. Increase our longevity!

—RIGVEDA 10/186

While there are combinations in a horoscope indicating affliction to the native, there are others that indicate cancellation of that affliction. It is imperative, therefore, on the part of an astrologer not to create any panic by pronouncing ill results without considering factors that cancel an affliction. Arishta Bhanga, or the cancellation of Arishta, thus forms an essential part of horoscopic study.

It may, however, be pointed out that a typical combination for Arishta Bhanga must involve two components:

(a) the presence of an affliction; and

(b) the cancellation of this affliction.

The classical texts always use strong expressions. Many combinations for Arishta Bhanga are ascribed beneficial results, good health, long life and so on. However, by Arishta Bhanga we are inclined to consider only a *qualitative improvement* in the existing affliction. Thus, when there is an affliction to the chart, a combination for its cancellation neutralises this affliction. Whether this tends to produce decidedly positive results remains questionable.

It has been pointed out earlier that malefic influences on the lagna/lagna lord, the Moon, and the quadrants in different manners produce affliction. It will be seen that when there is a predominance of benefic influences, the afflictions disappear or get cancelled.

CLASSICAL COMBINATIONS FOR ARISHTA BHANGA

Once again, the main sources for these classical combinations are Parashara and Varahamihira. In addition, some material has been taken from the *Sri Ranbir Jyotirmahanibandha* and the *Manasagari*. All these combinations must be applied judiciously and not literally. It is best to integrate these combinations with the operating dashas in order to obtain the best results.

1. Jupiter alone, in strength, posited in the lagna destroys all evil.

   Note : A strong Jupiter in the lagna is considered the most potent single factor in overcoming planetary afflictions. It has been said that Mercury in lagna overcomes one thousand defects; Venus in a similar situation overcomes ten thousand blemishes; Jupiter in lagna takes care of a hundred thousand afflictions in the horoscopic chart.
2. Any of the strong Mercury, Jupiter and Venus when located in one of the quadrants (houses 1, 4, 7 or 10) destroys all Arishta.
3. Strong lagna lord in a quadrant removes planetary afflictions.
4. A strong lagna lord unaspected by malefics, and aspected by benefics in quadrants, destroys all affliction and provides progressively increasing prosperity and long life.
5. The Moon in the 6th or the 8th house becomes a protector of the native born during daytime (from sunrise to sunset) in Krishna Paksha (the waning phase of the Moon), or during night time (from sunset to sunrise) in Shukla Paksha (the waxing phase of the Moon).
6. All planets located in Sheershodaya signs (signs 3, 5, 6, 7, 8 and 11) at the time of birth remove affliction.
7. Rahu in the 3rd or the 6th or the 11th house aspected by a benefic removes affliction instantaneously. Arishtas also vanish if Rahu is located in signs Mesha, Vrisha or Karka coinciding with the lagna.
8. Malefics located in the vargas (signs in the divisional charts)

of benefics, aspected by benefics which are themselves in benefic vargas: in this situation too, afflictions disappear.

9. When the rising sign belongs to a benefic, the benefics in the chart are strong, and the malefics are weak, Arishtas tend to disappear.
10. All Arishtas disappear when the Moon, though located in the 6th or the 8th house, is in the Drekkana of Mercury or Jupiter or Venus.
11. Afflictions get cancelled when malefics are surrounded by benefics, and the benefics are located in quadrants or trines.
12. Lagna lord in the lagna aspected by all other planets removes affliction. Similarly full Moon aspected by all the other planets neutralises affliction.
13. Benefics in houses 6, 7 and 8 unassociated with malefics remove affliction.

    Note : This forms a benefic *Lagnadhi Yoga* which is highly protective; it is comparable to a *Chandradhi Yoga* which too is beneficial.

14. A strong lagna lord in the 11th house or 3rd house or a quadrant removes affliction, ensures good health and promises long life.
15. Full Moon, hemmed between benefics, removes affliction. It becomes particularly beneficial if also aspected by Venus.
16. The Sun in the 12th house for Tula lagna ensures a longevity of a hundred years.
17. Jupiter - Mars conjunction or the aspect of Jupiter on Mars cancels all affliction and is favourable for the native's mother.

    Note : This is too general. It is important to keep in mind the houses involved in this combination and the houses owned by Jupiter and Mars in relation to a given lagna.

18. Malefics in houses 4 or 10, hemmed between benefics, and the benefics located in quadrants or trines: This situation proves auspicious for the father of the native.
19. Great afflictions vanish when a full Moon is exalted or in

its own house, in the vargas of friendly planets or in its own vargas, aspected by benefics and unaspected by malefics.

20. The location of Jupiter in Karka or Dhanu or in Meena, and in lagna or a quadrant or a trine, removes affliction.
21. When there are several benefic yogas in a horoscope, they remove affliction.

ARISHTA BHANGA : Some Examples

Chart VII-1

Chart VII-1 shows the Moon with Rahu in the 8th house. The Moon is not in a benefic Drekkana. However, it is a full Moon. The lagna lord Mars is conjunct with the Sun, Ketu and the 8th lord Mercury. It is within one degree of Mercury and defeated in planetary warfare by it. The only saving factor is the presence of Jupiter in Meena in the fifth house, aspecting the lagna as also occupying the 10th house from the Moon (forming the benefic Gajakesari Yoga). The native contracted poliomyelitis during early childhood and developed paralysis of both the lower limbs from the level of the hip joints. It may be noted here that one of the malefic Drekkanas (as mentioned under the chapter on Arishtas) rises in the lagna although aspected by its own lord. It is also aspected by Saturn (make a Drekkana chart to see this). This affliction is normally said to cause death by the 7th year of birth. Instead it caused an incurable disability around that age.

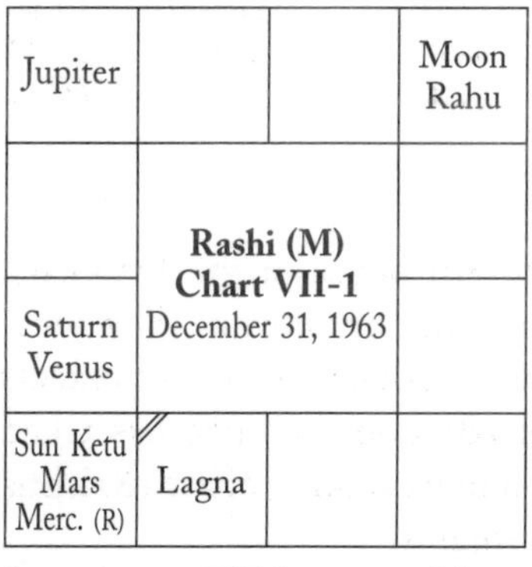

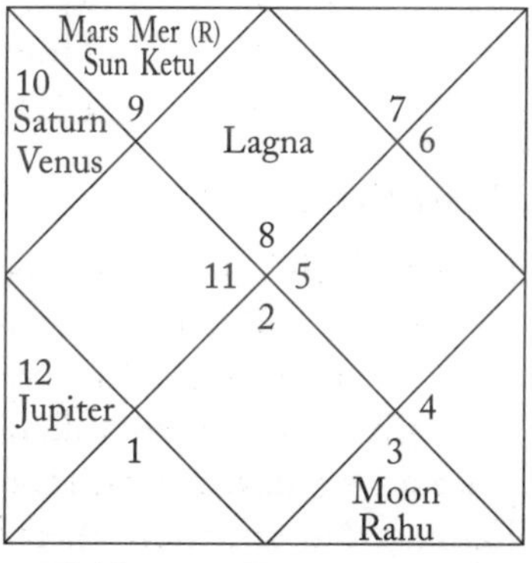

Lagna	08°56'	Mars	26°17'	Venus	15°32'
Sun	15°11'	Mercury (R)	25°23'	Saturn	26°58'
Moon	22°02'	Jupiter	17°18'	Rahu	17°56'

There is thus only a partial cancellation of the affliction. As has been already indicated, an Arishta Bhanga implies a *qualitative improvement* only.

Chart VII-2

A more complete cancellation of affliction is manifest in chart VII-2. Here, the Moon is in the 8th house aspected by Saturn, the 8th lord, from the 6th house. The lagna lord, though placed in the 3rd house, a benefic factor, is associated with the Sun and aspected by Saturn. However, the Moon is placed in a benefic Drekkana, i.e., that of Venus. There is an aspect of Jupiter on Mars and also on the lagna. The most effective cancellation of affliction is offered by the fact that the birth occured at night time in Shukla Paksha, the waxing phase of the Moon.

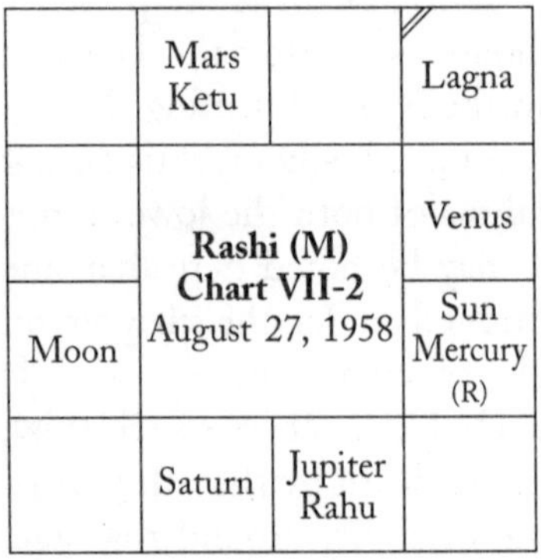

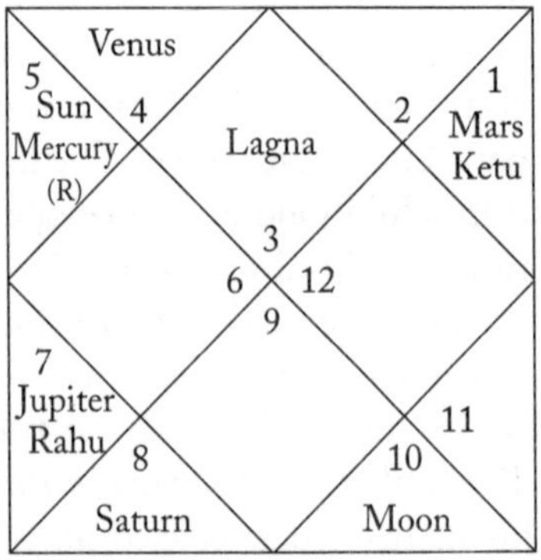

Lagna	26°00'	Mars	27°19'	Venus	19°56'
Sun	09°50'	Mercury(R)	04°01'	Saturn	25°49'
Moon	12°24'	Jupiter	04°44'	Rahu	00°14'

Chart VII-3

In chart VII-3, the Moon is in the 8th house in the Drekkana of the Sun, and is unaspected by malefics or benefics. The presence of the Moon in the 8th house unaspected by any planets generally produces no affliction. In addition the birth has taken place during daytime with the Moon in its waning phase (Krishna Paksha). No affliction, therefore, remains.

It is thus understandable that a careful study of cancellation of affliction in a chart is essential. When the affliction is more

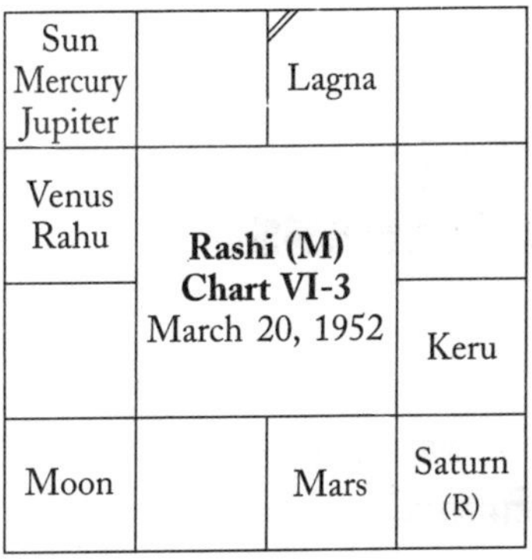

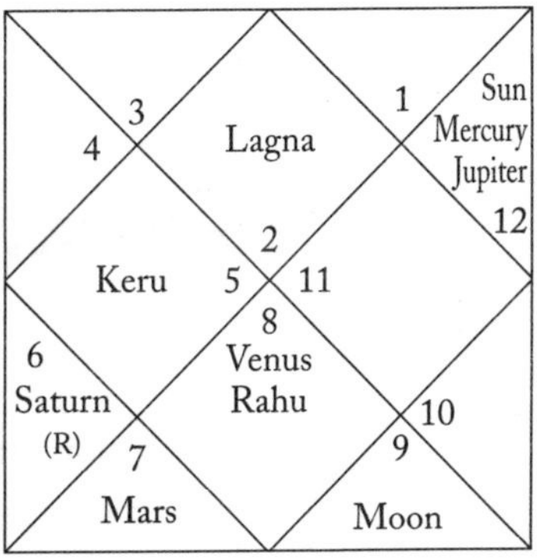

Lagna	28°29'	Mars	25°07'	Venus	11°17'
Sun	06°22'	Mercury	24°37'	Saturn (R)	19°23'
Moon	21°03'	Jupiter	27°20'	Rahu	07°04'

severe and cancellation inadequate, some adverse results will accrue though death may not occur. When there is a complete or adequate cancellation of affliction, only minor health problems may be indicated. Only when there are several adverse factors operating in a chart, those too without the presence of combinations for cancellation of affliction, should the astrologer conclude an untoward outcome.

CHAPTER EIGHT

CONGENITAL ILLNESS

जन्मान्तरकृतं पापं व्याधिरूपेण बाधते।
तच्छान्तिरौषधैर्दानैर्जपहोमसुरार्चनैः।।

Sin committed in a previous birth torments (the native) with ill health. This needs pacification by medication, charity, chanting of hymns, Homa (offerings to the Fire) and worship (of gods).

—AYURVEDA

Congenital ailments are of special interest to the medical person. Often they need prompt and specialised treatment. Inadequately treated, they may result in permanent disability to the patient. Many of these ailments are incurable or only partly curable, offering great challenges in their management.

For the astrologer it is a virgin area. Little research has been done in this field. During the study and analysis of a horoscope, generally no attention is paid to the state of health of the native at the time of birth. This oversight often leads to several pitfalls in predictive astrology. An attempt is being made here to present certain principles on the basis of which it will be possible to detect congenital ailments from the study of horoscopic charts. Some hints about the curability or otherwise of these ailments will also be available. It is, however, appropriate to stress that there is much more to congenital ailments than can be presented in one chapter of a book. Only some basic principles as applicable to actual horoscopes of patients are being elucidated.

The Relevant Principles

We have already discussed the combinations for Balarishta as well as for Arishta Bhanga in the preceding chapters. Those principles are highly valid if applied judiciously, with a lot of flexibility. A literal application is generally fraught with failure. In this section stress is being laid on the dasha scheme, or the scheme of operational periods, playing its role at the time of birth. *The dashas are a highly advanced system of Vedic astrology. These are of use in the timing of events.* It stands to reason, thus, that if an adverse dasha is operating at the time of birth, it is producing adverse results in respect of the newborn child. If an adverse dasha is indicating ill health or disease at the time of birth, the child is already suffering from disease at the time of birth. Thus, an adverse dasha scheme operating at the time of birth would generally indicate a congenital illness. If an adverse dasha starts sometime after birth, then the child is born healthy but suffers ill health later; that is not a congenital disease! So, the main principles for the determination of a congenital illness are:

(i) Dashas (major and sub-periods) of natural malefics at the time of birth.

(ii) Dashas of malefics for a particular lagna operating at the time of birth.

Note : Malefic and benefic planets have already been discussed.

(iii) Dashas of planets associated with malefics.

(iv) Dashas of planets associated with the lagna or lagna lord; and of those related to adverse houses, like the 6th or the 8th or the 12th.

(v) Inherent weakness of the lagna or the lagna lord.

(vi) Affliction to the Moon causing a Balarishta.

(vii) Presence or absence of combinations for cancellation of affliction.

Note : Of particular significance are the aspect of a strong Jupiter on the lagna, the lagna lord or the Moon, the presence of natural benefics in the quadrants, and the absence of natural malefics in the quadrants.

Chart for the Time of Conception

It has been suggested that a chart erected for the time of conception would throw greater light on the health of the foetus in its intrauterine life. The planetary lords for the ten lunar months that the foetus spends inside the mother, from the time of its conception till its birth, in their respective order, are:

Venus, Mars, Jupiter, Sun, Moon, Saturn, Mercury, lord of the lagna, Moon and Sun.

Affliction of any of these indicates adverse influences on the growth of the foetus during the respective months.

It may, however, be pointed out that it is difficult to ascertain the exact moment when conception takes place. Only a highly careful approach in determining the time of conception may yield results.

CONGENITAL ILLNESS : Some Examples

Ten basic charts are being discussed without going into the divisional charts. These ten examples are being presented in a progressively increasing severity of affliction. Two dashas, the Vimshottari and the Yogini, are being employed. The major, sub and sub-sub periods (MD, AD, PD) have been calculated for the time of birth in the case of the Vimshottari dasha while the major and sub-periods (MD and AD) have been calculated in the case of the Yogini dasha.

Chart VIII-1

The Vimshottari dasha (MD / AD/PD) operating at the time of birth was Sat-Jup-Moon. Saturn is the lord of the 12th house; Jupiter is the exalted but retrograde lagna lord in the Rahu-Ketu

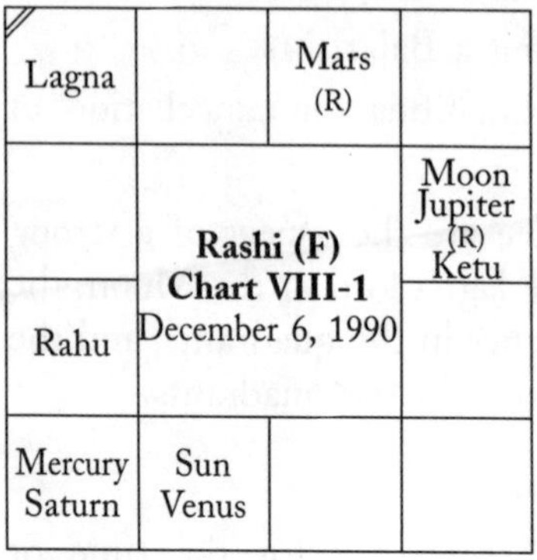

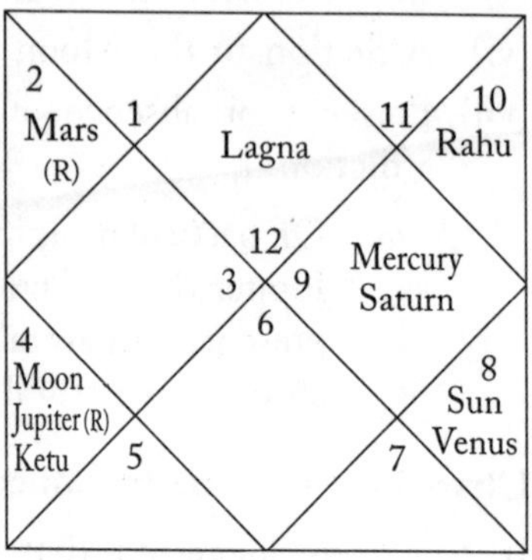

Lagna	16°14'	Mars (R)	08°35'	Venus	28°47'
Sun	20°13'	Mercury	11°13'	Saturn	29°07'
Moon	16°10'	Jupiter (R)	19°19'	Rahu	05°10'

axis (RKA) while the Moon, strong in its own house, is situated with the lagna lord in the RKA. Mars aspects the MD lord whereas Ketu associates with the AD and PD lords.

The Yogini dasha was Dhanya-Pingala (Jup-Sun). The Sun is the lord of the 6th house joined by the lord of the 8th, Venus, and aspected by Mars. A strong Jupiter, however, also aspects the Sun, as it does the lagna.

The native suffered from a lumbo-sacral meningomyelocoele which was cured after a simple operation.

Chart VIII-2

The native suffered from congenital heart disease which was surgically curable; a major surgical procedure was, however, required.

Vimshottari dasha : Sat-Moon-Jup. Saturn is the 8th lord in the 8th house in RKA. The Moon is debilitated in the 6th house, associated with the Sun and aspected by the 6th lord Mars from the 12th house. Jupiter is a maraka for this lagna and is retrograde. Saturn and Jupiter are under the influence of Ketu while Mars aspects the Moon.

Yogini dasha: Bhramari-Siddha (Mar-Ven). Mars is the 6th lord located in the 12th house, and aspects the lagna lord, the Moon, as also the sub-lord Venus. Venus is the lord of the 12th house also.

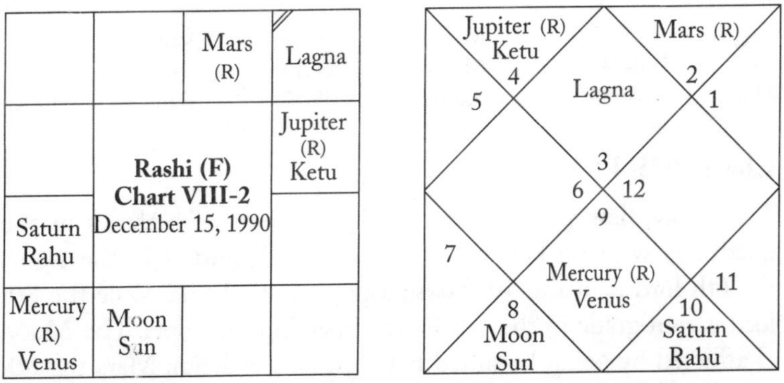

Lagna	01°28'	Mars (R)	05°59'	Venus	10°16'
Sun	29°31'	Mercury (R)	16°13'	Saturn	00°04'
Moon	11°20'	Jupiter (R)	19°28'	Rahu	04°42'

Chart VIII-3

The native had an undescended testis on the left side which required surgical removal.

Vimshottari dasha : Mars-Mercury-Venus. Mars is the 6th lord in the 8th house; Mercury is the lagna lord in the 7th house, in the RKA, aspected by Saturn, the 8th lord. Venus is the 12th lord in the 7th house aspected by Saturn.

Yogini dasha : Pingala-Ulka (Sun-Saturn). The Sun is in the 7th house associated with the lagna lord and the 12th lord, in the RKA, while the 8th lord Saturn aspects it.

Note : It may be noted here that while Mars and Ketu indicate surgical treatment, Saturn in addition indicates the removal of an organ.

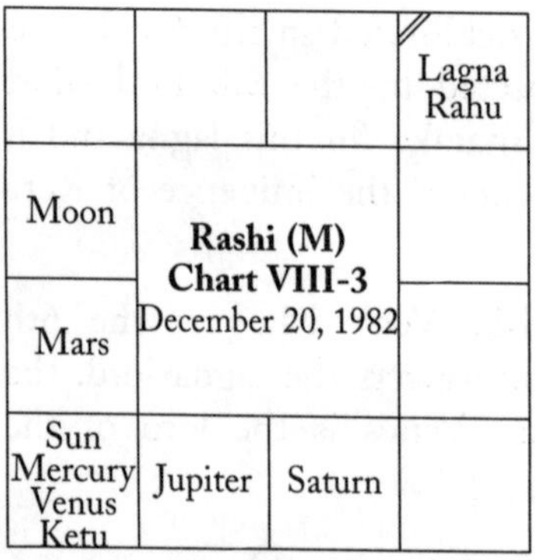

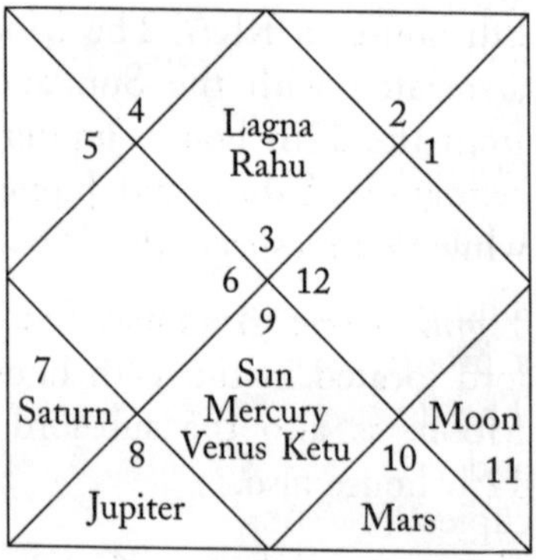

Lagna	23°02'	Mars	14°25'	Venus	16°04'
Sun	04°43'	Mercury	21°13'	Saturn	08°24'
Moon	00°34'	Jupiter	05°15'	Rahu	10°39'

Chart VIII-4

The major flaw in this chart is the presence of malefics in the quadrants with no benefics there. The 12th lord is in the lagna, the 6th lord is in the 4th house aspecting the lagna while the 8th lord is retrograde in the 7th house aspecting the lagna. The Moon is afflicted by being hemmed between two malefics. Mars the 8th lord, also aspects the lagna lord. The aspect of Jupiter from the 9th house is the saving factor. The child suffers from Down's syndrome, his mental age far less than his chronological age.

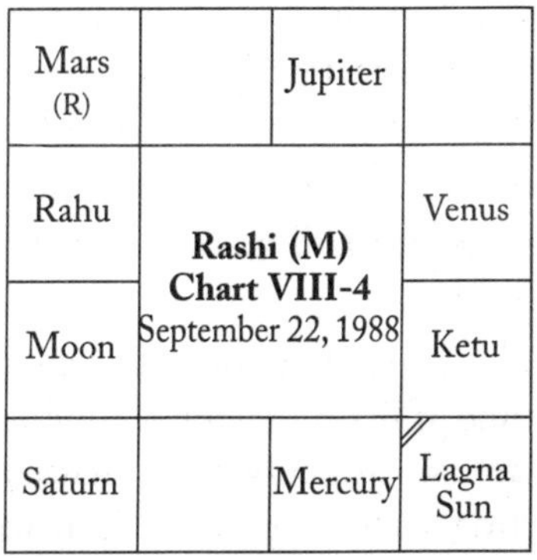

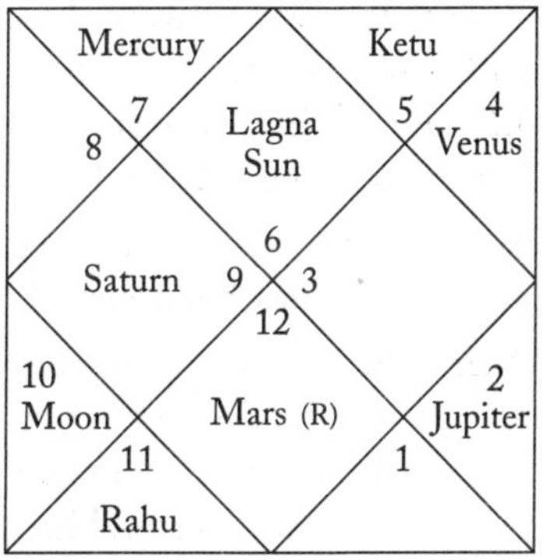

Lagna	03°38'	Mars (R)	13°16'	Venus	22°20'
Sun	05°44'	Mercury	01°10'	Saturn	02°39'
Moon	15°53'	Jupiter	12°25'	Rahu	20°20'

Vimshottari dasha: Moon-Saturn-Saturn. Saturn is the 6th lord aspecting the lagna. The Moon is a malefic, being the 11th lord, and afflicted in the 5th house.

Yogini dasha: Mangala-Ulka (Moon-Saturn); similar to the Vimshottari dasha.

Chart VIII-5

The native suffers from muscular dystrophy, which is generally a progressive disease. All malefics are situated in the 6/12 axis. The lagna lord is exalted in the 5th house but it is retrograde and aspected by the 8th lord Venus. A debilitated planet occupies the lagna.

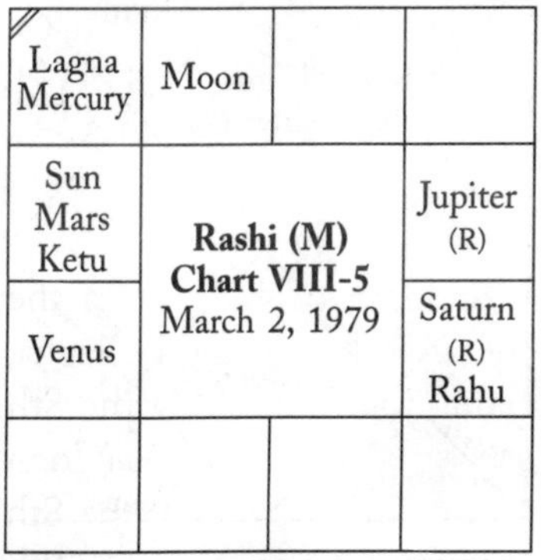

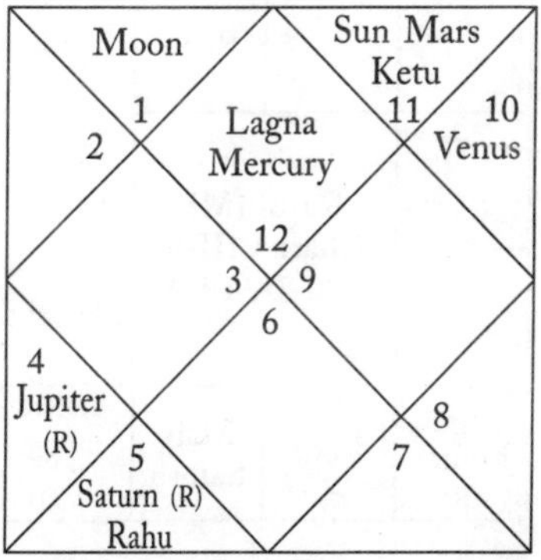

Lagna	25°02'	Mars	08°12'	Venus	04°35'
Sun	17°23'	Mercury	03°48'	Saturn (R)	16°57'
Moon	04°03'	Jupiter (R)	06°20'	Rahu	23°57'

Vimshottari dasha : Ketu-Moon-Mars. Ketu is in the 12th house with Mars as well as the 6th lord, and is aspected by a retrograde 12th lord. The Moon is in a maraka house. Mars is in the 12th house with the 6th lord and aspected by the 12th lord.

Yogini dasha : Bhramari-Ulka (Mars-Saturn). The role of Mars and Saturn has been already discussed.

Note : Severity of a disease generally depends upon the extent of affliction. When there is one afflicting factor, a curable disease results. When there are two afflictions, the malady is more severe. Three afflicting factors generally lead to an incurable disease. Mars here has triple affliction. It is involved in the RKA; it is associated with the Sun; it is aspected by Saturn.

Chart VIII-6

This is a case of severe cyanotic congenital heart disease which could only be partially rectified following surgery.

Vimshottari dasha : Jupiter-Venus-Mars. Jupiter is the retrograde lagna lord in the lagna. Venus is the 6th lord in the 8th house associated with the Sun and aspected by Saturn. Mars is the 12th lord associated with Saturn.

Yogini dasha : Pingala-Ulka (Sun-Saturn). The Sun is located in the 8th house along with the 6th lord, aspected by Saturn which is the AD lord and a malefic for this lagna.

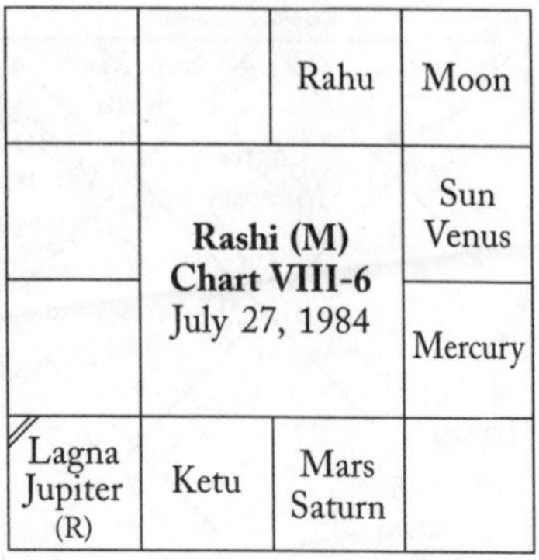

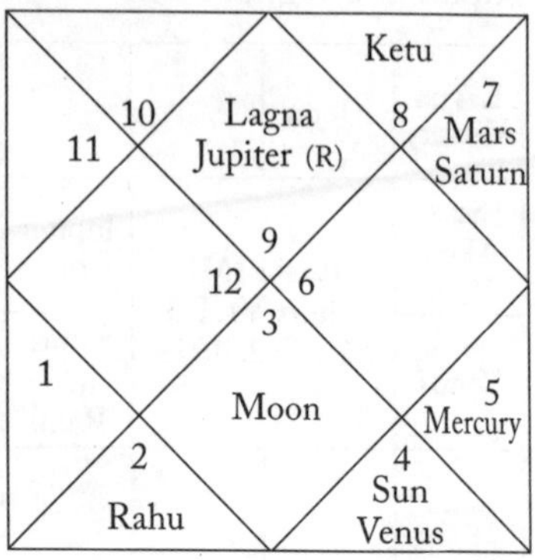

Lagna	08°32'	Mars	26°22'	Venus	22°25'
Sun	10°58'	Mercury	07°46'	Saturn	16°15'
Moon	27°16'	Jupiter (R)	11°10'	Rahu	09°51'

Note: Jupiter as the lagna lord in the lagna offers little protection as it is retrograde. It is further under the aspect of a malefic Saturn. Only partial recovery thus ensued.

Chart VIII-7

She suffers from renal rickets, a disease affecting the skeleton because of a deficiency of Vitamin D.

Vimshottari dasha: Mercury-Saturn-Venus. Mercury is the 8th lord. Saturn, a malefic, occupies the lagna in RKA, along with the lagna lord and 6th lord, Mars, and a debilitated Moon. Venus is the 12th lord.

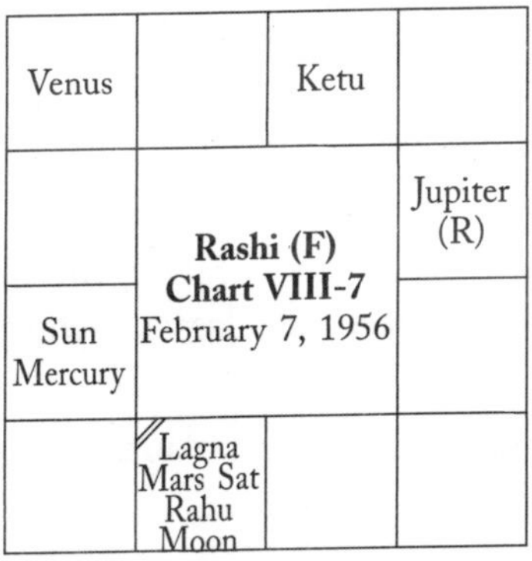

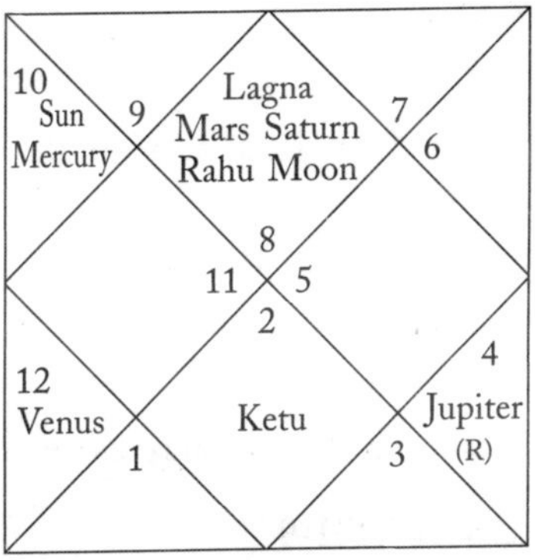

Lagna	15°30'	Mars	22°21'	Venus	01°25'
Sun	23°49'	Mercury	04°30'	Saturn	08°34'
Moon	28°50'	Jupiter (R)	04°30'	Rahu	22°09'

Yogini dasha : Bhadrika-Bhramari (Mercury-Mars). Mercury has been discussed already. Mars is the highly afflicted lagna lord, and the 6th lord, in the lagna.

Note : Mars is exactly on the same degree as Rahu and, therefore, grossly afflicted. An incurable ailment has been the result.

Chart VIII-8

He suffers from spondylo-epiphyseal dysplasia, a disorder of the skeletal system resulting in extremely short stature (approx. three feet).

Vimshottari dasha : Jupiter-Saturn-Rahu. Jupiter is the lagna lord in the 12th house associated with the 8th lord Venus. Saturn

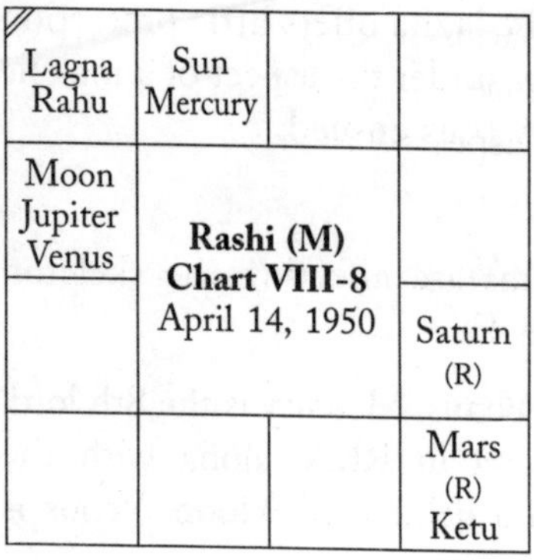

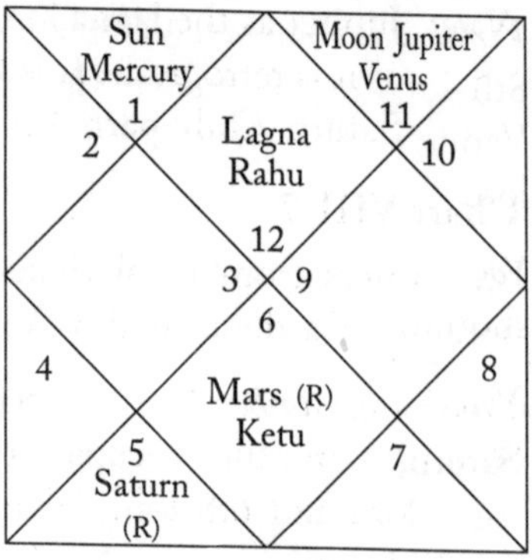

Lagna	16°16'	Mars (R)	01°21'	Venus	14°00'
Sun	00°19'	Mercury	17°00'	Saturn (R)	20°11'
Moon	23°26'	Jupiter	06°35'	Rahu	14°16'

is the 12th lord, retrograde in the 6th house. Rahu is situated in the lagna.

Yogini dasha : Bhramari-Ulka (Mars-Sat). Mars is retrograde in the 7th house along with Ketu, and aspects the lagna. Saturn has been discussed above.

Note : Rahu is fairly close to the cusp of the ascendant.

Chart VIII-9

The native suffers from Vitamin D–resistant renal rickets. Calcification of both kidneys and high blood pressure have resulted as a consequence of his treatment.

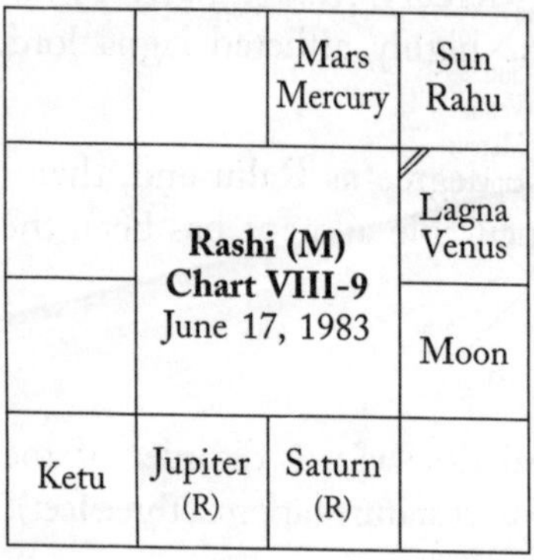

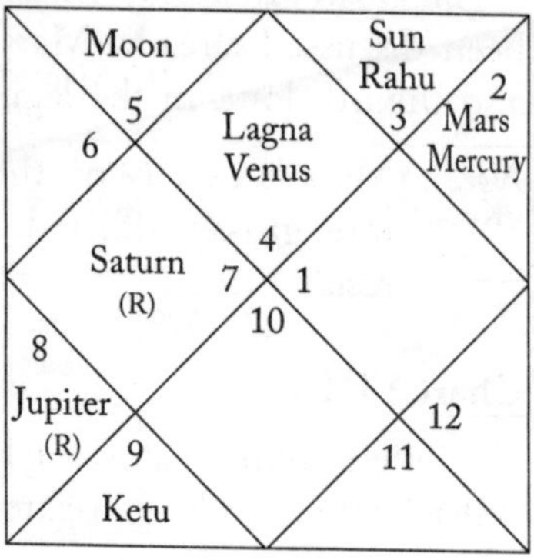

Lagna	15°53'	Mars	28°08'	Venus	17°08'
Sun	01°47'	Mercury	10°12'	Saturn (R)	04°16'
Moon	22°55'	Jupiter (R)	09°59'	Rahu	01°22'

Vimshottari dasha : Ven-Sat-Ven. Saturn is the malefic 7th and 8th lord, retrograde in the 4th house and aspecting the lagna. Venus is posited in the lagna and aspected by a retrograde 8th lord Saturn as well as by retrograde 6th lord Jupiter.

Yogini dasha: Ulka-Siddha (Saturn-Venus). Same as the Vimshottari dasha.

Note : The Sun on the same degree as Rahu in the 12th house indicates suffering for his father also (Chart VIII-8 above).

Chart VIII-10

This child had Thalassaemia major, a blood disorder which eventually proved fatal for him.

Vimshottari dasha : Mars-Mars-Saturn. Mars is a maraka, placed in a maraka house. Saturn is in RKA and aspects the lagna.

Yogini dasha : Sankata - Sankata (Rahu-Rahu). Rahu behaves as Saturn. Situated in the 4th house in Simha, it also behaves as the Sun which is associated with the 6th and the 8th lords, Venus and Jupiter. Venus is also the lagna lord.

Note : This chart has inherent weakness in it. There are no effective benefics in quadrants or the trines. Three malefics occupy the 4/10 axis. More importantly, the lagna lord Venus is on the same degree as the highly

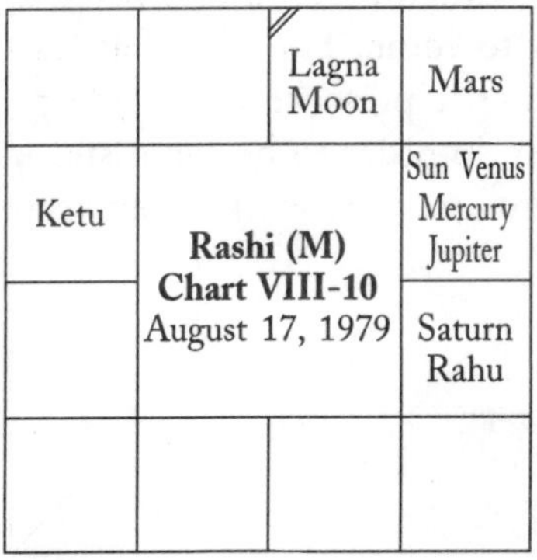

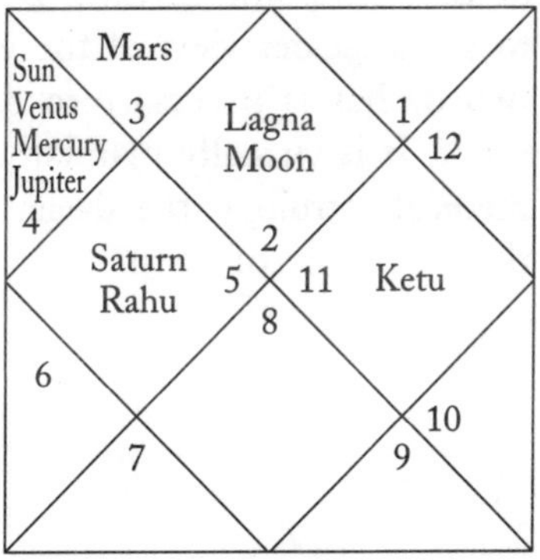

Lagna	17°38'	Mars	11°22'	Venus	27°20'
Sun	29°44'	Mercury	11°31'	Saturn	20°37'
Moon	23°44'	Jupiter	27°12'	Rahu	14°59'

malefic eighth (and eleventh) lord Jupiter; Venus is the loser here in planetary warfare. As lagna lord, Venus is also subject to a powerful Papakartari yoga, being hemmed between malefics.

Conclusion

Congenital ailments generally occur in the wake of malefic dasha periods, operating at the time of birth, involving the 6th house, the 8th house, the 12th house, the lagna and their lords. If there is an inherent weakness of the lagna or the lagna lord, the affliction becomes manifold. A strong Jupiter aspecting or associating with the Moon or the lagna is a protective factor. The retrogression of planets is generally adverse for health.

Involvement of planets in mutual warfare is also important. Subjugation of the lagna lord is an important factor. It may be remembered here that although the concept of planetary warfare is not applicable to the luminaries as well as to Rahu and Ketu in the strictest technical sense, any close proximity of planets to each other is to be considered important. Too close a proximity to the Sun or to Rahu or Ketu can damage any planet and produce adverse results in terms of health.

Mars and Ketu, and sometimes Saturn, involving the dasha lords operative at the time of birth tend to indicate surgical treatment. Cures result when affliction is small and benefic influences dominate. It is important to integrate the combinations of Balarishta and Arishta Bhanga with the dasha system so as to get a clearer view of the events to come. The use of at least two dashas is necessary to confirm the presence of an adverse event. It is virtually mandatory that, in order to be successful in medical astrology, the dasha scheme must be worked out from the very time of birth.

CHAPTER NINE

SOUND AND UNSOUND HEALTH

नैनं छिन्दन्ति शस्त्राणि नैनं दहति पावकः।
न चैनं क्लेदयन्त्यापो न शोषयति मारुतः।।

Weapons cleave it not, nor does fire burn it. Water moistens it not, nor does wind dry it up.

—GITA II-23

It is a well known medical principle that when a number of people are exposed to an infective illness, only a particular number contract that illness. Others tend to escape unaffected. During the most virulent epidemics, there are several people who remain untouched. In the case of hereditary diseases too, not all the children of the affected parents suffer. Several medical explanations have been put forward to explain this. The most pertinent explanation, amongst others, is the inherent resistance of a human being to an infective illness.

The proneness to disease varies from person to person. Not only is the virulence of a microbe important in causing a disease but also a poor resistance of the host and a suitable environment in his body. Those who suffer from debilitating disease, malnutrition or diabetes, for example, fall an easy prey to varying ailments. A well-nourished healthy individual, protected against infective illnesses by vaccination or other means, doesn't easily contract illness. The inherent body resistance and a lack of suitable environment for bacterial growth are important factors in protection against illness. The case of a microbiologist who consumed a culture of the cholera bacilli (containing billions of bacteria responsible for producing cholera) in the presence of an audience of scientists, and still did not suffer the illness, is an example not to be forgotten.

Medical astrologers need to keep the examples of medical science in mind. There are indications which show a sound health in one chart and unsound health in another. In a 'healthy' chart, an ordinarily malefic dasha will pass unnoticed, and only an extremely malefic dasha will prove adverse. In another chart indicating poor health, an ordinarily malefic dasha or a malefic transit may cause major upsets in health. It is thus vital, for an astrologer, to determine the inherent resistance of a chart against ill health.

The various factors which decide good or bad health are being briefly discussed below. The principles mentioned here need to be extended, as far as possible, to the divisional charts also.

Indications for Sound Health

The various factors that lead to good health are being mentioned below.

1. *Strong lagna* :

   The lagna is the single most important constituent of a horoscope. Planets are only subservient to the lagna. The lagna indicates the state of health of an individual. A lagna is strong in the following circumstances:

   (a) *Vargottama*, i.e., the sign rising in the lagna is the same as the Navamsha lagna. Vargottama is a special state of strength.

   (b) *Benefic occupation* : Natural benefics like Jupiter, Venus and unafflicted Mercury in the lagna are indicative of sound health. When the natural benefics also own good houses like the trines, they become still better.

   (c) *Benefic aspect* : Aspect of benefics on the lagna is an additional desirable factor.

   (d) *Occupation by the lagna lord* : Any house, when occupied by its own lord, tends to prosper and its indications get encouragement. The lagna being indicative of health becomes strong when occupied, or aspected, by its own lord.

   (e) *Raja yogas in the lagna* : Raja yogas are combinations of beneficence. The effects of various Raja yogas depend to a large extent on the houses involved by them. When Raja yogas form in the lagna, they strengthen the lagna and promote health.

2. *Strong lagna lord* :

   Whatever is indicated by a house is equally indicated by its lord. A house tends to prosper when its lord is strong and well placed. A planet gains strength when it is:

   (a) Exalted;

   (b) Vargottama, i.e., placed in the same sign in both the rashi chart and the Navamsha chart;

   (c) In its own house;

   (d) In the house of a friend;

   (e) Placed in a quadrant or a trine or 2nd house or 11th house;

   (f) Associated with or aspected by benefics or friendly planets; or

   (g) Participating in the formation of Raja yogas.

3. *Benefic 'Durudhara' around the lagna or the lagna lord* :

   Technically, a Durudhara yoga has been described as forming in relation to the Moon. When there are planets (other than the Sun) in the 2nd and the 12th houses from the Moon, a Durudhara yoga is said to form. It is supposed to be a beneficial yoga promising prosperity and comforts. When caused by benefics, it is productive of good results.

   A benefic Durudhara would form around the lagna or the lagna lord when benefic planets occupy the second and the twelfth positions from them. This could also be called as a *Shubha-Kartari yoga*, meaning that the lagna or the lagna lord is hemmed between benefics. Any house or planet hemmed between benefics tends to gain strength and produce benefic results.

4. *Unafflicted Moon* :

   A strong Moon is important for health and longevity. Several Arishta yogas have already been described in connection with the affliction of the Moon. A strong, unafflicted, Moon is also good for a sound mental health. A benefic Durudhara around the Moon is a positive factor for good physical and mental health of the native.

5. *Malefics in houses 3, 6 and 11* :
   A very potent factor for good health is the presence of malefics in the otherwise adverse houses, viz., 3, 6 and 11. The malefics in these houses provide physical strength, destruction of ailments and resistance against disease.

6. *Benefics in the trines* :
   The placement of benefics in the trines is also good for health.

7. *Benefics in the quadrants* :
   The quadrants are the pillars of a horoscope. Benefics as lords of the quadrants have not been praised by the classical writers of astrology, but their placement in the quadrants is highly desirable for a sound health. It may, however, be pointed out here that *benefics, when retrograde, do not provide any protection against disease. Instead they promote ill health.*

8. *Saturn in the eighth house* :
   Eighth house is the house of longevity. Saturn is the significator for longevity. According to an astrological dictum, the presence of a significator in its concerned house tends to destroy the indications of that house. For example, the Sun (significator for father) is adverse for father when located in the ninth house (house for father); the Moon (significator for mother) is adverse for mother when in the 4th house (house for mother); Mars (significator for brother) is adverse for brothers when in the third house (house for siblings). Saturn, however, is an exception. When placed in the eighth house, Saturn promotes good health and long life.

9. *Nature of the signs* :
   The twelve zodiacal signs, by their very nature, either resist against or succumb to disease. The fiery signs (i.e., signs 1, 5, 9) have the best resistance against disease and show prompt recovery. Next in order fall the earthy signs (i.e., signs 2, 6, 10) which have a fair amount of resistance. Airy signs (i.e., signs 3, 7, 11) come next in order. Those most susceptible to disease are the watery signs (i.e., signs 4, 8, 12); they have

relatively poor resistance against disease and show slow recovery once they contract it.

10. *Strong eighth lord* :
    A strong lord of the eighth house ensures good health.
11. *Strong Atma Karaka* :
    In the Jaimini system of astrology, the Atma Karaka is a planet which is the farthest advanced in a sign. A strong and well-placed Atma Karaka ensures good health.

    The Sun could be taken as the equivalent of the Atma Karaka in the Parashari system. The Sun stands for energy and vitality. If the Sun is strong in a chart, good health is generally ensured.
12. *Placement of Gulika/Mandi*:
    Gulika is the son of Saturn and is as malefic as, or worse than, the father. Gulika, like all other malefics, is good for health only in houses 3, 6 and 11; that too when it does not involve the Moon or the lagna lord. Gulika and Mandi may be taken as identical for all practical purposes.
13. *Houses 1 and 8 in Sarvashtakavarga* :
    Ashtakavarga is a system of working out the strength or weakness of various houses and planets on a numerical basis. It is an elaborate system which can be employed with a high degree of accuracy in conjunction with dashas and transits. The Sarvashtakavarga gives information about the total strength of individual houses in numerical terms, as contributed by the various planets. When the lagna and the 8th house are strong, according to the Sarvashtakavarga, it is an indication for sound health.

It is not necessary that all the above factors should be present in any one chart to ensure good health. Obviously, the more of them in a given chart, the better the health.

Indications for Ill Health

Combinations for ill health are the reverse of those indicating good health. They are being briefly mentioned below.

1. *Weak lagna* :
   A lagna becomes weak under the following circumstances:

(a) Occupation by malefics.

(b) Aspect of malefics, both natural as well as the lords of adverse houses.

(c) Presence of a debilitated planet in the lagna.

(d) Presence of adverse yogas in the lagna.

2. *Weak lagna lord* :

A lagna lord becomes weak when it is:

(a) Debilitated;

(b) Combust;

(c) In the house of an enemy;

(d) In an adverse house like the 6th or the 8th or the 12th.

(e) Associated with or aspected by malefics.

3. *Malefic 'Durudhara' around the lagna or lagna lord* :
Presence of malefic planets in the 2nd and 12th from the lagna or the lagna lord is bad for health. It can also be called as the *Paapa-Kartari yoga*, which literally means being hemmed between malefics.

4. *Afflicted Moon* :
Ill placement of the Moon, its debilitation or affliction by malefics, or a malefic Durudhara around it, is adverse for health.

5. *No malefics in houses 3, 6 and 11*:
An absence of malefics in these houses is a weak point which must be neutralised by other benefic combinations to ensure a sound health.

6. *Malefics in the trines* :
The trines are not the desired houses for malefics.

7. *Malefics in the quadrants* :
As opposed to benefics, the natural malefics are not bad as lords of the quadrants. But they are quite adverse when located in the quadrants. They are worse still if they are retrograde.

8. *Benefics in the eighth house* :
The eighth house is the house of chronicity and incurability. Benefics in the eighth house are wasted benefics; they would be more useful elsewhere

9. *Weak eighth lord* :
   Just as a strong lord of the eighth house is good for health, a weak and afflicted eighth lord proves adverse.

10. *Weak Atma Karaka* :
    A weak Atma Karaka or a weak Sun do not generally favour good health.

11. *Placement of Gulika/Mandi*:
    When Gulika is placed in the quadrants or trines, it produces adverse results. Its association with the lagna, the lagna lord, the Sun or the Moon does not augur well for health.

12. *Houses 1 and 8 in Sarvashtakavarga* :
    When these houses are weak according to the Sarvashtakavarga chart, poor health is indicated.

It must be emphasised here that ill health should not be predicted on the basis of one single factor. Several of these must be present to lead to proneness to disease. The presence of adverse factors must be suitably balanced against factors promising good health.

Indications for Cure or Recovery

All of us tend to suffer from ill health sometime or the other. The following factors generally indicate cure or recovery from ill health.

1. *Strong lagna* :
   The lagna is the single most important factor in the maintenance of health. A strong lagna and a strong lagna lord ensure recovery from disease.

2. *Strong 6th lord* :
   The strength of the 6th house and its lord promises a good body resistance and, therefore, recovery from illness.

3. *Favourable dasha* :
   Favourable major and sub-periods (MD and AD) ensure recovery from illness. The concept of the *subsequent dasha* is thus of significance. When a disease producing dasha is operating, if the subsequent dasha is favourable, it indicates recovery; if the subsequent dasha is unfavourable, it indicates no recovery or even complications. When several subsequent dashas are adverse one after the other, no recovery occurs.

4. *Favourable transit* :
   When transits indicate good results, recovery from disease occurs.
5. *Jupiter's aspect* :
   Jupiter is the best and the most potent natural benefic. When it aspects the dasha lords, either in the birth chart or during its transit, it favours recovery and good health.

Chart IX-1

This Chart belongs to a patient of progressive muscular dystrophy leading to difficulty in walking, and getting up from lying or sitting position.

The lagna lord is also the 8th lord placed in the 7th house in association with the Sun, and the 6th lord Mercury. A malefic Saturn aspects this combination. Three natural malefics, viz., the Sun, Mars and Saturn, are located in the quadrants. Of the two benefics in the quadrants, Mercury is the adverse 3rd and 6th lord and retrograde, while Jupiter is the 12th lord and debilitated.

That the disease is congenital is indicated by the Vimshottari dasha of Mars-Venus-Jupiter at the time of birth. Mars is the 8th lord (as also the lagna lord) associated with the 6th lord and aspecting the lagna. Venus is a maraka (lord of the 2nd and 7th houses), debilitated in the 6th house. Jupiter is the debilitated 12th lord associated with another malefic. The Moon is afflicted by Ketu and debilitated in the Navamsha.

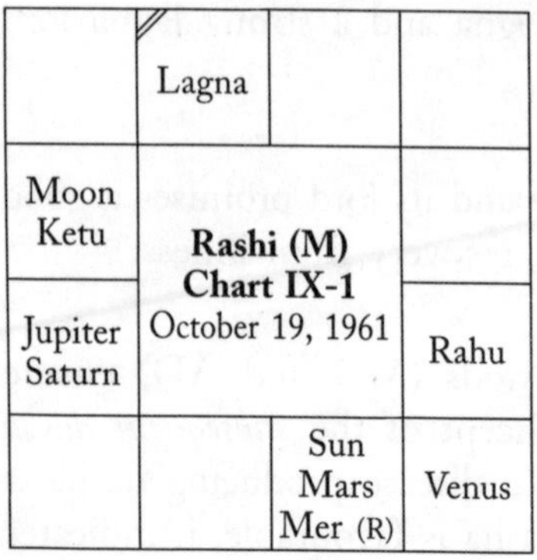

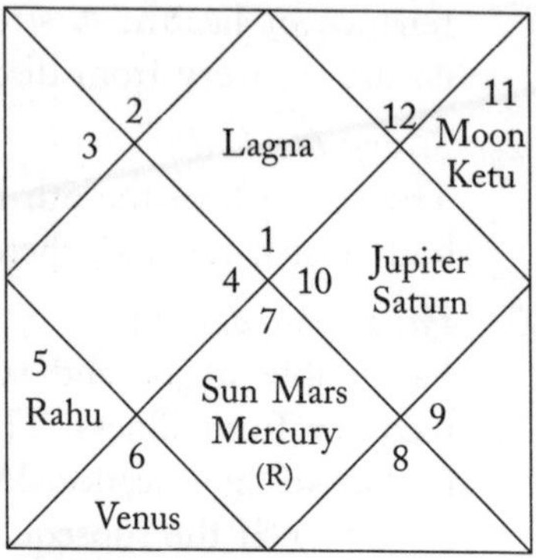

Lagna	29°35'	Mars	18°49'	Venus	08°28'
Sun	02°37'	Mercury (R)	09°44'	Saturn	00°18'
Moon	04°02'	Jupiter	05°04'	Rahu	02°06'

The Yogini dasha at birth was Pingala-Siddha (Sun-Venus). The Sun is debilitated in the 7th house in association with the 6th lord and the 8th lord, aspected by Saturn. Venus, debilitated in the 6th house, has already been commented upon.

Chart IX-2

Three malefics and the 12th lord Moon are located in the quadrants. The lagna is subjected to a Paapa-Kartari yoga. A malefic retrograde Saturn afflicts the lagna and the Moon.

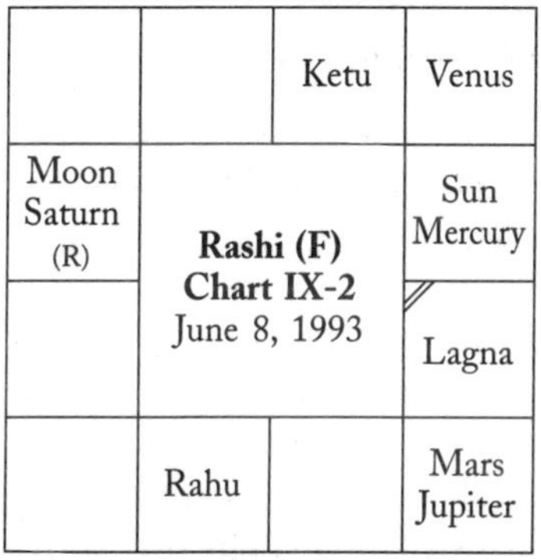

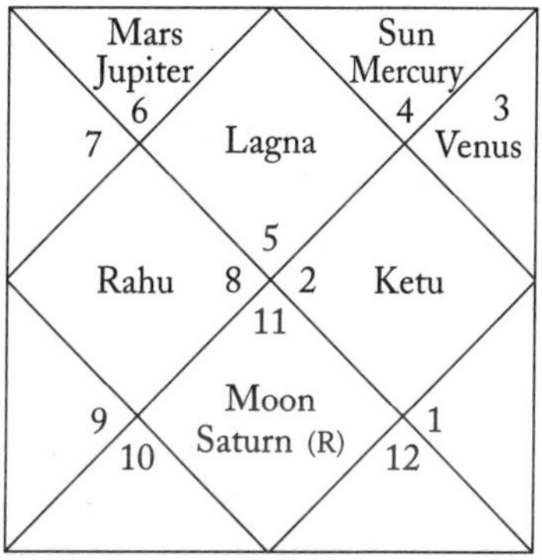

Lagna	11°32'	Mars	02°30'	Venus	10°59'
Sun	19°52'	Mercury	00°45'	Saturn (R)	04°13'
Moon	29°58'	Jupiter	06°46'	Rahu	16°06'

The native, a female child, has bilateral eye disease from the very birth. The Vimshottari dasha at the time of birth was Jup-Moon-Jup. Jupiter is the 8th lord, while the Moon is the 12th lord in the 7th house associated with the retrograde 6th lord Saturn.

In the Yogini dasha, Bhramari-Sankata (Mars-Rahu) was running. Mars is associated with the 8th lord Jupiter in the second, a maraka, house. Rahu in the 4th house is aspected by a retrograde Saturn, the 6th and 7th lord. Rahu in any case represents Saturn.

It will thus be seen that an inherent weakness in a chart leads to disease when a malefic dasha is also in operation. The horoscope is the static promise for an individual. The dasha is the dynamic factor which decides the time of fructification of a promise.

CHAPTER TEN

ONSET AND OUTCOME OF DISEASE

व्याधेरनिष्टसंस्पर्शाच्छ्रमादिष्टविवर्जनात् ।
दुःखं चतुर्भिः शारीरं कारणैः सम्प्रवर्तते ।।

Disease, undesired happenings, excessive physical labour, and dissociation from the objects of desire — these four cause physical torments.

—MAHABHARATA, ARANYA PARVA, CH.2, SL.22

The subject of the onset and outcome of disease is the most important area of medical astrology. It is natural for a consultor to be concerned about his health. When a patient is a consultor, he is also concerned about the outcome of his ailment. It may also be of concern to the medical man to know about the course a patient's ailment is likely to take. What is most important, however, is the fact that a medical astrologer can forecast the occurrence of a disease months and years in advance when the native may be in the soundest of his health and his physician may not even be able to dream of an illness for him.

The medical practitioner of today encounters disease in a passive manner. A patient or his relative comes to him and narrates his problem. The physician examines the patient and on the basis of his findings proceeds to conduct certain investigations to confirm his clinical diagnosis. Next follows the treatment which could be strictly medical or involve surgery also. The role of a medical astrologer starts before a person falls ill. The astrologer can work out the planetary periods that are adverse for a native's health. During the illness, the astrologer can determine the course of illness and the likely outcome. Unfortunately in his present state of astrological knowledge, he cannot make a sound medical diagnosis, a job which is best left to the modern day physician.

The narration that follows has been aimed to make an astrologer understand the period of illness for a native and the outcome of his illness. Simple astrological principles as laid down by the sage Parashara are being applied, in a scientific manner, to actual horoscopic charts of patients. As is understandable, no stress is being laid on the actual diagnosis of the disease which has, however, been mentioned for the interest of the reader. This chapter is an extension of the research work of the author, titled 'Disease: Its Onset and Outcome' published in the *Advanced Techniques of Astrological Predictions, Vol. I* edited by K.N. Rao.

THE RELEVANT ASTROLOGICAL PRINCIPLES

The uniqueness of Vedic astrology lies in its ability to time events by the use of dashas or operational periods. There are scores of dasha systems in Vedic astrology. The two most common dashas employed in India are the Vimshottari and the Yogini.

While any one dasha would give equally sound results when properly employed, the simultaneous use of two dashas provides greater confirmation and accuracy of predictions. These dashas are to be employed in the rashi chart as also the relevant divisional charts.

I. The Vimshottari Dasha

It is a cycle of 120 years with all nine planets having specific number of years allotted to them.

1. In order that an event may be timed with any degree of accuracy, it is appropriate to calculate the Vimshottari dasha from Mahadasha (MD, or the major period) through Antardasha (AD, or the sub-period) upto Pratyantardasha (PD, or the sub-sub-period). The MD gives a broad timing; the AD narrows it down; the PD indicates the actual precipitation of an event.
2. The disease as commonly understood is an affliction of the body. In a horoscopic chart, the body is represented by the lagna as well as the lagna lord. It is logical to assume that the state of the lagna and the lagna lord in the rashi chart as well as the divisional charts should reflect the state of health of the native.

3. The sage Parashara has mentioned certain Ashubha (malefic and generally adverse) and Maraka (death inflicting) planets for each lagna. When the dasha of a planet adverse to a particular lagna is in operation, it would tend to adversely affect the health of a person, in other words leading to proneness to disease. Thus the MD, AD and PD of the malefics as well as the death inflictors are the periods to be watched in regard to health.
4. The adverse influence would be more pronounced if the lords of the MD, AD and PD are in any way connected with the lagna or the lagna lord. The underlying principle is that since the lagna and the lagna lord represent the body, any link of a benefic or a malefic dasha lord with the lagna or the lagna lord would favourably or unfavourably influence health.
5. The adverse results get further accentuated if the lagna, the lagna lord and the lords of the MD, AD and PD get afflicted by natural malefics. Further aggravation results from their association with the Trika (6, 8, 12) houses or Trika lords.
6. Dashas of planets falling in or owning the 22nd Drekkana or the 64th Navamsha are also adverse.
7. Rahu-Ketu axis (RKA) falling on the lagna, the lagna lord, or the dasha lords is an adverse factor. Also, Rahu behaves as Saturn and Ketu as Mars.
8. Benefic influences on the lagna, the lagna lord and the dasha lords tend to decrease or neutralise affliction.

II. The Yogini Dasha

The Yogini dasha is a cycle of thirty-six years. It is thus possible that a disease may occur in the first or the second or even the third cycle of Yogini dasha. In the present context, the Yogini dasha has been employed as a confirmatory tool to the Vimshottari dasha. For a detailed application of it, the reader is referred to the *Applications of Yogini Dasha* by Jhanji and Sharma.

1. In the case of the Yogini dasha, the MD and AD must be calculated.
2. Since the eight different Yoginis have eight different planets

as their lords (Rahu and Ketu here work as one unit) any particular MD or AD is taken as the MD or AD of the planet owning that Yogini.

3. To these MD and AD lords, the same principles of analysis are applied as to the Vimshottari dasha lords.

III. The Divisional Charts

For medical astrology, the rashi, the Navamsha, the Drekkana and the Dwadashamsha must be used. The condition of the lagna, the lagna lord and the dasha lords must be judged in the rashi chart as also the various divisional charts.

IV. The Inherent Strength

The inherent strength of a chart, besides the strength of the lagna and the lagna lord, must be judged from the following:

1. Benefics in quadrants: They provide the best protection. Malefics here indicate ill health.
2. Malefics in houses 3, 6 and 11 provide strength, stamina and resistance to disease. Benefics in these houses only waste their beneficence.
3. Retrograde planets: Retrograde benefics in quadrants do not provide any protection and in fact lead to disease, during their MD/ AD/ PD. The malefics under similar situations are worse.

   Note : It is the natural malefics and benefics that are being considered here.

Method of Application of Astrological Principles

In order to apply the principles mentioned above, to actual horoscopes, a methodical approach as detailed below is suggested.

1. *The operative dasha* : Find out if the MD, AD and PD lords (or only MD and AD lords in case of Yogini dasha) are malefic or otherwise to the lagna concerned.
2. *Dasha relation with the lagna/ lagna lord* : See if the particular dasha lords have any relationship with the lagna or the lagna lord. The points to be considered here are:

(a) Dasha of a planet in the lagna;

(b) Dasha of a planet aspecting the lagna;

(c) Dasha of the lagna lord itself;

(d) Dasha of a planet associated with the lagna lord;

(e) Dasha of a planet aspecting the lagna lord.

When an adverse dasha lord associates with the lagna or the lagna lord in any of the ways described above, the health of the individual is adversely affected.

3. *Malefic influence* : The influence (by conjunction, aspect, exchange, etc.) of natural malefics or the Trika houses or the Trika lords on the MD, AD and PD lords as well as on the lagna and the lagna lord, is an additional adverse factor.

4. *The importance of the RKA* : The Rahu-Ketu axis is an important factor in causing disease. As has already been pointed out, Rahu gives the results of Saturn and Ketu of Mars. In addition, Rahu and Ketu give results of the lords of signs wherein they are placed and of planets associating with them. Involvement of any dasha lords in the RKA increases the maleficence of such dasha lords.

5. *The divisional charts* : The dasha lords must be thoroughly examined in the divisional charts also. The following factors need attention in this regards.

   (a) Ownership, by a dasha lord, of the lagna or the house occupied by the lagna lord.

   (b) Placement of the dasha lords in relation to the lagna or the lagna lord. For example, the dasha lords located in the 6th, 8th or 12th from the lagna or the lagna lord in a divisional chart suffer affliction.

   (c) Ownership by dasha lords, of adverse houses, like the 6th, the 8th or the 12th, in the divisional chart, or their association with lords of such houses;

   (d) Aspect or association of malefics like Mars and Saturn, or benefics like Jupiter, is also important.

   (e) Involvement of the dasha lords in RKA increases their malevolence.

(f) Any connection of the dasha lords with the sign coinciding with the ascendant of the rashi chart further accentuates the influence of a particular dasha on the health of the native.

6. *Protective influences* : A horoscope which is inherently strong does not indicate any suffering to the native in the wake of an ordinarily adverse dasha. Benefics in the quadrants and malefics in the houses 3, 6 and 11 are important in this regard besides, of course, the inherent strength of the lagna and the lagna lord. Retrogression of planets is generally bad for health. The dashas of retrograde planets must be watched carefully.
7. *The dasha sequence* : It is ever important to see the nature of dasha sequence. An adverse dasha followed by a benefic dasha indicates recovery from disease. On the other hand, when the subsequent dasha is also adverse, the disease goes on and may get complicated. When malefic periods follow one after the other, there is no cure but only continuous suffering or even death.
8. *Extent of severity* : The severity of an illness depends on the extent of malefic influences on the lagna, the lagna lord and the dasha lords. Malefic transits of planets also aggravate illness whereas benefic transits herald relief.

APPLICATION OF PRINCIPLES : Examples

The above mentioned principles are now being applied to actual cases. Cases of lesser severity are being dealt with first while those with more severe or lethal ailments have been discussed in the later part of this narration.

Chart X-1

This chart belongs to a young child who had a torsion of his left testis when he was in his 5th year. To save him from developing a complete gangrene of his testis, he was operated on April 28, 1994.

Three benefics (Mercury, Jupiter, Venus) and a retrograde malefic (Saturn) occupy the quadrants. Rahu in the 6th house is aspected by Jupiter. It is a case of a day birth with the Moon in

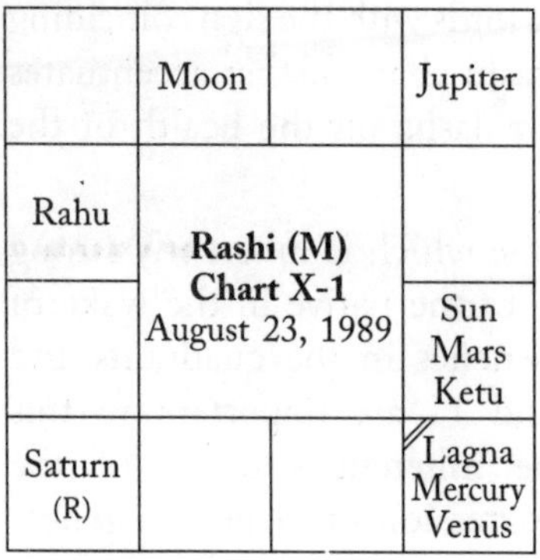

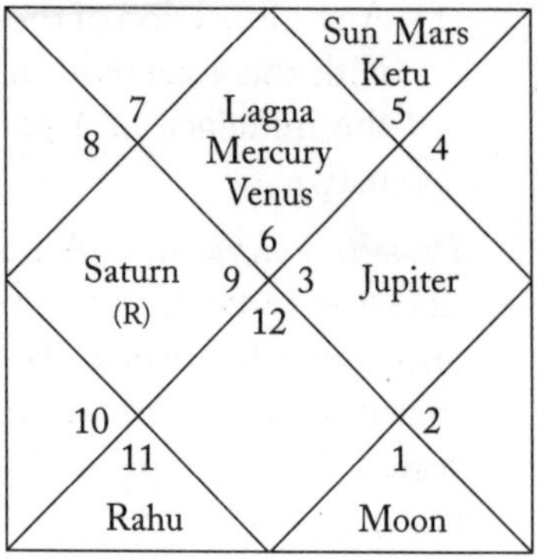

Lagna	02°50'	Mars	18°39'	Venus	12°15'
Sun	06°14'	Mercury	02°40'	Saturn (R)	13°53'
Moon	27°24'	Jupiter	10°41'	Rahu	02°05'

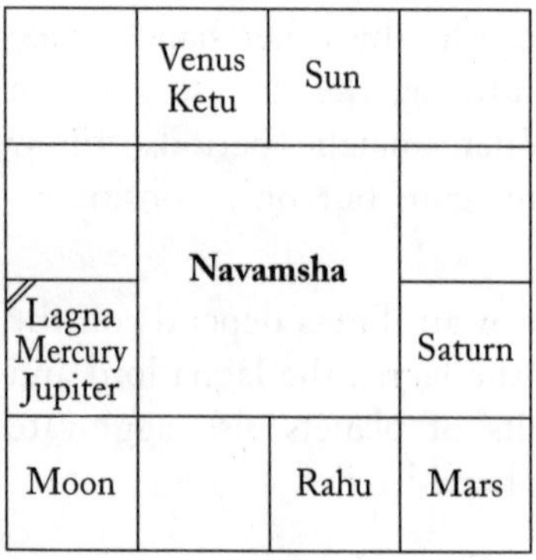

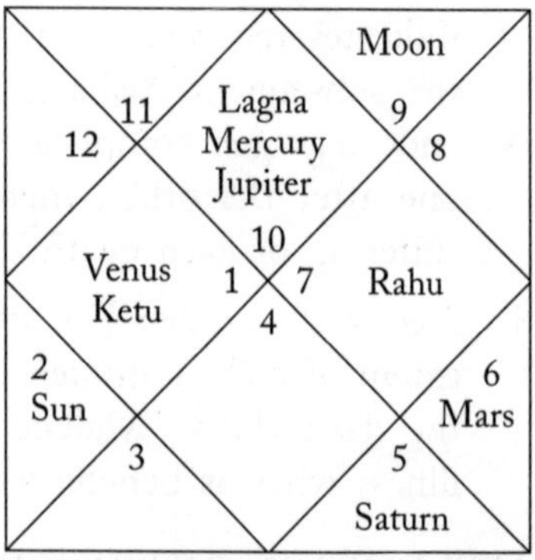

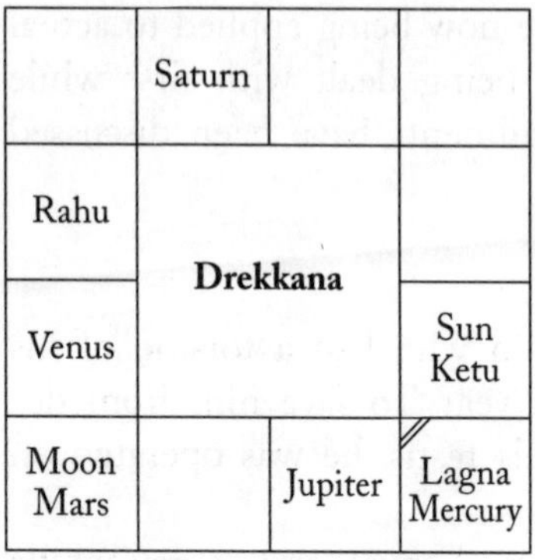

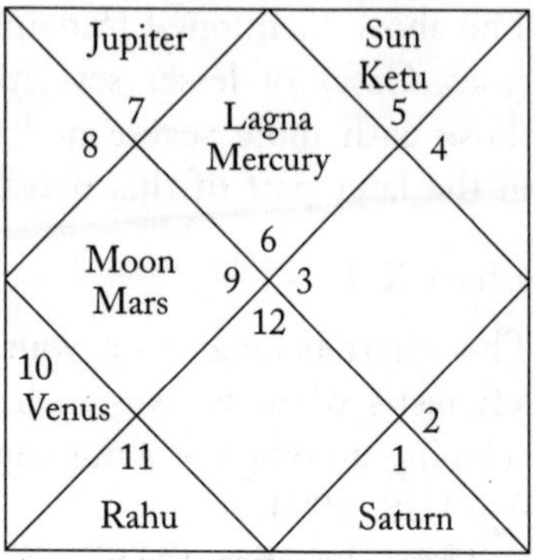

a waning phase. The lagna lord is exalted in the lagna. A rectifiable weakness lies in a debilitated planet occupying the lagna in

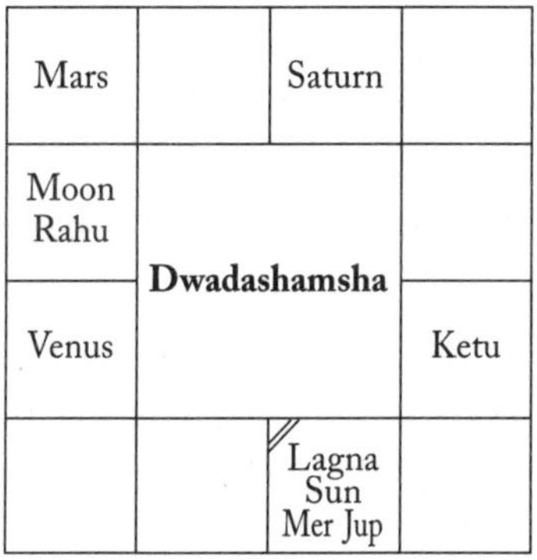

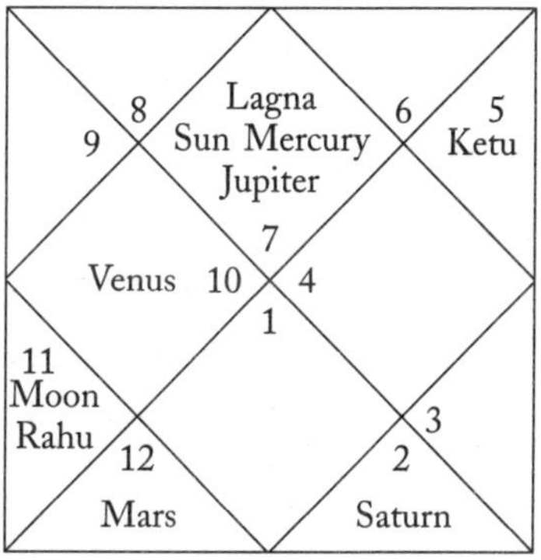

association with the lagna lord. A retrograde Saturn, itself aspected by Jupiter, aspects the lagna from the 4th house. All divisional charts show predominant benefic influence on the lagna.

Vimshottari dasha : Sun-Venus-Venus from April 25, 1994 to June 25, 1994.

The Sun (MD) is the lord of the 12th house (hospitalisation) associated with Ketu and the 8th lord Mars. In the Navamsha it is the 8th lord aspected by Saturn, the lagna lord, from the 8th house. The Drekkana chart shows the Sun with Ketu in the 12th house. In the Dwadashamsha, the Sun is debilitated in the lagna and aspected by a malefic Mars.

Venus (AD and PD) is associated with the lagna lord in the lagna and aspected by a retrograde 6th lord Saturn. In the Navamsha, Venus is in the RKA aspected by Mars. In the Drekkana, Venus is aspected by Saturn, the 6th lord, from the 8th house. In the Dwadashamsha, Venus is the lagna lord.

Yogini dasha : Ulka-Bhramari (Saturn-Mars) from October 24, 1993 to June 24, 1994.

Saturn (MD) is the 6th lord, retrograde, aspecting the lagna and the lagna lord. Saturn occupies the 8th house in the Navamsha chart. In the Drekkana, Saturn is debilitated in the 8th house. In the Dwadashamsha, Saturn is again in the 8th house.

Mars (AD) is the 8th lord, in RKA, in the 12th house along with the 12th lord. Mars doesn't associate with the lagna or the lagna lord. For the Navamsha chart too, Mars is an adverse lord but under benefic influence. In the Drekkana chart, Mars is the adverse 8th lord, again not related to the lagna or the lagna lord.

It occupies the 6th house of the Dwadashamsha and aspects the lagna which, however, is under predominantly benefic influence.

Note : (i) Repeated influence of Mars and Ketu indicates surgical treatment.

(ii) Predominantly benefic influence on the lagna and the quadrants ensures recovery. The subsequent PD of the Sun, however, is not all too beneficial and only partial or delayed recovery is indicated.

(iii) In the Yogini dasha, the subsequent AD of Bhadrika (Mercury) is also under the influence of a retrograde Saturn though it is under benefic influence in all divisional charts.

Chart X-2

This child was born with bilateral undescended testes. Both his testes were lying in the abdomen. On May 2, 1994, his testes were surgically brought down to the scrotum. The Vimshottari dasha operating at birth was Rahu-Sun-Merc, involving the lagna, the 8th house and the 6th house, thus indicating the presence of a congenital defect. The Yogini dasha at birth was Pingala-Sankata, equivalent to Sun-Rahu confirming the indications of the Vimshottari dasha.

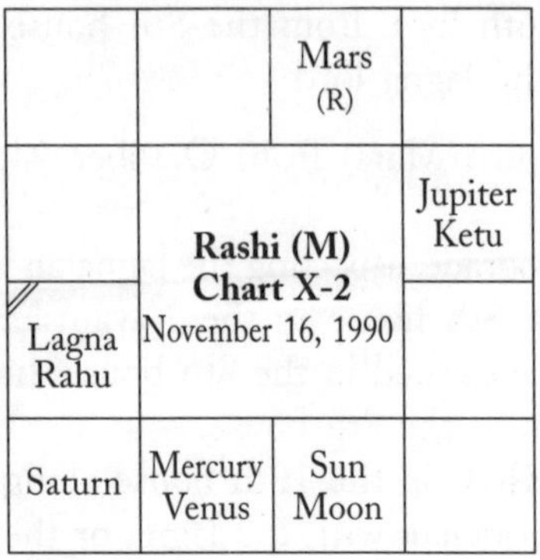

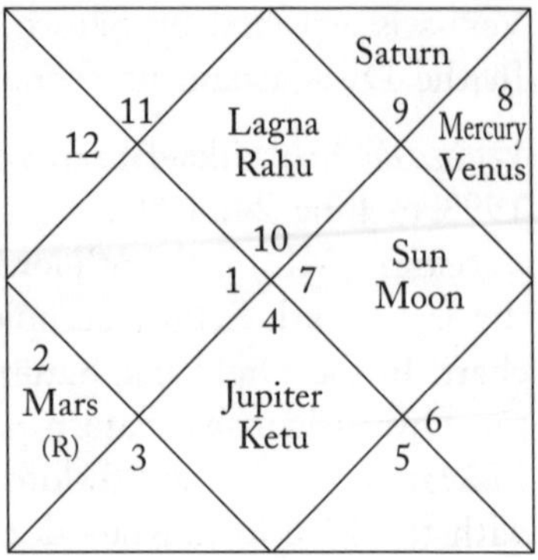

Lagna	17°48'	Mars (R)	15°53'	Venus	03°35'
Sun	29°55'	Mercury	14°12'	Saturn	27°17'
Moon	17°54'	Jupiter	19°33'	Rahu	06°46'

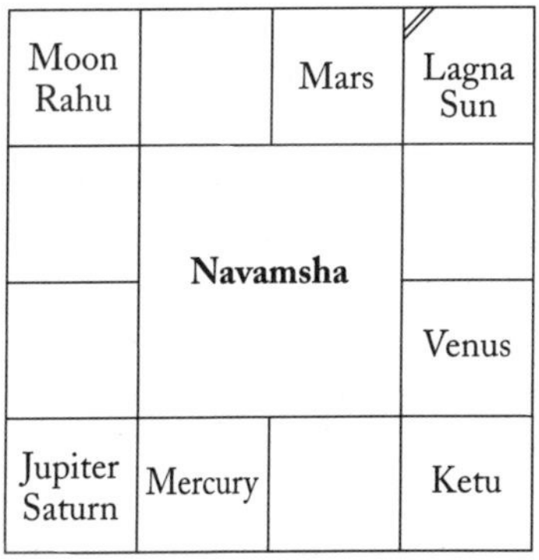

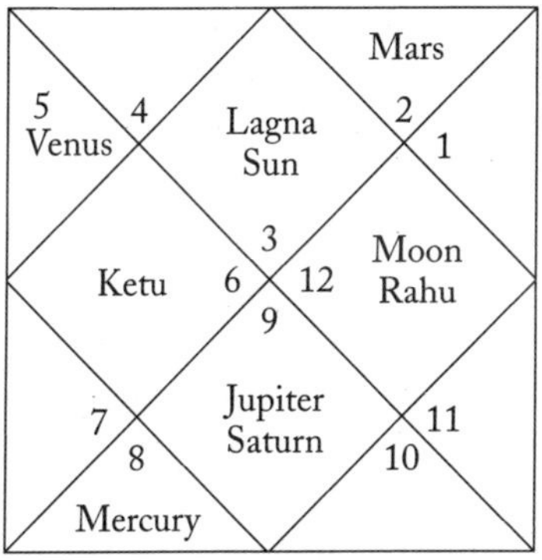

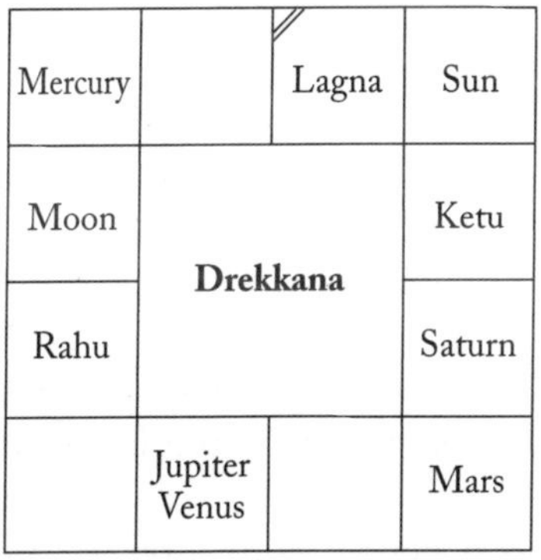

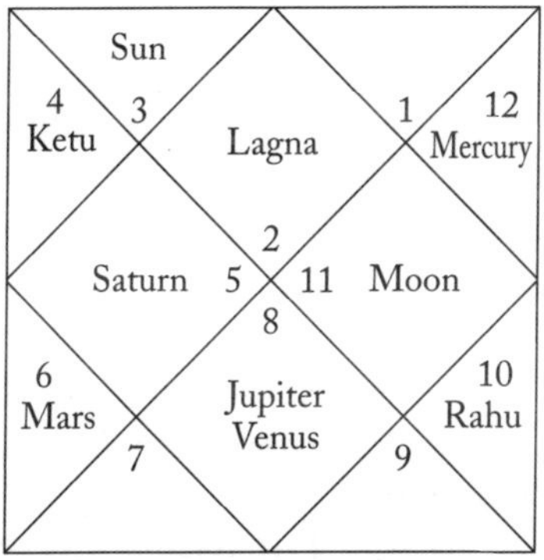

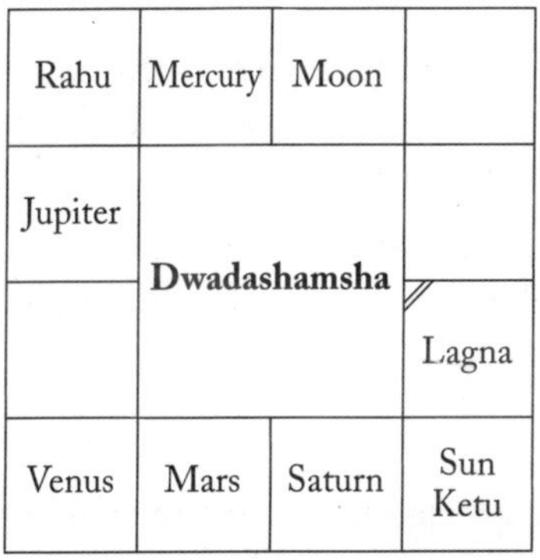

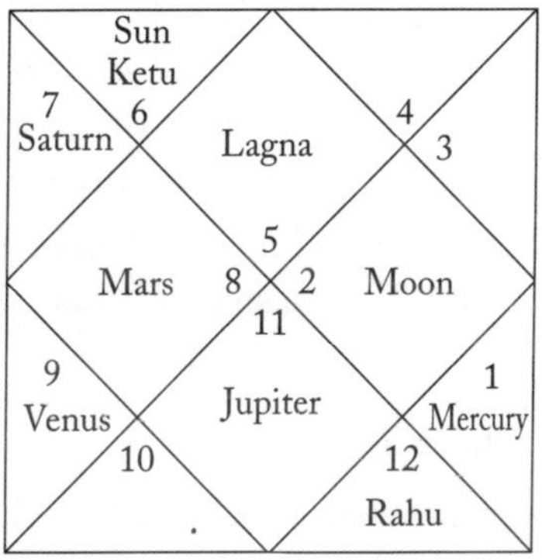

Vimshottari dasha : At the time of curative surgical treatment, the dasha running was Jupiter-Jupiter-Mercury. The MD and the AD lord Jupiter is a malefic lord in the RKA. It is, however, an exalted Jupiter and aspects the lagna from the 7th house. The PD lord Mercury is the 6th lord aspected by a retrograde Mars.

Mercury, however, is also the 9th lord and, in association with the 10th lord Venus, forms a benefic yoga which also receives the aspect of an exalted Jupiter.

In the Navamsha, Jupiter is associated with the 8th lord Saturn and aspects the lagna. Mercury is the lagna lord in the 6th house, aspected by the 6th lord Mars.

In the Drekkana, Jupiter is the lord of the 8th house associated with the lagna lord and aspecting the lagna. Mercury is debilitated and aspected by the 8th lord Jupiter as well as by Mars.

Jupiter happens to be the 8th lord in the Dwadashamsha chart also, and is aspected by Mars. Mercury is aspected by the 6th lord Saturn.

Yogini dasha: Bhramari-Bhramari (Mars-Mars) from March 9, 1994 to August 19, 1994. Mars as a retrograde malefic aspects the lagna lord Saturn in the 12th house.

In the Navamsha, Mars is the 6th lord aspecting the lagna lord Mercury located in the 6th house.

In the Drekkana, Mars is a malefic lord aspected by a debilitated Mercury, but has no direct relation with the lagna or the lagna lord.

In the Dwadashamsha, Mars is a benefic lord aspected by the 12th lord, the Moon.

Note : (a) It will be seen that a strong Jupiter aspects the lagna in all the divisional charts. The repeated role of Mars confirms surgical intervention.

(b) The subsequent PD of Ketu and the AD of Yogini dasha of Bhadrika (Mercury) are under Jupiterian influence.

Chart X-3

Two malefics and two benefics occupy quadrants in the chart of this frail girl who underwent surgical removal of appendix for recurrent appendicitis on September 29, 1993. The lagna lord is located in the eighth house in association with Jupiter.

Vimshottari dasha : Venus-Rahu-Saturn operated from August 24, 1993 to February 24, 1994.

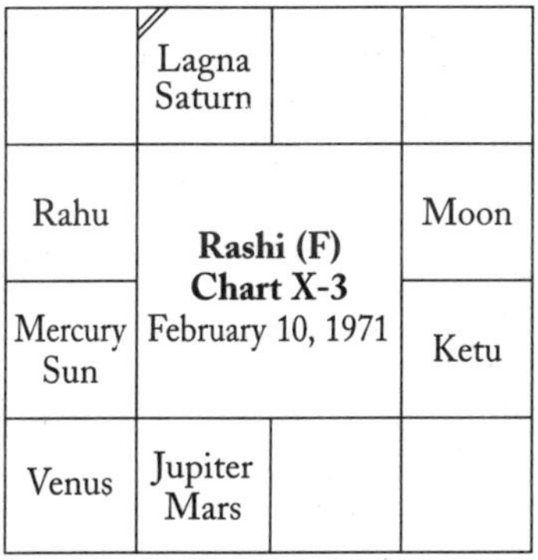

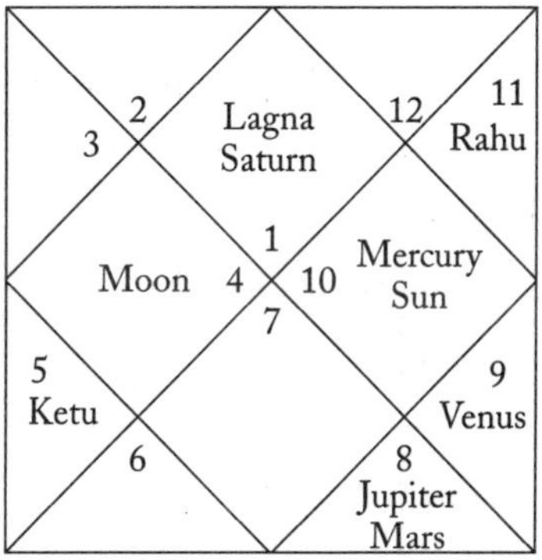

Lagna	15°01'	Mars	17°51'	Venus	11°36'
Sun	27°21'	Mercury	10°04'	Saturn	22°46'
Moon	24°07'	Jupiter	10°27'	Rahu	00°04'

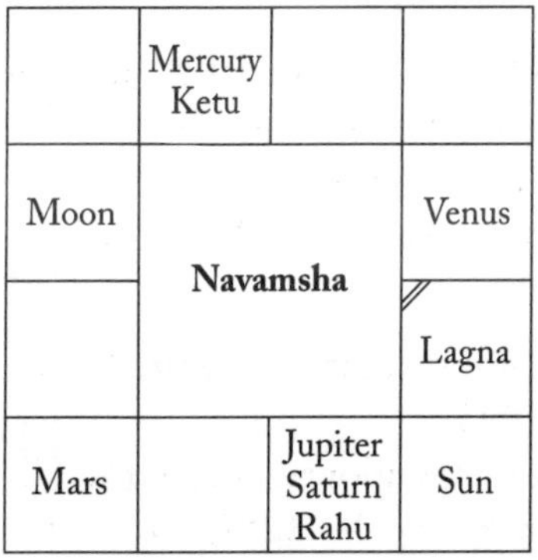

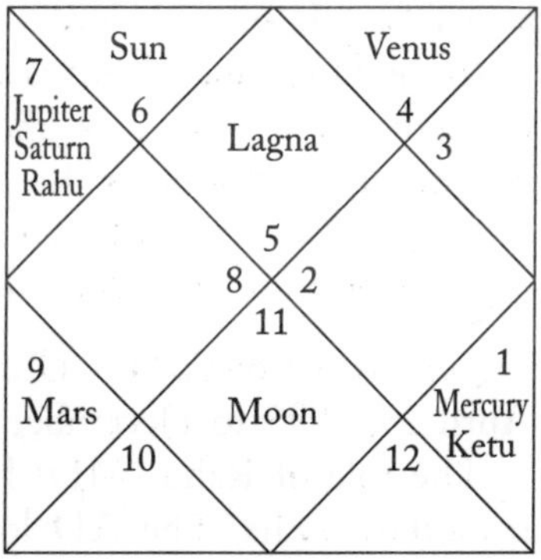

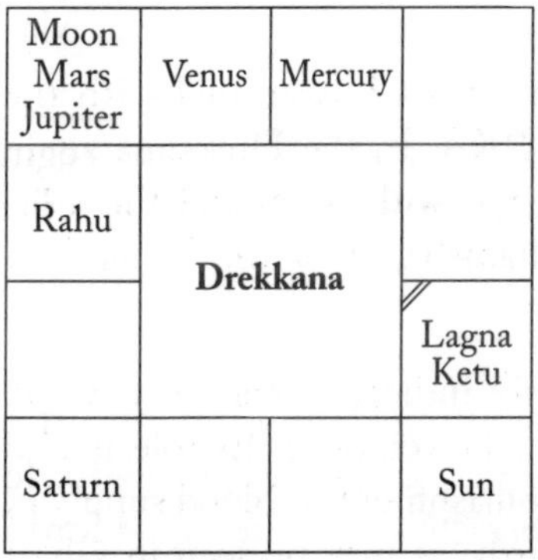

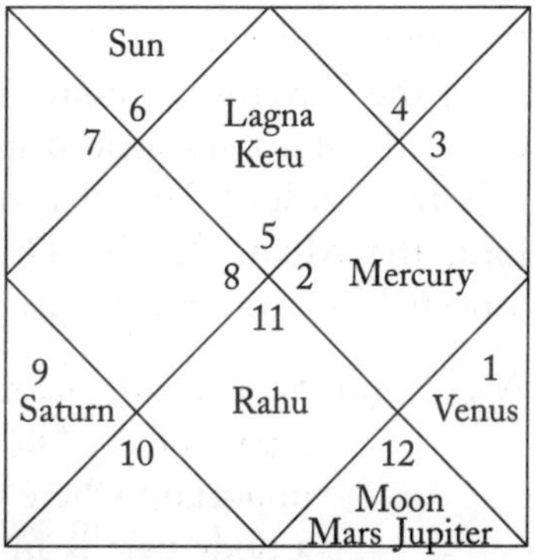

Venus (MD) is a maraka for Mesha lagna. Rahu (AD) behaves as Saturn and is aspected by the 8th lord, Mars, from the 8th house. Saturn (PD) is a malefic, debilitated in the lagna.

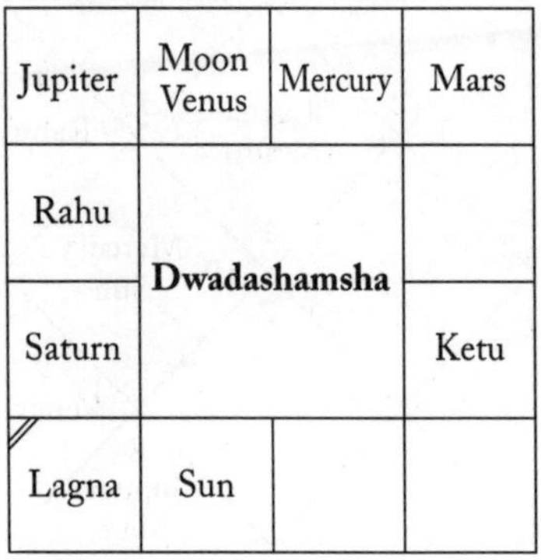

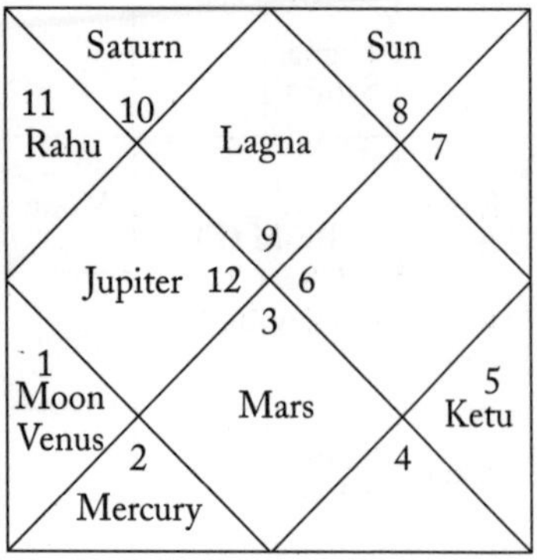

In the Navamsha, Venus is a malefic lord in the 12th house, aspected by the 6th lord Saturn and by Mars. Rahu in association with the 6th and the 8th lords is a malefic. Saturn too is a malefic 6th and 7th lord.

In the Drekkana, Venus is a malefic by lordship. RKA involves the lagna - 7th house axis, and Saturn aspects Rahu. Saturn itself is a malefic and aspects the lagna lord, the Sun.

In the Dwadashamsha chart, Venus, Rahu and Saturn are all malefics and under malefic influence.

Yogini dasha : Sankata - Dhanya (Rahu-Jupiter) operated from April 25, 1993 to December 25, 1993.

The role of Rahu (MD) has been mentioned under the Vimshottari dasha. The AD lord Jupiter is the 12th lord of the rashi chart placed in the 8th house with the 8th lord as well as the lagna lord Mars.

In the Navamsha, Jupiter is the 8th lord associated with the 6th lord Saturn and placed in the RKA. In the Drekkana again it is the 8th lord; here it is associated with Mars and the 12th lord, the Moon. In the Dwadashamsha, it is the lagna lord aspected by a malefic Saturn.

Note : (a) Saturn not uncommonly indicates treatment where a part of the body is to be removed. Its role is also important where the nourishment or blood supply of a body part is in jeopardy, as may be seen in Chart X-1 vide supra.

(b) The subsequent PD of Mercury is not too good though it is followed by Ketu which is better. It indicates delayed recovery. In Yogini, the subsequent AD of Bhramari is better.

Chart X-4

The native of this chart had his right kidney removed on April 8, 1996 since the kidney had developed hydronephrosis (a pathological distension or swelling because of obstruction) and had lost its function.

Vimshottari dasha : Saturn-Jupiter-Mercury was in operation from January 6, 1996 to May 16, 1996.

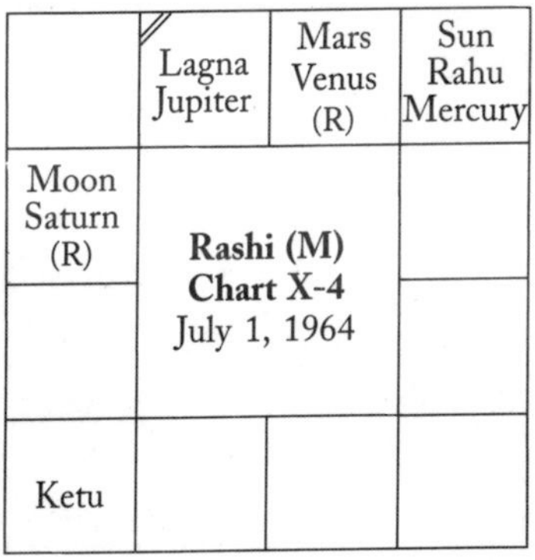

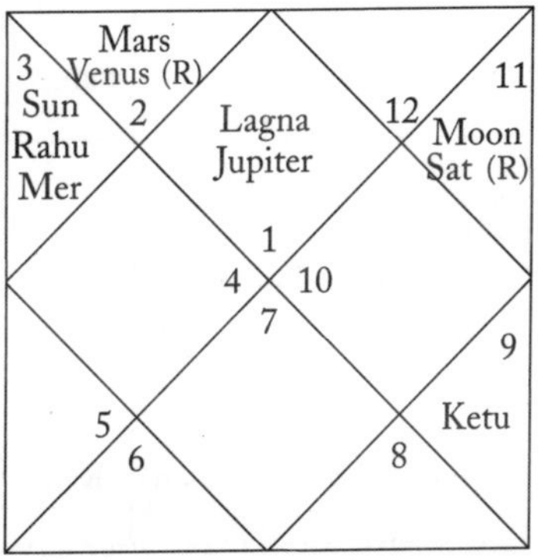

Lagna	26°16'	Mars	16°07'	Venus (R)	29°14'
Sun	15°42'	Mercury	20°01'	Saturn (R)	11°29'
Moon	21°24'	Jupiter	24°35'	Rahu	08°41'

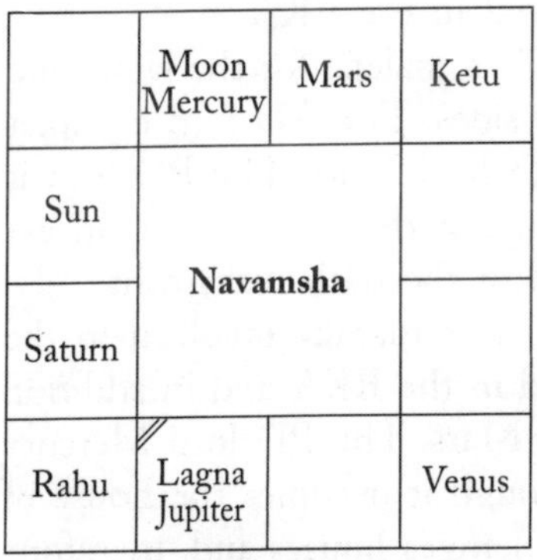

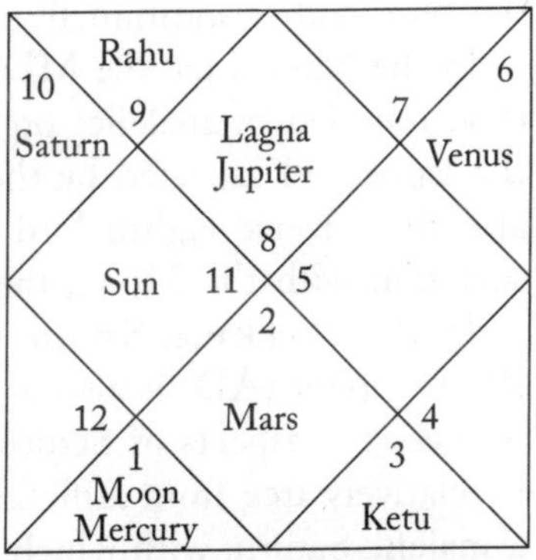

Saturn (MD) is a malefic for Mesha lagna. It aspects the lagna from the eleventh house. Its malefic potential increases as it happens to be retrograde. Jupiter (AD) is the twelfth lord

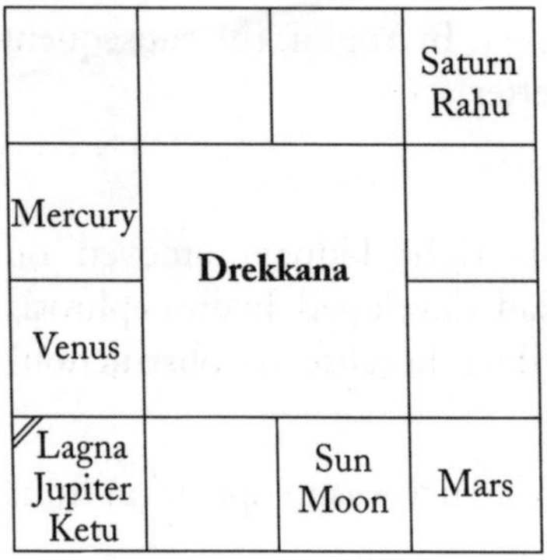

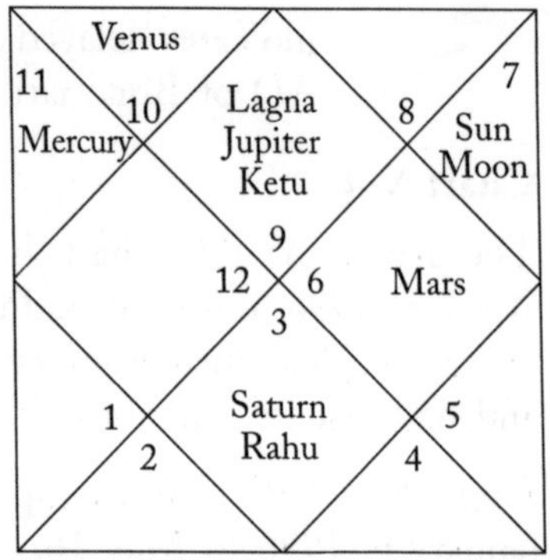

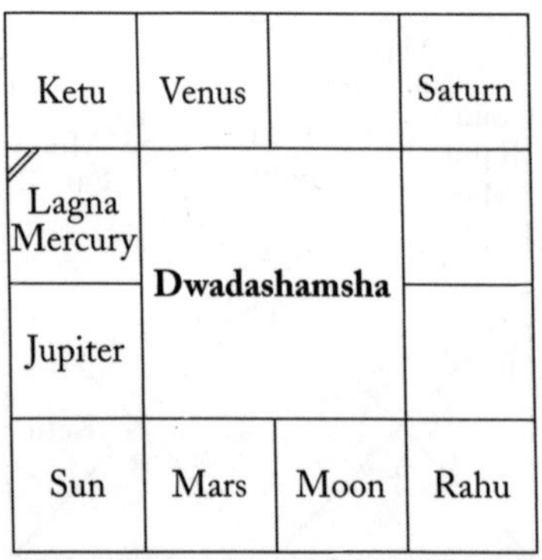

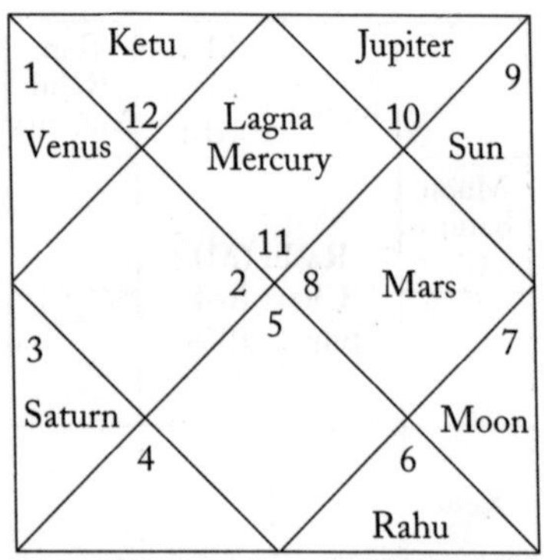

occupying the lagna and aspected by a retrograde, malefic Saturn. Mercury (PD) is malefic for Mesha lagna, being the lord of the third and the sixth houses. It is associated with a natural malefic, the Sun, and is additionally involved in the RKA.

In the Navamsha, the MD lord is a malefic for the lagna and is surrounded by malefics on both sides. The AD lord occupies the lagna and aspected by the sixth lord Mars. The PD lord is also the adverse eighth lord occupying the sixth house, in association with the Moon, the lord of the 64th Navamsha.

In the Drekkana, Saturn (MD) is a maraka involved in the RKA. Jupiter (AD) is also involved in the RKA and in addition receives the aspects of Saturn and Mars. The PD lord Mercury is relatively free from affliction though it occupies the house of a malefic Saturn, with which it exchanges houses and, therefore, gets linked.

In the Dwadashamsha, Saturn is the lagna lord aspected by the inimical Sun and Mars. Jupiter is a maraka debilitated in the twelfth house. Mercury is the eighth lord occupying the lagna and aspected by Mars. Note that here again, Mercury and Saturn exchange houses and thus get interconnected with each other.

Yogini Dasha : Pingla-Siddha (Sun-Venus) from March 9, 1996 to July 29, 1996.

The Sun (MD) is afflicted by its association with the sixth lord Mercury and the RKA. Venus (AD) is the retrograde maraka associated with the eighth lord Mars.

In the Navamsha, the Sun occupies an inimical sign while Venus is debilitated. There is no malefic association or aspect on the MD and AD lords. In the Drekkana, the Sun is debilitated and associated with the eighth lord Moon. Venus is a malefic occupying the sign of an afflicted Saturn. In the Dwadashamsha, the Sun receives the aspect of Saturn while Venus receives that of the sixth lord Moon.

Note :

(a) The presence of Jupiter in the lagna is a conspicuous feature of this chart. Since Jupiter lies fairly close to the lagna, it tends to occupy the lagna in most of the divisional charts. Jupiter here provides a lot of protection against ill health.

(b) Another important factor ensuring sound health is the presence of three malefics (Sun, Rahu and Saturn) in houses three and eleven. The retrogression of Saturn, however, is an adverse factor. The native made an uneventful recovery after surgery.

(c) In all ailments of the kidney, the Karaka Venus is likely to be variously afflicted, in the rashi chart and/or in the divisional charts. This feature will be noticed in other charts also, discussed in this chapter, where ailments related to kidney are mentioned.

(d) The subsequent PD of Ketu is better since Ketu occupies the ninth house with the healing aspect of Jupiter, the other aspects notwithstanding. In the Yogini dasha, the subsequent dasha of Sankata (Rahu) is better since Rahu in the third house must ensure recovery and good health. In the application of Yogini dasha, the Karaka seems to be of greater significance; in this case the dasha of the Karaka Venus (Siddha) caused the renal ailment.

Chart X-5

The native of this chart had a stone removed from his left kidney on June 11, 1992.

Vimshottari dasha: Saturn-Jupiter-Rahu from May 25, 1992 to October 12, 1992.

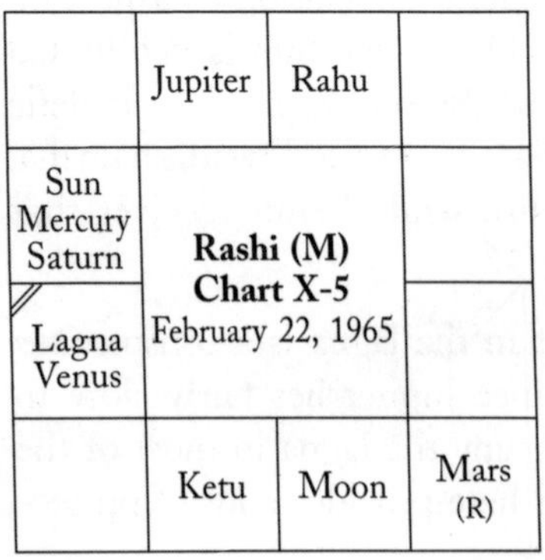

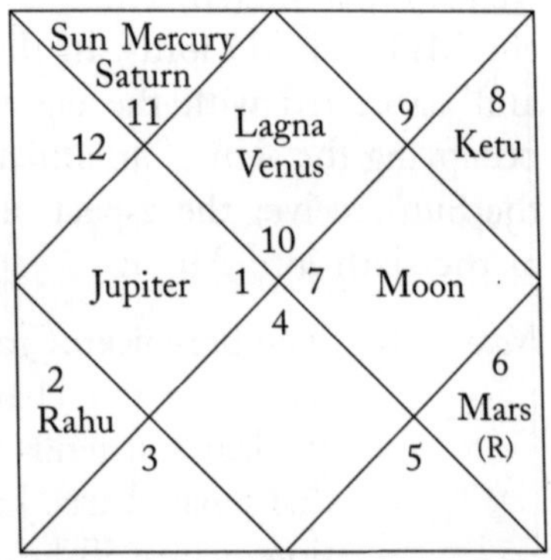

Lagna	21°19'	Mars (R)	00°58'	Venus	27°31'
Sun	09°48'	Mercury	08°03'	Saturn	13°41'
Moon	26°08'	Jupiter	25°40'	Rahu	26°32'

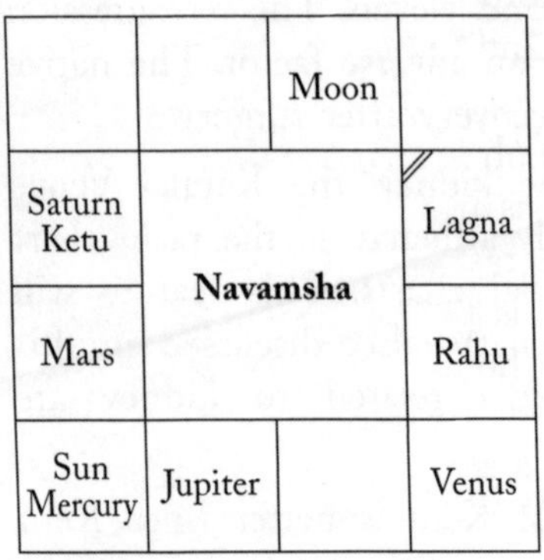

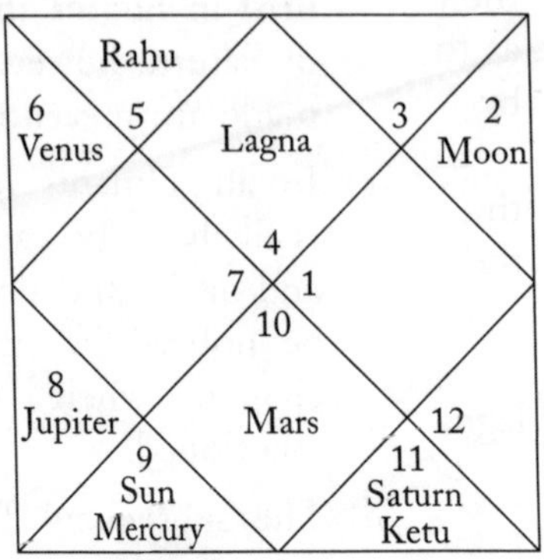

Saturn (MD) is the lord of the lagna placed in the 2nd house in association with the 6th and the 8th lords. Jupiter is a malefic lord aspected by Saturn and Mars. Rahu represents Saturn (the

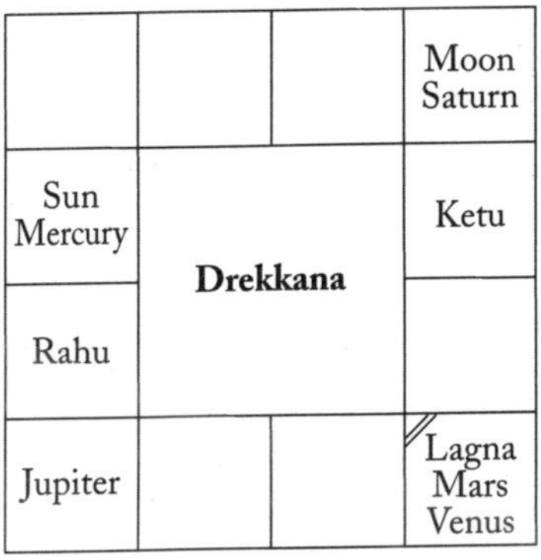

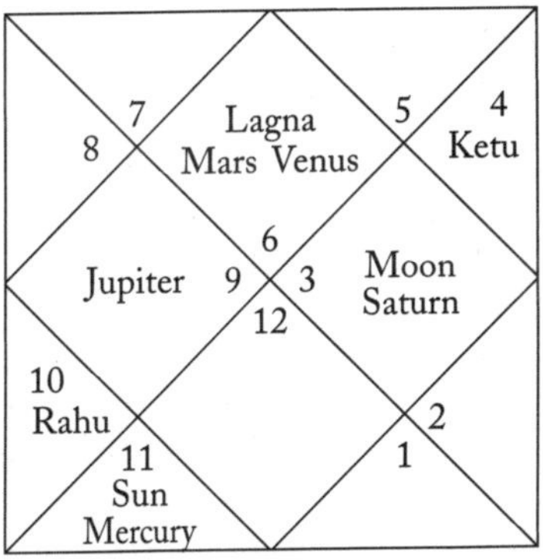

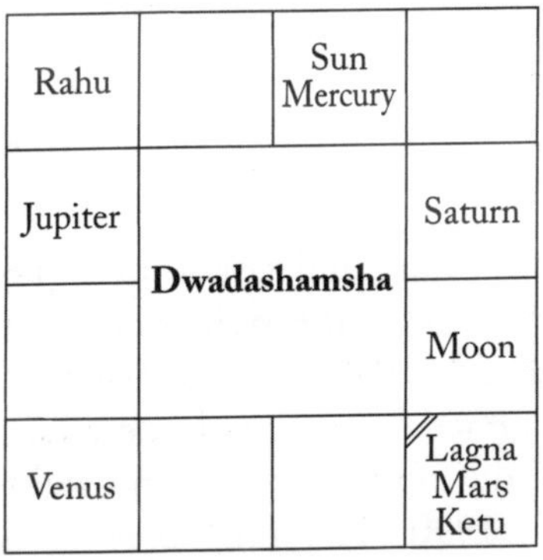

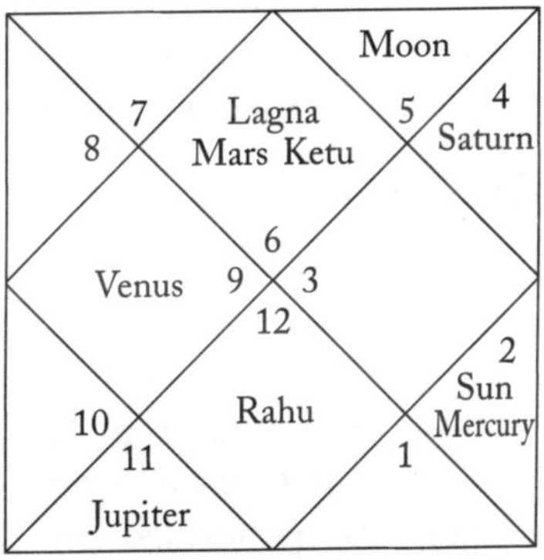

lagna lord) and Venus (which is posited in the lagna).

In the Navamsha, Saturn is a malefic lord in RKA located in the 8th house. Jupiter is the 6th lord aspecting the lagna as well as the lagna lord. Rahu is in the 2nd (a maraka house) aspected by Mars and Saturn.

In the Drekkana, Saturn is the 6h lord; Jupiter is aspected by the 6th and the 8th lords; Rahu is in the house of Saturn (in the same sign as the lagna of the rashi chart).

In the Dwadashamsha, Saturn is the 6th lord aspecting the lagna; Jupiter is placed in the 6th house; the RKA involves the lagna and Mars aspects Rahu.

Yogini dasha : Sankata - Bhramari (Rahu-Mars) from Nov 29, 1991 to Oct 19, 1992.

The role of Rahu (MD) has already been outlined.

Mars (AD) is retrograde malefic for the rashi chart. It aspects the lagna of the Navamsha chart. It happens to be the 8th lord in the lagna of the Drekkana chart. In the Dwadashamsha too, it is the 8th lord in the lagna, in the RKA aspected by Saturn.

Note : (a) In the rashi chart, three benefics occupy the quadrants. Jupiter also protects the lagna and the lagna lord in the Navamsha chart.

(b) The subsequent Vimshottari dasha (MD, AD and PD of Mercury) is the 6th lord dasha associated with the 8th lord, the Sun, and the lagna lord Saturn in the 2nd house. The subsequent Yogini dasha is Bhadrika whose lord is also Mercury. The native developed post-surgery complication of an incisional hernia. Mercury is also afflicted in the other divisional charts.

Chart X-6

This chart belongs to a young lady who underwent multiple surgical operations on her urinary system on the right side. The first operation was done on March 28, 1990 and consisted of removal of a stone from her right ureter. The second operation, consisting of surgical correction of the obstruction of the right kidney, was performed on June 9, 1990. The final operation, consisting of a transplantation of the right ureter into her urinary bladder, was performed on March 20, 1991. The patient has recovered since.

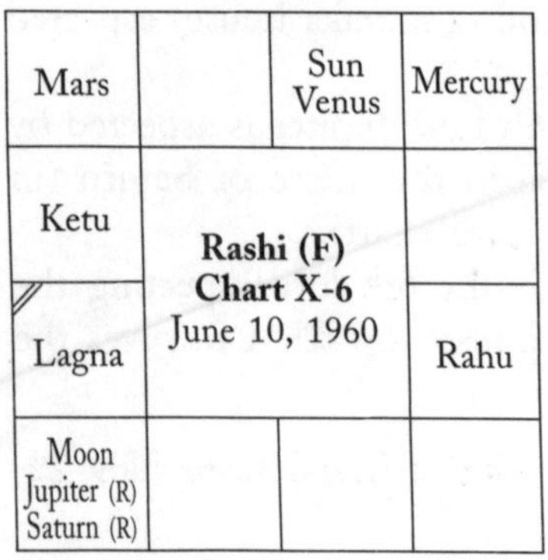

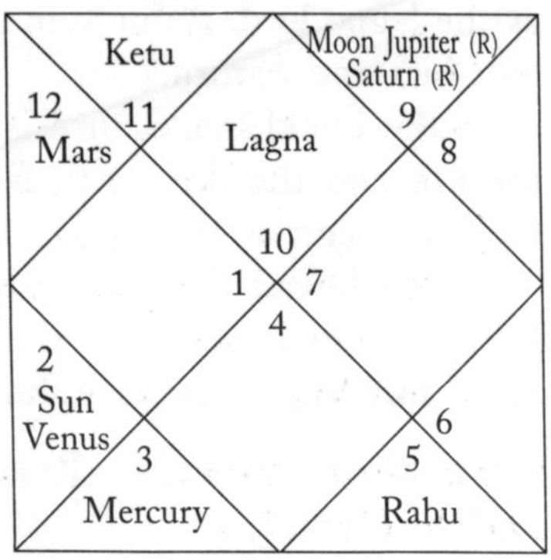

Lagna	12°31'	Mars	29°13'	Venus	23°13'
Sun	26°29'	Mercury	23°21'	Saturn (R)	23°40'
Moon	13°14'	Jupiter (R)	06°37'	Rahu	26°51'

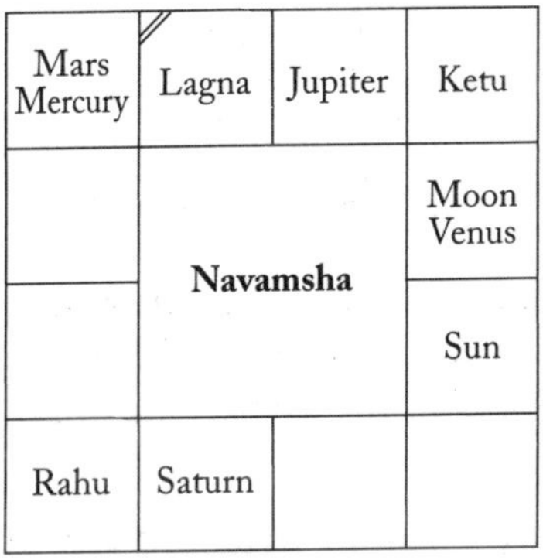

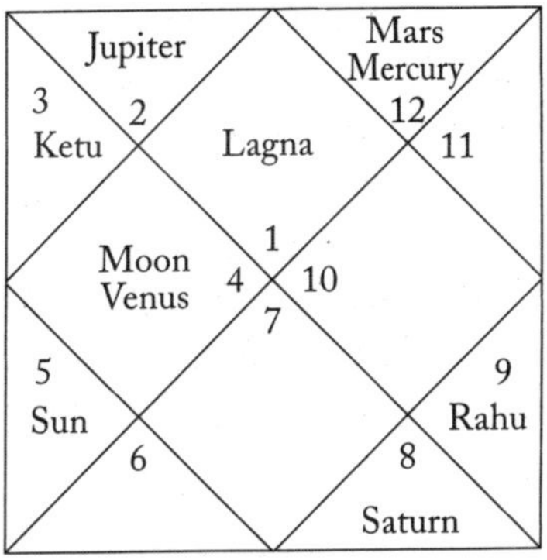

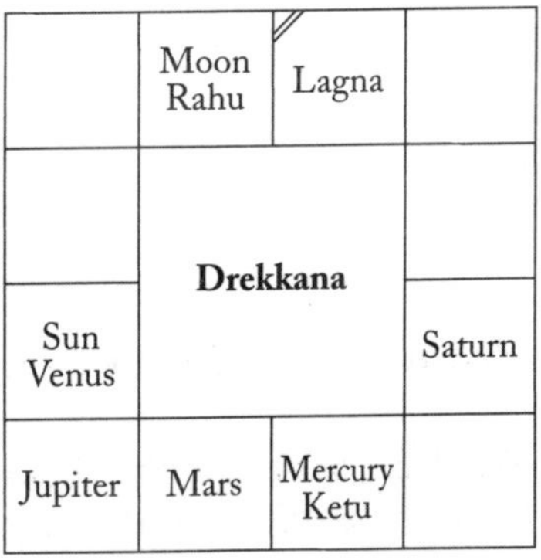

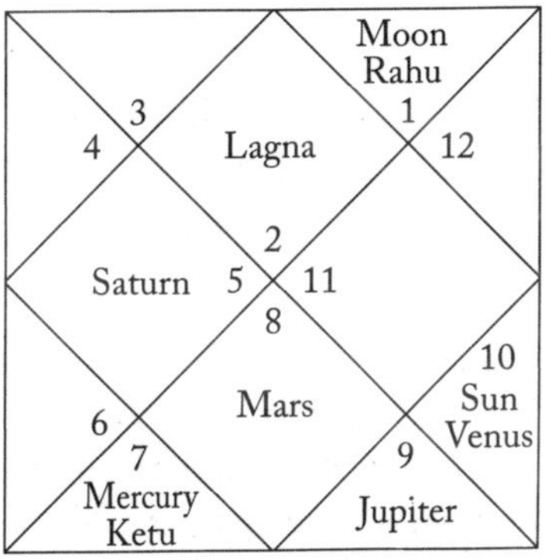

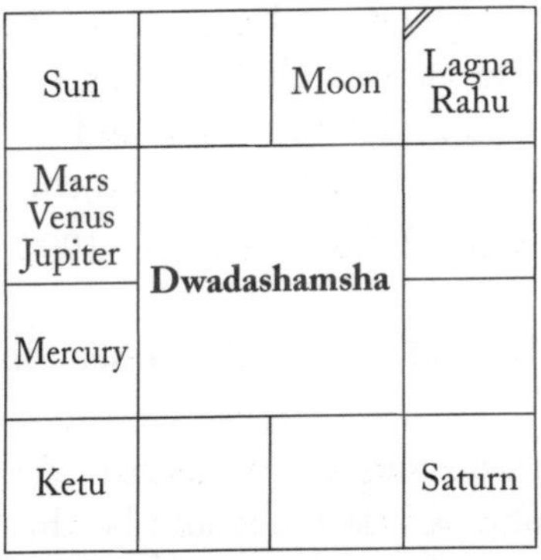

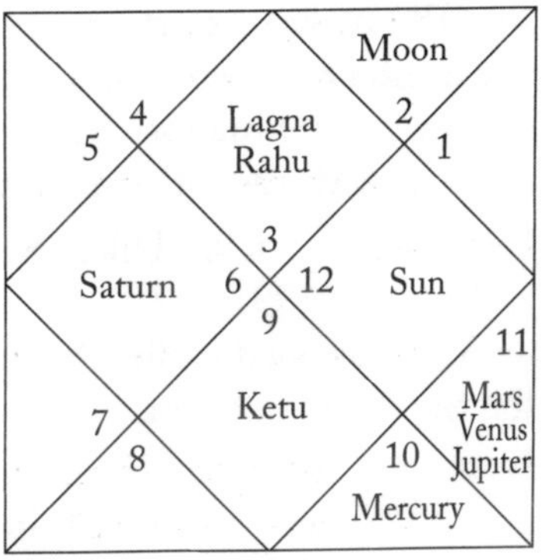

A. FIRST OPERATION:

Vimshottari dasha : Moon-Jupiter-Venus from January 25, 1990 to April 15, 1990

The Moon (MD) is a malefic lord in the 12th house associated with another malefic lord Jupiter (AD) and the lagna lord (natural malefic) Saturn. Venus (PD) is not too bad though associated with the Sun. In the divisional charts too, the dasha lords are variously afflicted.

Yogini dasha : Bhadrika-Bhramari (Mercury-Mars) from December 6, 1989 to June 26, 1990.

Mercury is afflicted, by Mars and Saturn, in the 6th house. It is afflicted by Mars in the Navamsha and by Saturn and RKA in the Drekkana, and is in the 8th house in the Dwadashamsha.

B. SECOND OPERATION:

Vimshottari dasha : Moon-Jupiter-Moon from May 9, 1990 to June 19, 1990.

The MD, AD and PD have already been explained.

Yogini dasha: Bhadrika-Bhramari (Mercury - Mars) from December 6, 1989 to June 26, 1990.

The same as already explained above.

C. THIRD OPERATION:

Vimshottari dashas : Moon-Saturn-Mercury from December 29, 1990 to March 20, 1991.

The MD remains the same. The AD lord, Saturn, is the lagna lord associated with the Moon and Jupiter. The PD lord Mercury is the 6th lord in the 6th house and has been referred to above. The PD of Ketu starts on the day of operation. Ketu too is not under much benefic influence in the various charts though it improves the situation. Saturn is a benefic for this lagna and associated with two other benefics; its period led to improvement.

Yogini dasha : Ulka-Ulka (Saturn-Saturn) from June 26, 1990, to June 26, 1991.

As mentioned earlier, Saturn (MD and AD lord) is a benefic for the Makara lagna.

Note : (a) After the third and curative surgical procedure, the subsequent PD, in Vimshottari dasha, would be that of Venus (i.e., Moon-Saturn-Venus). Venus is the yogakaraka for this ascendant. In addition, Venus loses its link with the lagna and the lagna lord though the 8th lord, the Sun, continues to afflict it to some extent.

(b) The subsequent AD in Yogini dasha is Siddha (again Venus).

Chart X-7

This native had multiple stones removed from his right kidney and ureter on Feb 9, 1994. The right kidney was virtually non-functioning and is likely to regain very poor function, if at all.

Vimshottari dasha : Sun-Ketu-Jupiter from January 27, 1994 to February 14, 1994.

The Sun (MD) is an adverse lord associated with another malefic lord and aspected by a retrograde Jupiter which is also the 6th lord. It is the 6th lord of the Navamsha, in the 6th house, associated with the 8th lord, and aspected by Mars. In the Drekkana too it is the 6th lord associated with the lagna lord. In the Dwadashamsha, it is aspected by the 6th lord Venus and a malefic Mars.

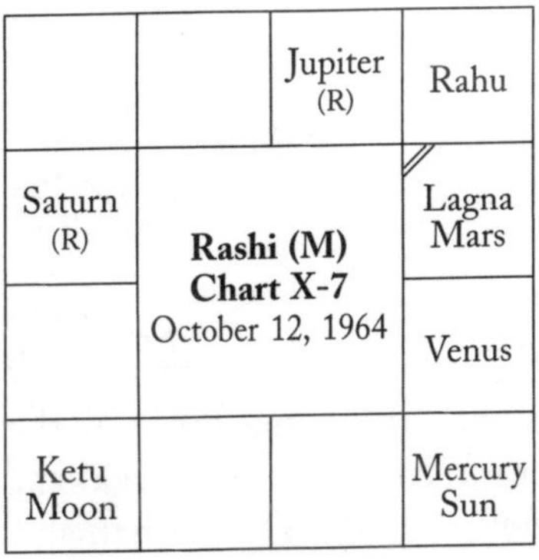

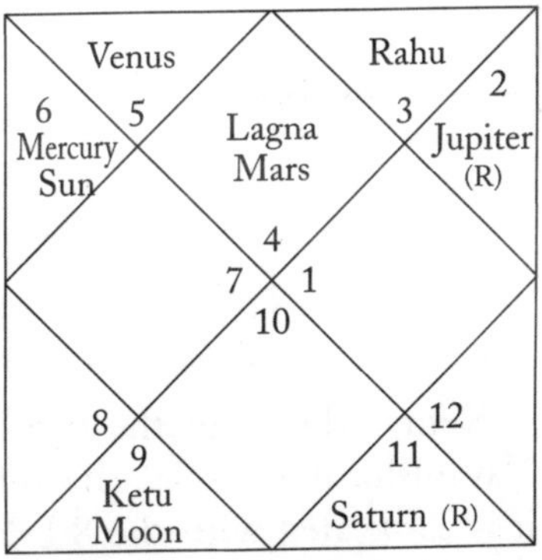

Lagna	26°41'	Mars	22°40'	Venus	13°35'
Sun	25°09'	Mercury	22°16'	Saturn (R)	05°21'
Moon	04°52'	Jupiter (R)	01°34'	Rahu	02°18'

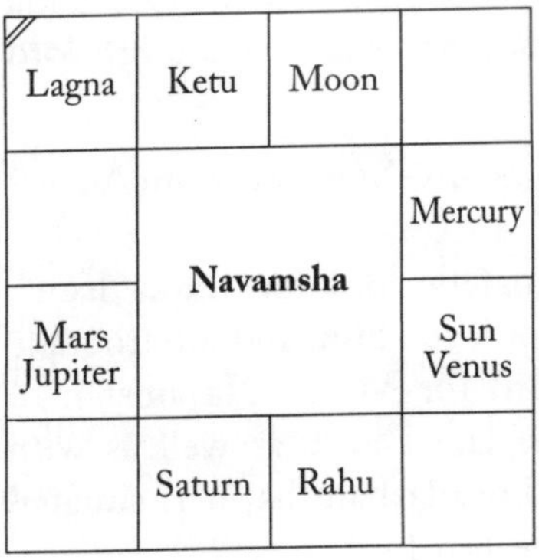

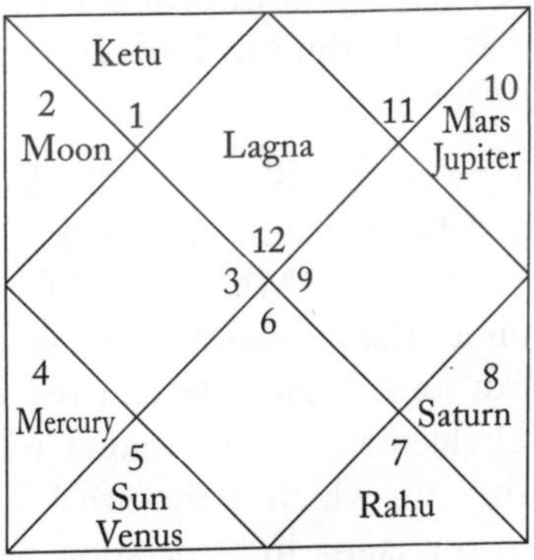

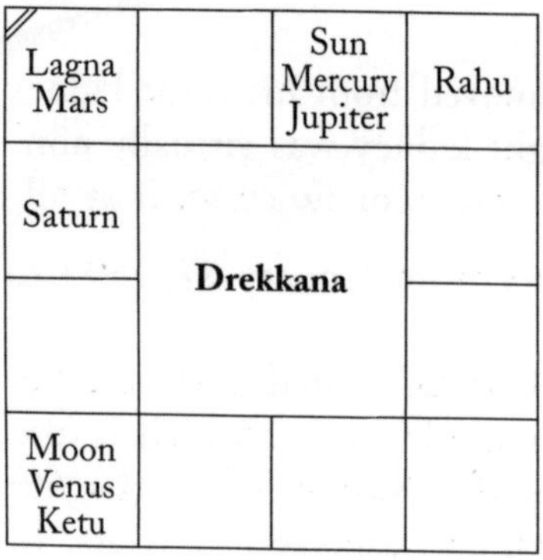

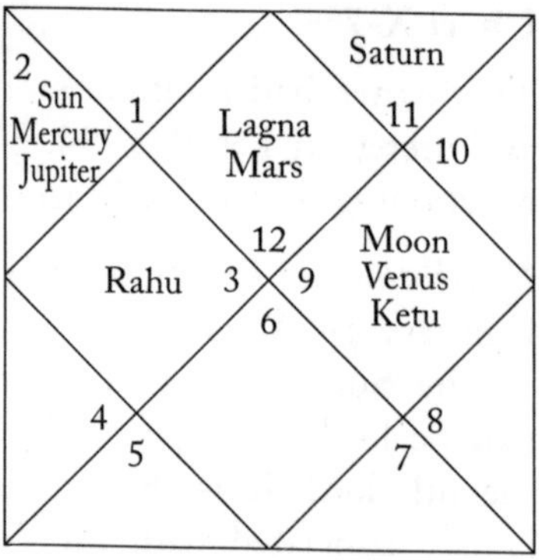

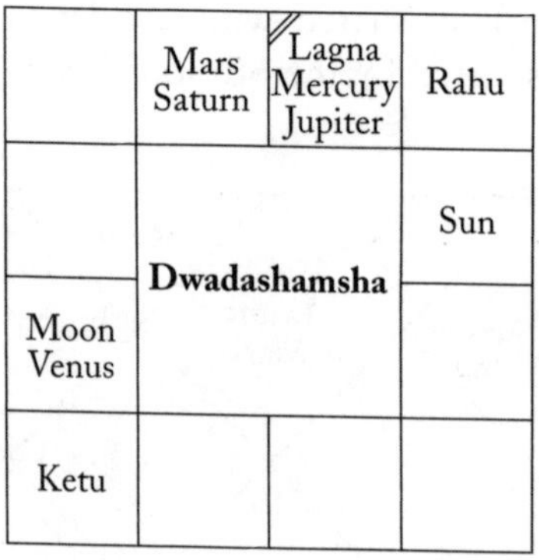

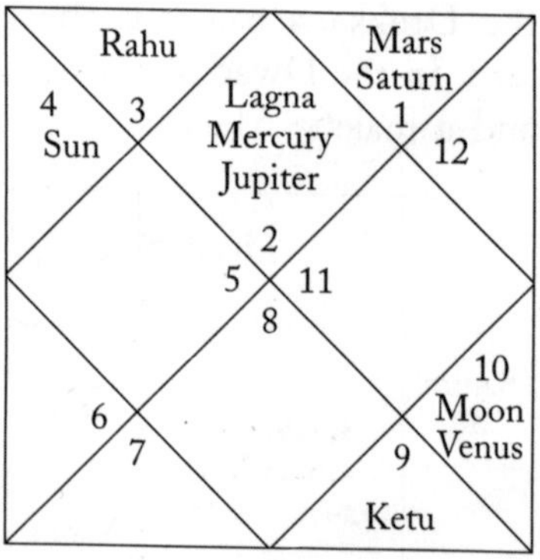

Ketu (AD) is in the 6th house with the lagna lord. In the Navamsha it is under the influence of Mars. In the Drekkana it is associated with the 8th lord Venus. In the Dwadashamsha, it is located in the 8th house.

Jupiter (PD) is the retrograde 6th lord. In the Navamsha it is debilitated, associated with Mars, aspected by Saturn as well as Mercury, both malefics for Pisces ascendant. In the Drekkana it is with the 6th lord. In the Dwadashamsha it is the 8th lord in the lagna.

Yogini dasha : Bhadrika-Bhadrika (Mercury-Mercury) from August 3, 1993 to April 13, 1994.

Mercury (MD and AD) is a malefic lord for Karka lagna, under the influence of the second lord, the Sun, and a retrograde 6th lord, Jupiter. It is a malefic lord for Meena Navamsha. In Drekkana, it is associated with the lagna lord, as well as with the Sun which is the 6th lord. In Dwadashamsha, it is situated in the lagna in association with the 8th lord.

Note : (a) The subsequent sequence of Vimshottari PD's (Saturn, Mercury) followed by the MD of Venus all appear to offer no relief.

(b) In the Yogini dashas also, the subsequent AD sequence is Ulka (Saturn), Siddha (Venus), Sankata (Rahu), etc.

Chart X-8

The native of this chart went for a simple surgical procedure of removal of the gall bladder (for stones) on January 20, 1993. He, however, went into complications and has developed a persistent bile leakage from his abdomen. Three malefics, two of them debilitated, occupy the quadrants. The only benefic, Mercury, occupying the lagna along with a debilitated Sun, is retrograde.

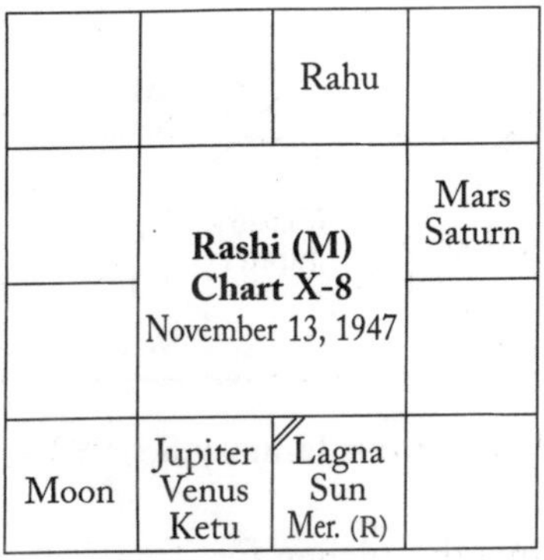

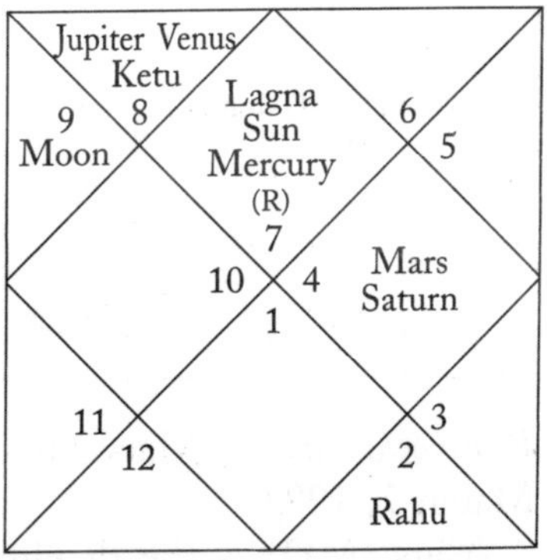

Lagna	29°47'	Mars	29°22'	Venus	14°56'
Sun	26°42'	Mercury (R)	12°43'	Saturn	29°07'
Moon	02°56'	Jupiter	11°09'	Rahu	00°13'

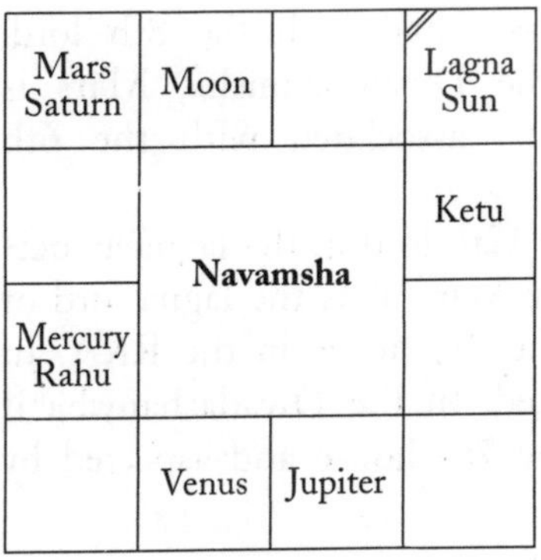

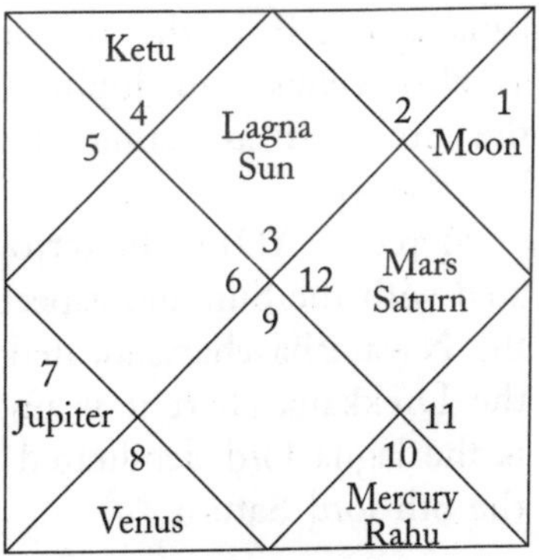

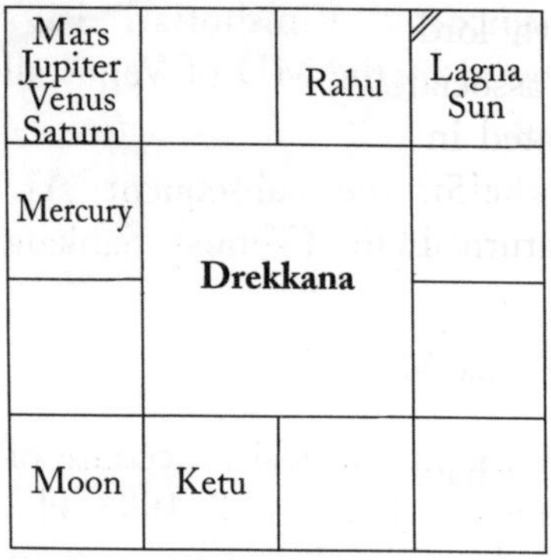

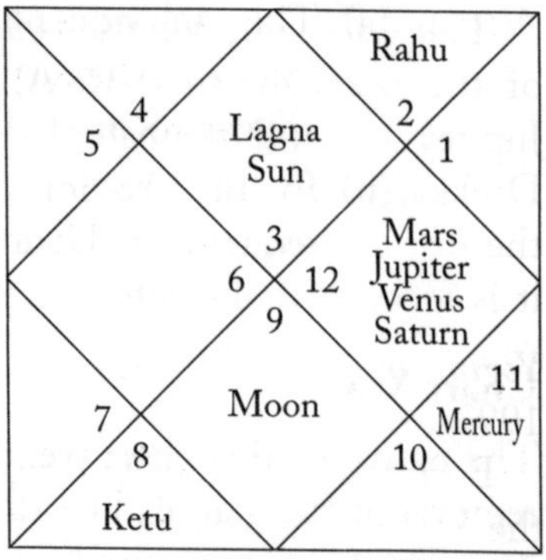

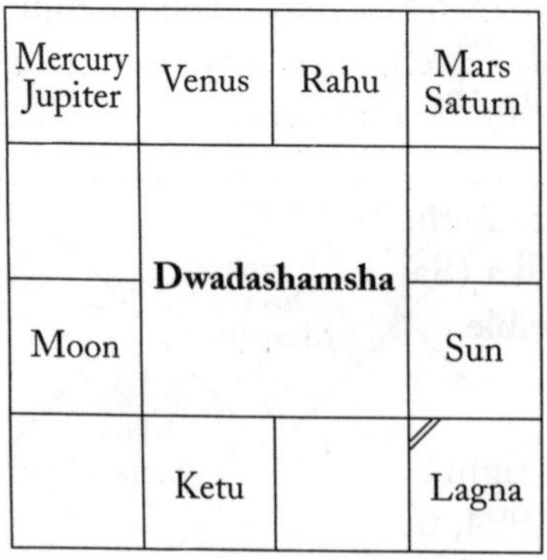

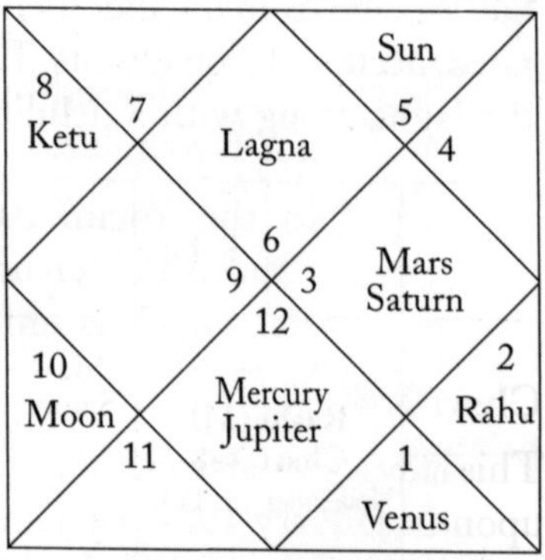

Vimshottari dasha: Mars-Mercury-Venus from January 8, 1993 to March 7, 1993.

Mars (MD) is the debilitated maraka planet for Tula lagna on a degree-to-degree conjunction with Saturn. Jupiter's aspect on Mars provides some relief. Mars is the 6th lord of the Navamsha associated with the eighth lord. In the Drekkana again, it is the 6th lord associated with the 8th lord, as also Venus and Jupiter. In the Dwadashamsha, Mars is the 8th lord aspecting the lagna, associated with the 6th lord Saturn.

Mercury (AD) is the retrograde 12th lord in the lagna associated with the Sun and aspected by Mars. It is the lagna lord of the Navamsha chart, located in the 8th house in the RKA. In the Drekkana chart it is unafflicted. In the Dwadashamsha it is the lagna lord debilitated in the 7th house and aspected by the 6th lord Saturn

The PD lord, Venus, is the 8th lord (and the lagna lord) of the rashi chart, in RKA, and associated with the 6th lord Jupiter. In the Navamsha it is located in the 6th house. In the Drekkana it is the 12th lord (and the 5th lord) associated with the 6th lord Mars and 8th lord Saturn. In the Dwadashamsha, it is located in the 8th house.

Yogini dasha : Siddha-Bhramari (Venus-Mars) from August 18, 1992 to May 28, 1993.

Both the MD and AD dasha lords have been discussed under the Vimshottari dasha.

Note : (a) The Vimshottari PD's in the MD of Mars are quite small. The AD sequence would be Ketu (after Mercury), followed by Venus, the Sun, etc. All these are not favourable.

(b) In the Yogini dasha too, the sequence of AD is Bhadrika (Mercury), Ulka (Saturn), Siddha (Venus), etc., which is unfavourable.

Chart X-9

This lady suffered from cancer of the right breast. She was operated upon in January 1984. By January 1994, the disease had recurred and disseminated with absolutely no chance of any relief.

Vimshottari dasha : Venus-Ketu-Moon from January 21, 1984 to April 26, 1984 was the period for surgical treatment.

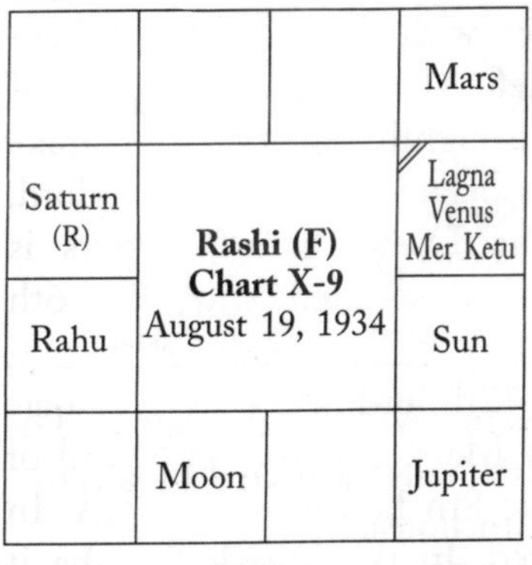

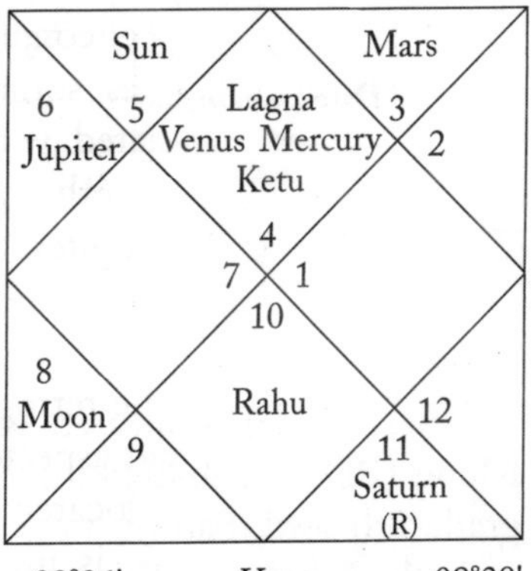

Lagna	08°08'	Mars	29°36'	Venus	08°39'
Sun	02°18'	Mercury	23°39'	Saturn (R)	01°45'
Moon	12°16'	Jupiter	26°41'	Rahu	18°17'

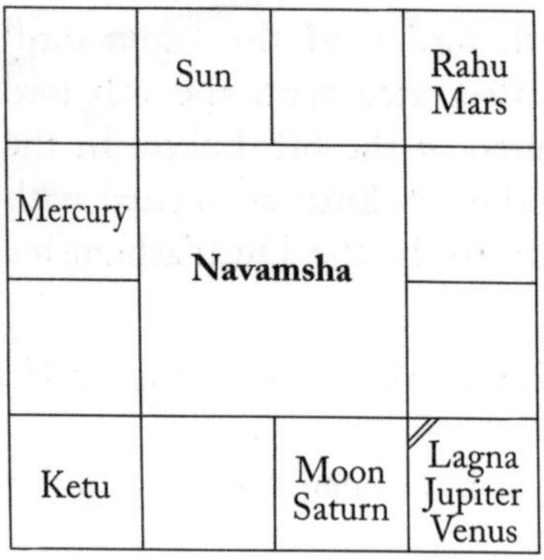

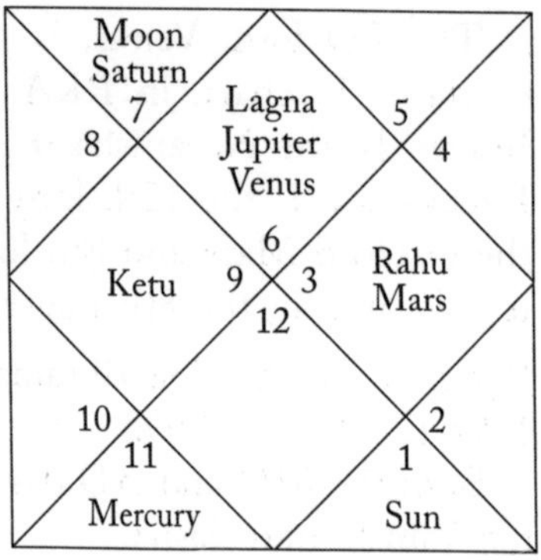

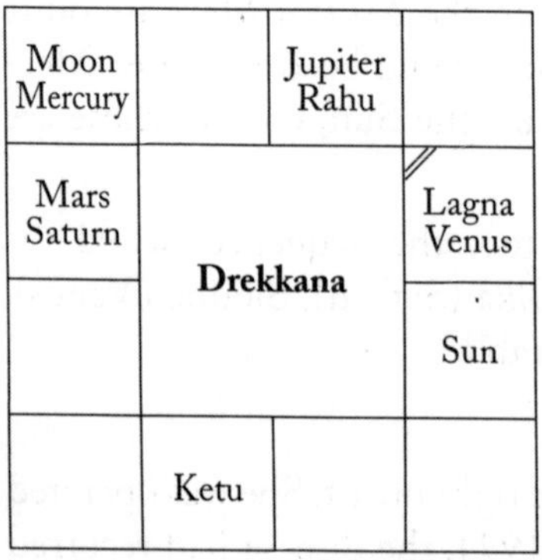

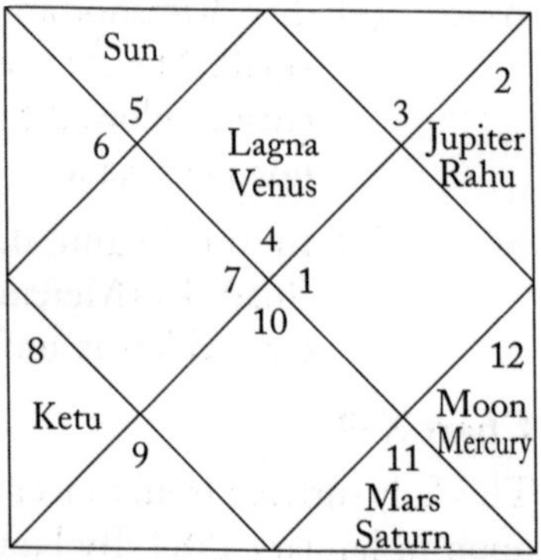

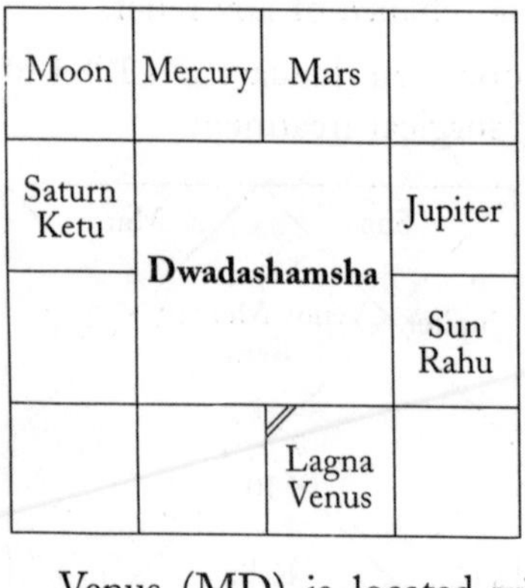

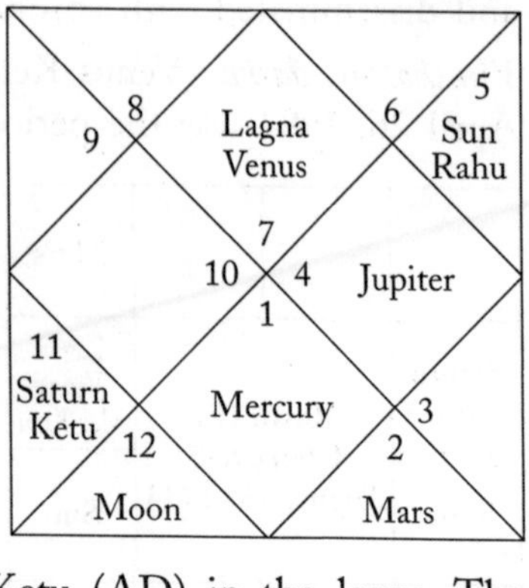

Venus (MD) is located with Ketu (AD) in the lagna. The Moon (PD) is debilitated in the 5th house aspected by a retrograde 8th lord, Saturn, from the 8th house.

In the Navamsha, Venus and Ketu are under the influence of the 8th lord Mars, while the Moon is associated with the 6th lord Saturn and aspected by the 12th lord, the Sun, from the 8th house.

In the Drekkana, Venus is a malefic lord in the lagna; Ketu is aspected by the 8th lord Saturn from 8th house; the Moon is associated with a debilitated malefic lord Mercury.

In the Dwadashamsha, Venus is the lagna lord in the lagna and, though also the 8th lord, is capable of strengthening the lagna. Ketu is in the 5th house associated with the 4th and 5th lord Saturn and aspected by the Sun. The Moon is in the 6th house but under Jupiter's influence. Three benefics occupy the quadrants in the Dwadashamsha.

The native remained fairly alright in the Sun's major period. The Sun is quite strong in all the divisional charts. Her condition deteriorated in the MD of the Moon. In January 1994, she was found to have disseminated metastases when the dasha running was Moon-Jup-Sat (December 30, 1993 to March 16, 1994). The Moon (MD) has already been discussed. Jupiter (AD) is a malefic lord in all the charts, under Mars' influence in the rashi, Navamsha and Drekkana. Saturn (PD) is an adverse lord, retrograde, and variously afflicted in all the divisional charts. After the MD/ AD of Moon-Jup would follow Moon-Sat which indicates no relief.

Yogini dasha : Siddha-Sankata (Venus-Rahu) was running from April 24, 1983 to November 14, 1984 when the operation was performed.

Venus has already been discussed. Sankata also represents Ketu which too has been discussed.

At the time of dissemination of disease, the running dasha is Sankata-Ulka (Rahu/Ketu-Saturn). This is also adverse as has been discussed earlier.

Note : Malefic dashas followed by malefic dashas clearly indicate no relief.

Chart X-10

This native suffered from acute leukemia (a form of blood cancer) and died of his disease on February 7, 1989, within six months of its detection.

Vimshottari dasha : Rahu-Mercury-Jupiter operated from October 24, 1988 to February 27, 1989.

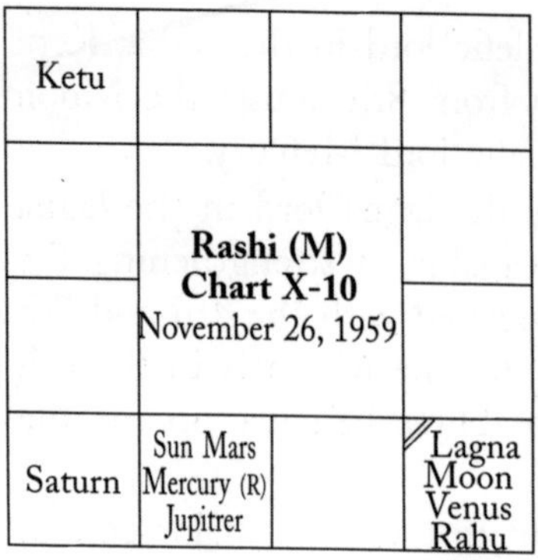

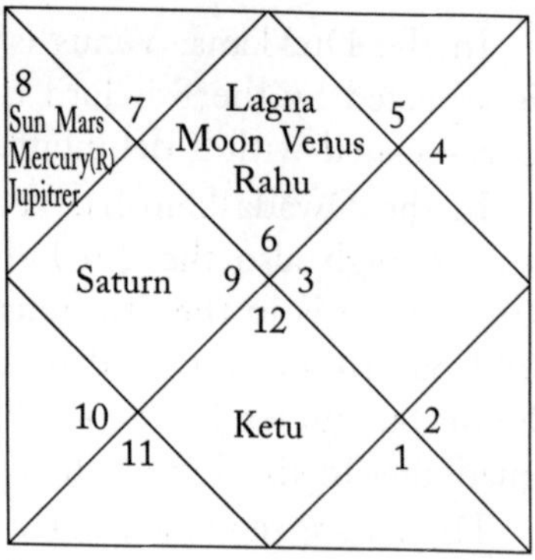

Lagna	14°40'	Mars	01°09'	Venus	23°23'
Sun	09°34'	Mercury (R)	06°10'	Saturn	12°02'
Moon	05°12'	Jupiter	17°21'	Rahu	08°36'

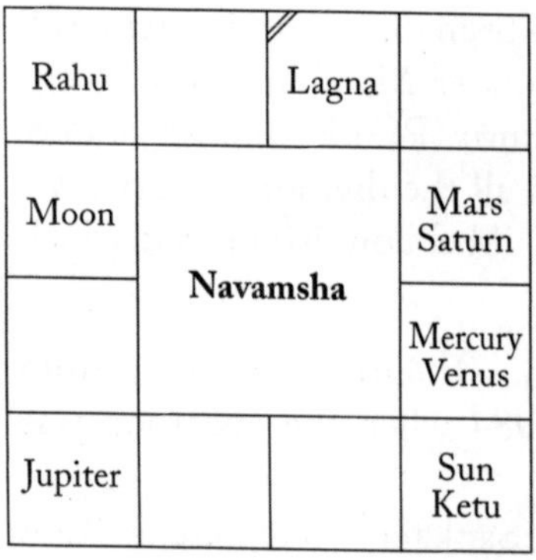

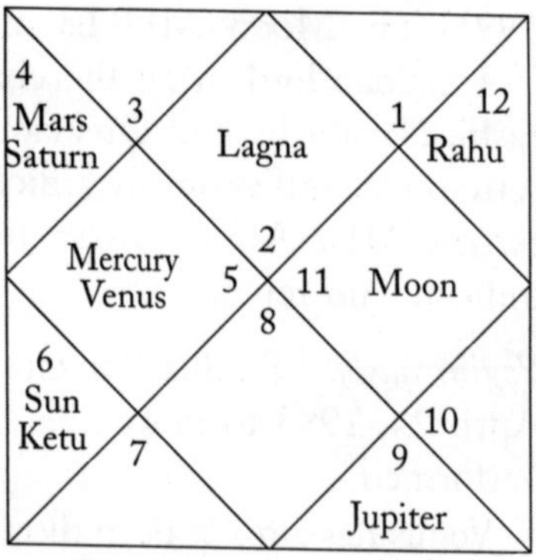

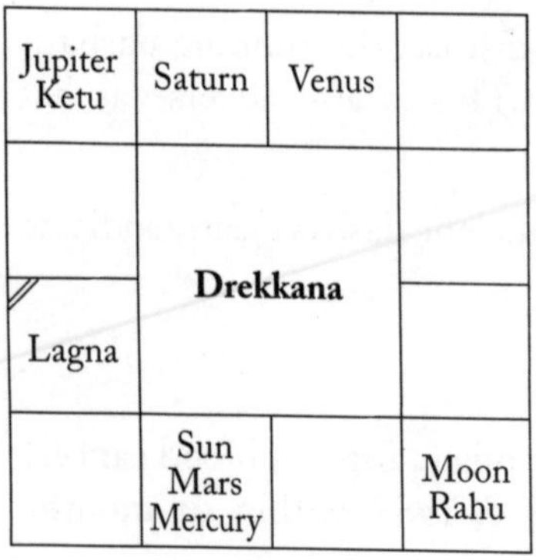

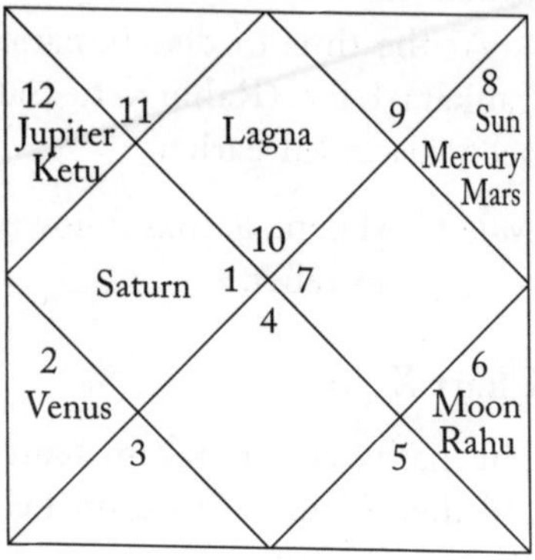

The MD, AD and PD lords are all afflicted and related by position or aspect to the lagna or the lagna lord. A debilitated

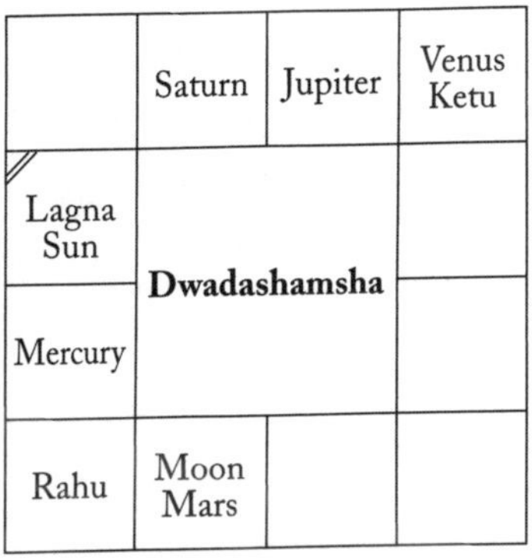

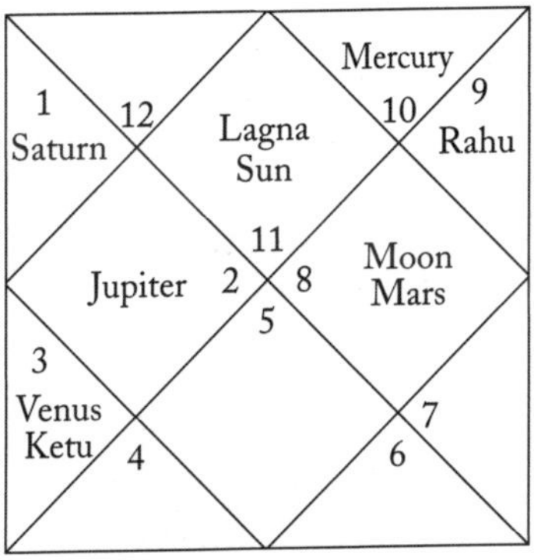

Venus in RKA, aspected by the 6th lord Saturn, inhabits the lagna.

The MD, AD and PD lords are themselves malefic for the various divisional charts wherein they are all variously afflicted.

The subsequent PD lord Saturn is also malefic and afflicted all over.

Yogini dasha : Ulka-Pingala (Saturn-Sun) from February 3, 1989 to June 3, 1989.

Both Saturn (MD) and the Sun (AD) are malefic either by lordship or by association in the rashi as well as the divisional charts. The subsequent AD of Dhanya (Jupiter) has already been described as adverse.

Note : The lagna lord is retrograde and combust, associated with a combust eighth lord and a combust Jupiter.

Chart X-11

This native suffered from what is known as a periampullary carcinoma (a cancer involving the bile duct, the pancreatic duct and the 2nd part of the duodenum). He underwent surgical resection of the growth on November 17, 1989. The disease subsequently spread to his liver and he died in June 1992.

Vimshottari dasha : Mercury-Saturn-Venus was running at the time of surgery from July 18, 1989 to December 29, 1989.

Mercury (MD) is the malefic lord in the RKA associated with another two malefics, Mars and the Sun. Saturn (AD) is another malefic lord in the 12th house. Venus is the 6th lord located in the lagna. The MD, AD and PD lords are all adverse in the

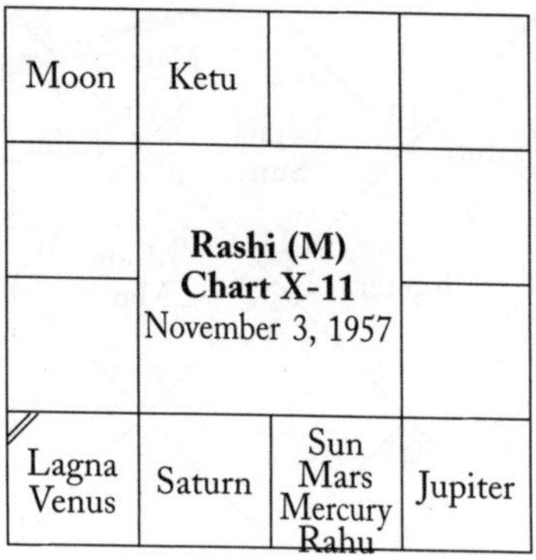

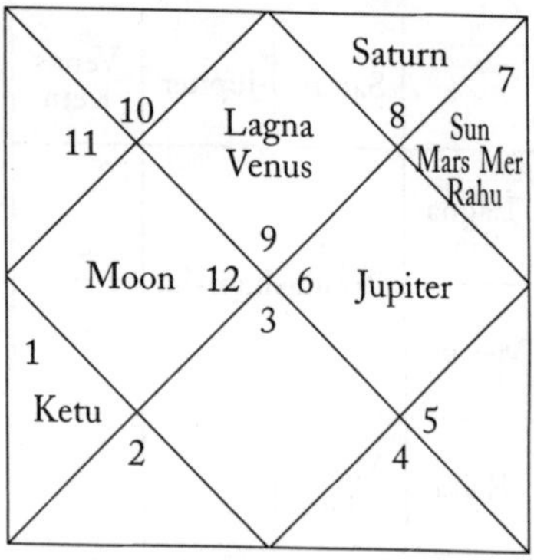

Lagna	15°17'	Mars	03°20'	Venus	04°21'
Sun	17°49'	Mercury	24°23'	Saturn	19°28'
Moon	05°08'	Jupiter	25°06'	Rahu	17°17'

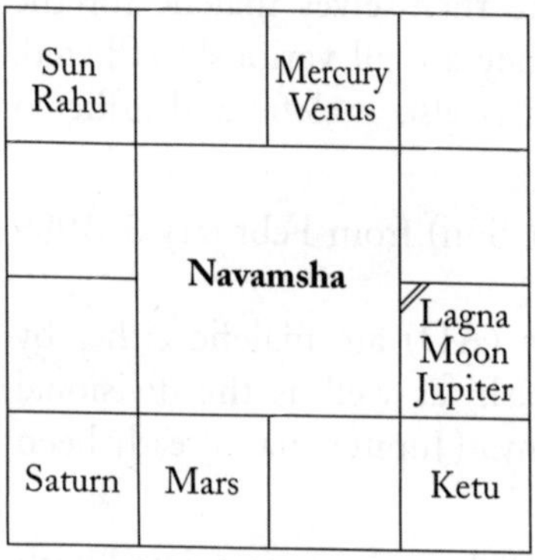

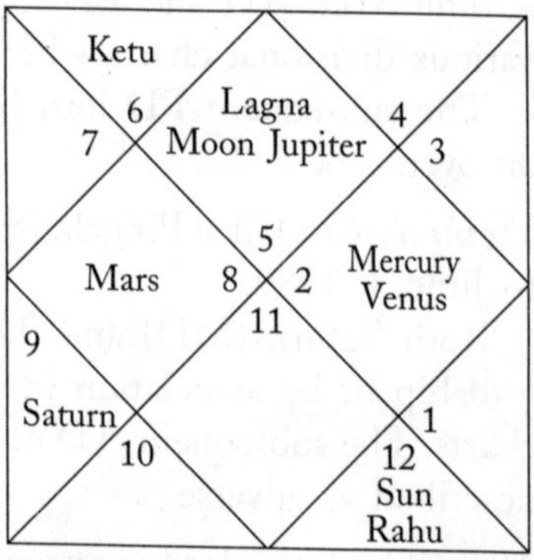

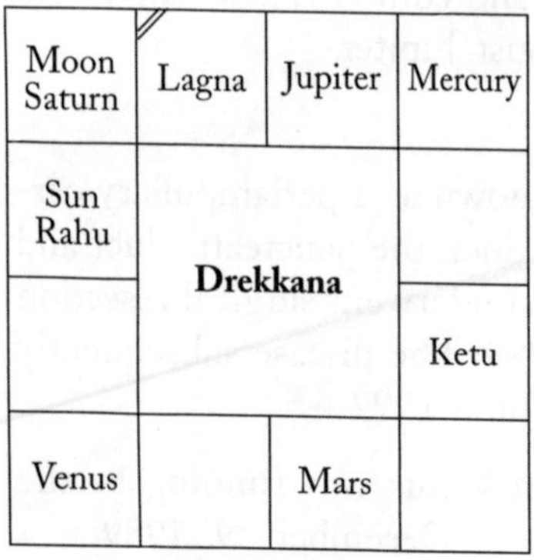

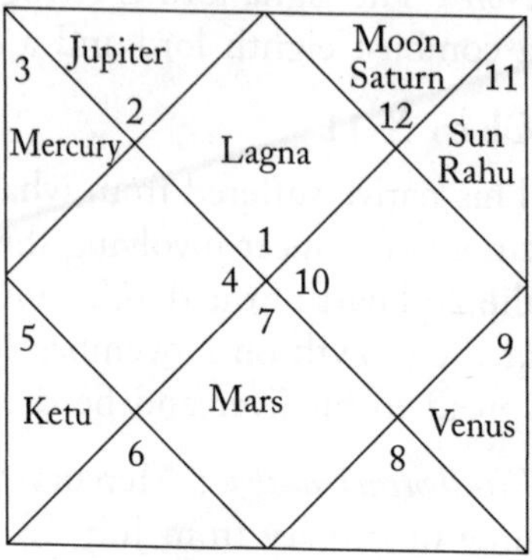

divisional charts either because of adverse lordship or of malefic association or aspect.

Death occured in Ketu-Venus-Saturn (running from June 6, 1992 to August 12, 1992).

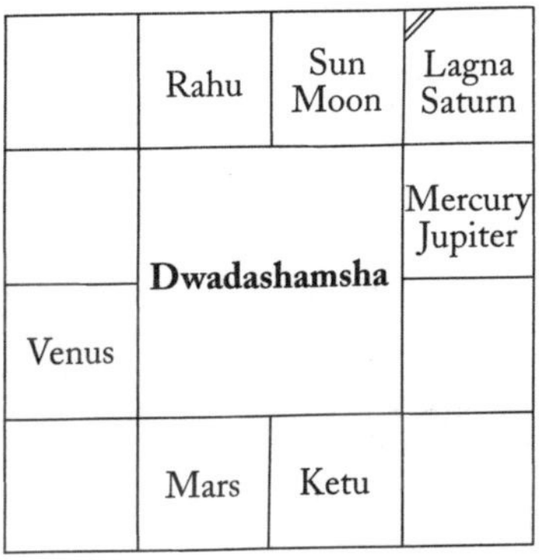

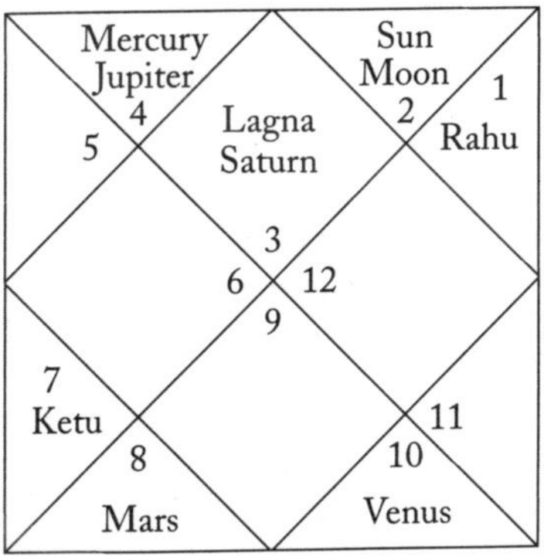

Ketu (MD) is a part of the RKA and aspected by the Sun, Mars and a malefic Mercury. Ketu is also afflicted by the degree-to-degree aspect of the Sun. Venus and Saturn have been discussed already.

Yogini dasha : Bhramari-Bhadrika (Mars-Mercury) operated from August 12, 1989 to March 2, 1990.

Mars (MD) is under heavy malefic influence, including the RKA, in the rashi chart. It is aspected by malefic lords in the Navamsha. In the Drekkana and the Dwadashamsha, it is the 8th and the 6th lord respectively.

The role of Mercury (AD) has been discussed under the Vimshottari dasha.

At the time of death it was Bhramari-Sankata (Mars-Rahu/Ketu); both have been discussed above.

Note : Mars happens to be the lord of the 22nd Drekkana as also the 64th Navamsha.

Chart X-12

This chart is being discussed in greater details to highlight certain subtler aspects of astrology. The native suffered from chronic myeloid leukemia (another form of blood cancer) of which she died on May 9, 1990.

Vimshottari dasha: Jupiter-Jupiter-Mercury operated from March 20, 1990 to July 9, 1990.

The MD and AD lord Jupiter is a malefic for this lagna and aspected by two malefics Saturn and Mars. Mercury (PD) is too

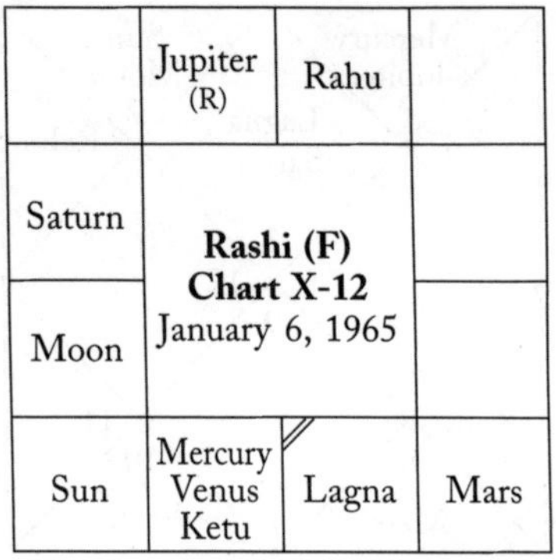

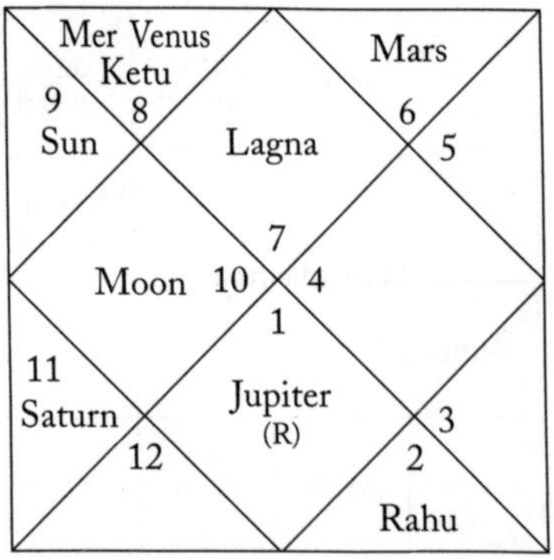

Lagna	19°04'	Mars	01°42'	Venus	28°31'
Sun	21°56'	Mercury	28°58'	Saturn	08°23'
Moon	24°08'	Jupiter (R)	22°47'	Rahu	29°26'

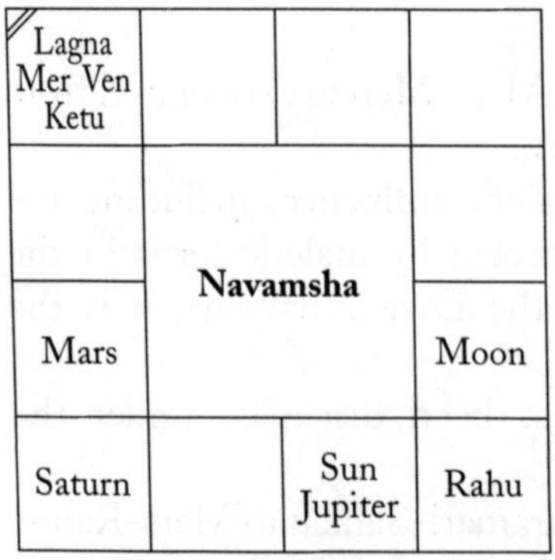

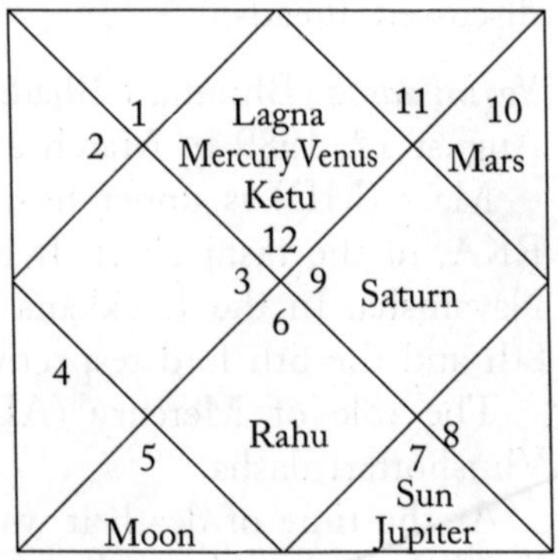

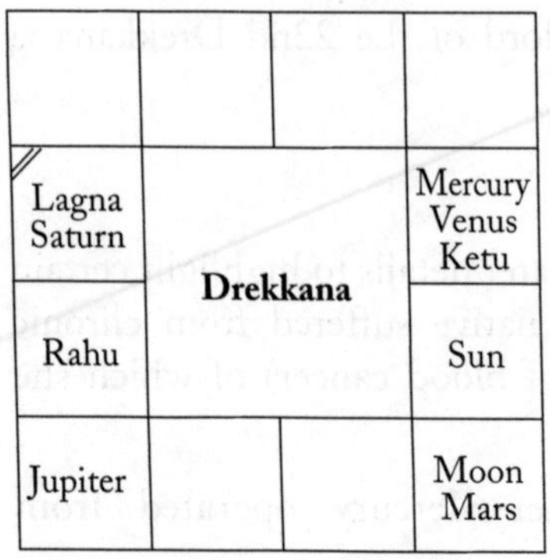

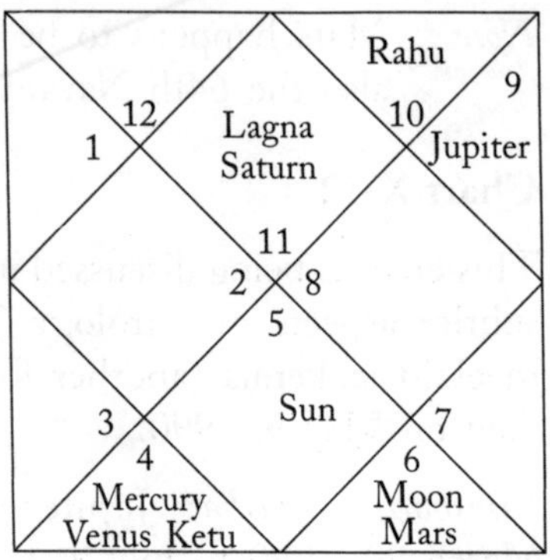

close to the lagna lord as well as Ketu. Saturn aspects the lagna lord and the PD lord also. Jupiter is retrograde.

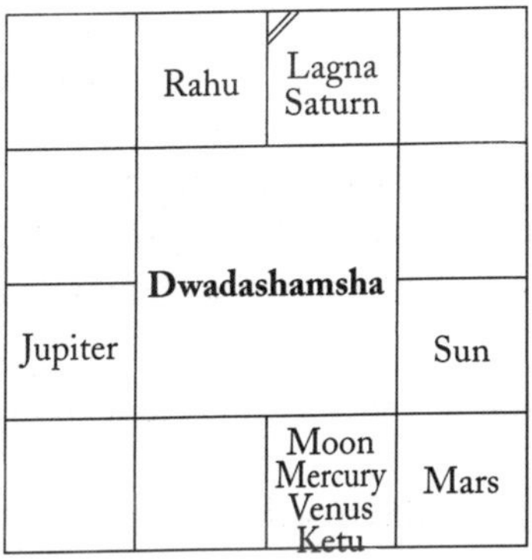

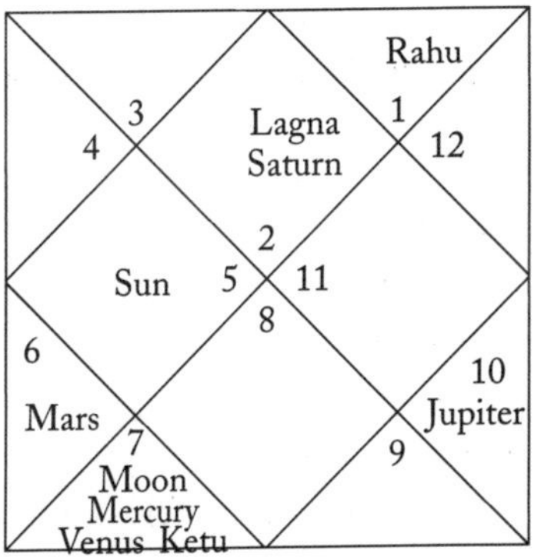

In the Navamsha, Jupiter (MD and AD) is lagna lord in the 8th house associated with the 6th lord. Mercury (PD) is debilitated in the lagna in the RKA, and associated with the 8th lord.

In the Drekkana as well as the Dwadashamsha, both Jupiter and Mercury have adverse lordship and are variously afflicted.

The next dasha of Jupiter-Jupiter-Ketu is adverse too. Ketu is too close to the lagna lord and is also aspected by Saturn.

Yogini dasha : Siddha - Bhadrika (Venus-Mercury) from October 3, 1989 to September 23, 1990.

Venus (MD) is the lagna lord in the RKA aspected by Saturn. It is afflicted in all the divisional charts. The role of Mercury (AD) has already been discussed.

Now we propose to discuss this event from a different angle. Do the charts of one's blood relations indicate the same event? If yes, how? Let us see!

The Father's Chart

The rashi chart **(Chart X-13)** and the Saptamsha chart (the 1/7 division which indicates progeny) are of significance here. The fifth house of the rashi chart, and the lagna and the 5th house of Saptamsha chart are the relevant houses.

Vimshottari dasha: Jupiter-Rahu-Venus in operation from May 1, 1990 to September 25, 1990.

Jupiter (MD) is the debilitated 5th lord in the 3rd house, and occupies the lagna of the Saptamsha chart, being the 8th lord aspected by Mars.

Rahu (AD) involves the lagna in the rashi chart, and occupies the 12th house of Saptamsha under the aspect of a malefic Saturn.

Venus (PD) is the lord of the 5th house from Jupiter (the significator for children), in RKA, and associated with its 8th lord, the Sun. It is an adverse lord for the Saptamsha, debilitated and aspected by Mars.

Yogini dasha : Sankata - Siddha (Rahu-Venus) from August 21, 1989 to March 11, 1991.

Both MD and AD lords have been discussed above.

The Mother's Chart

The same event is seen from the mother's chart **(chart X-14)**.

Vimshottari dasha : Venus-Venus-Saturn from April 14, 1990 to October 24, 1990.

Venus (MD and AD) is the 8th lord aspecting the 5th house of rashi chart and involved in the RKA. Saturn (PD) is the 5th lord in the 8th house and aspects the 5th house. In the Saptamsha chart, Venus is the lord of the 5th house in the lagna. Saturn (PD) as the lord of the lagna aspects the adverse combination of Mars and Rahu in the 5th house.

Yogini dasha : Siddha - Siddha (Venus-Venus) from May 2, 1990 to September 12, 1991.

The role of Venus has already been discussed.

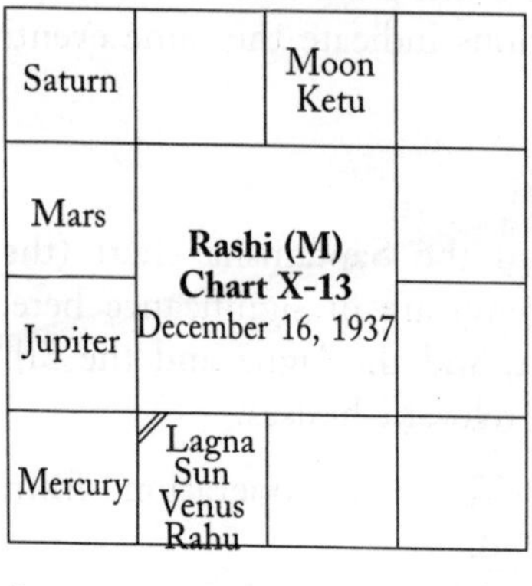

Rashi (M)
Chart X-13
December 16, 1937

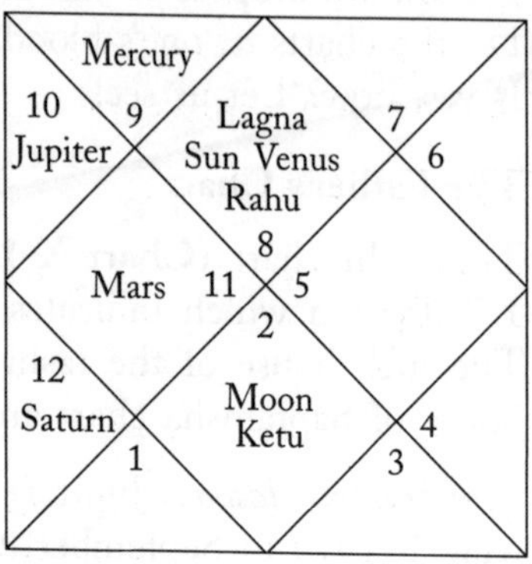

Lagna	13°02'	Mars	02°40'	Venus	18°37'
Sun	27°31'	Mercury	20°38'	Saturn	05°33'
Moon	05°02'	Jupiter	06°07'	Rahu	12°02'

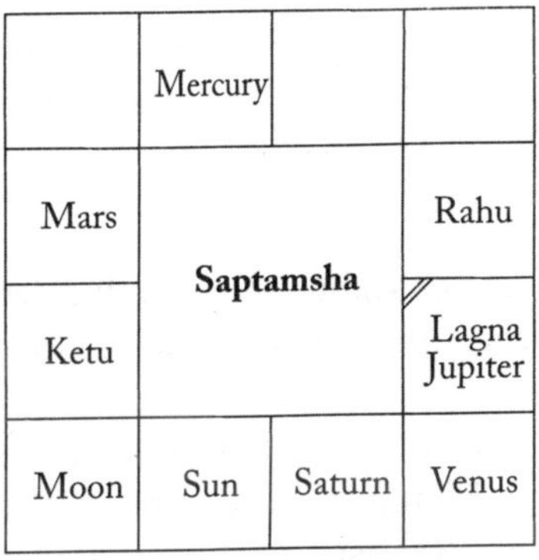

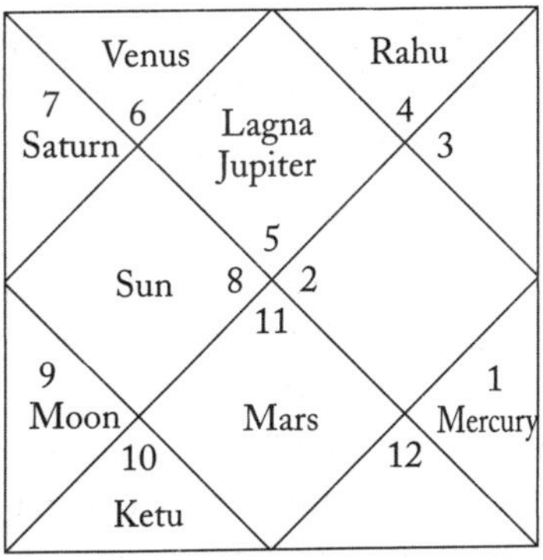

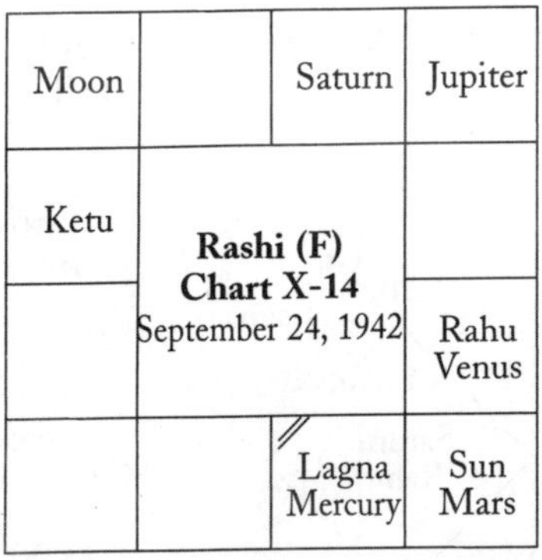

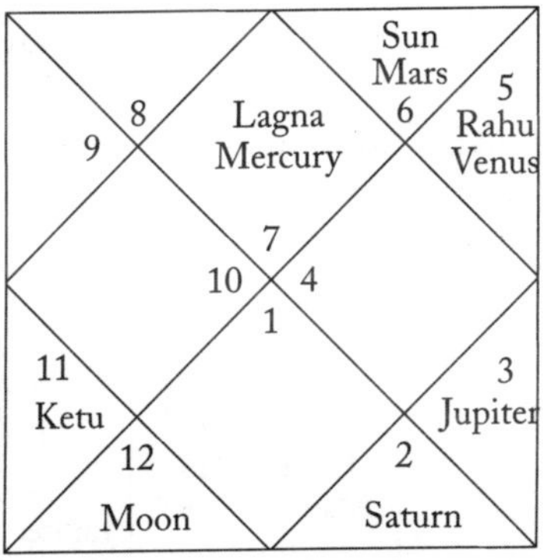

Lagna	13°02'	Mars	11°18'	Venus	23°40'
Sun	07°22'	Mercury	01°52'	Saturn	19°28'
Moon	01°19'	Jupiter	28°29'	Rahu	11°10'

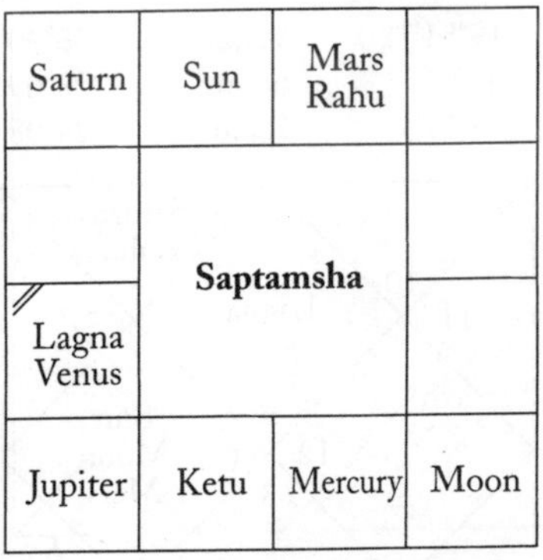

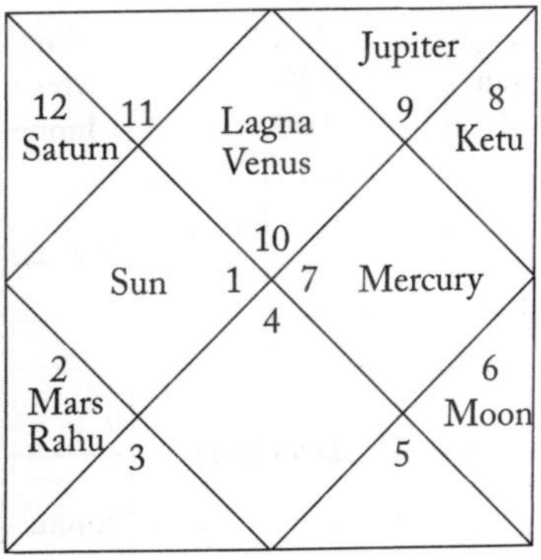

The Horoscopes of Siblings

The horoscopes of two younger siblings of the native are also being discussed. The relevant divisional chart here is the Drekkana while the relevant houses are the 3rd in both the rashi and the Drekkana, as also the lagna of the Drekkana.

Chart X-15

This chart shows the *Vimshottari dasha* of Rahu-Mercury-Jupiter (May 2, 1990 to September 4, 1990) running at the time of elder sister's death.

Rahu (MD) is associated with the 3rd lord Saturn in both the rashi and the Drekkana charts. Mercury (AD) aspects the lagna of the Drekkana chart. Jupiter (PD) aspects the 3rd house in both the rashi and the Drekkana charts.

The *Yogini dasha* of Bhadrika-Bhadrika (Mercury-Mercury) operated from January 11, 1990 to September 21, 1990. The role of Mercury has been discussed above.

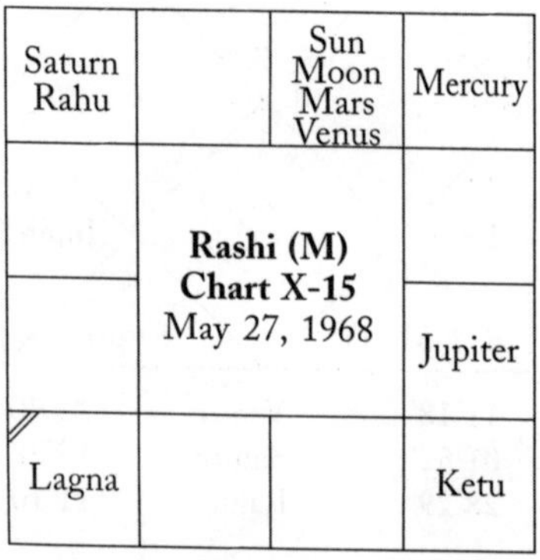

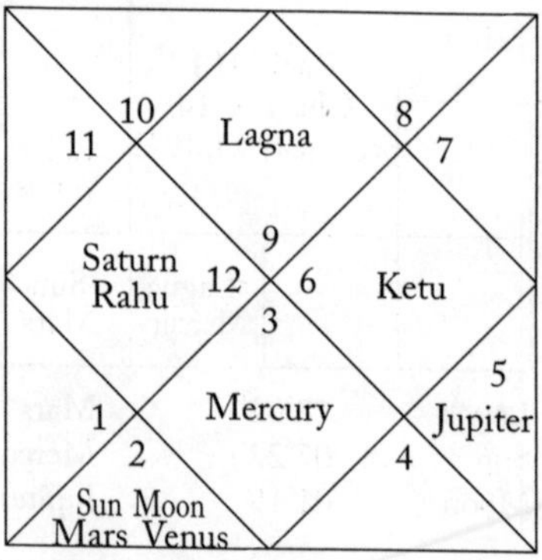

Lagna	03°12'	Mars	19°51'	Venus	06°30'
Sun	12°57'	Mercury	05°06'	Saturn	28°09'
Moon	16°26'	Jupiter	04°17'	Rahu	24°08'

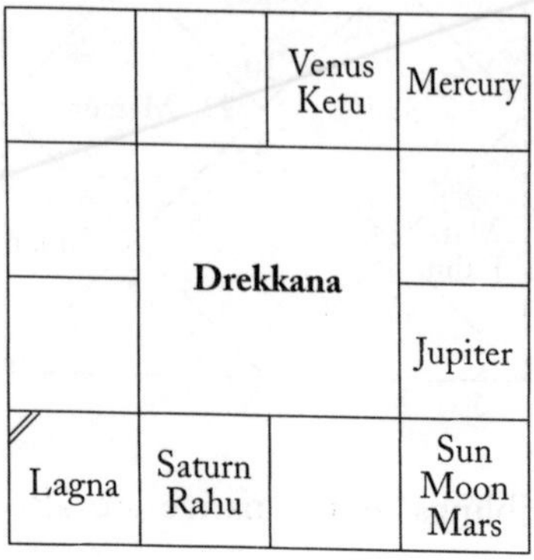

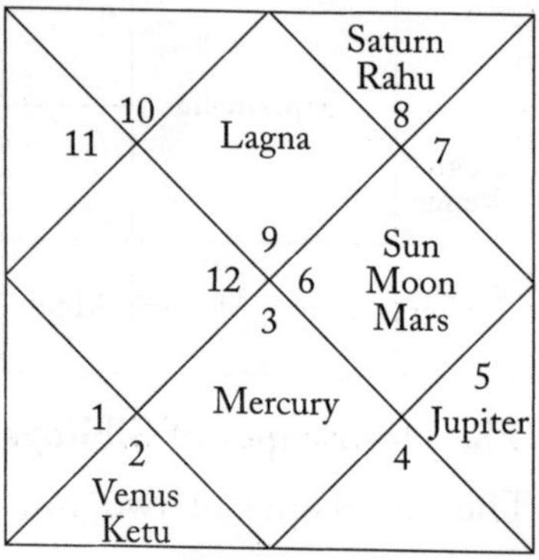

Chart X-16

This has the *Vimshottari dasha* of Rahu-Saturn-Saturn from March 4, 1990 to August 16, 1990.

Rahu (MD) represents Saturn which, as the AD and PD lord also, and as a malefic 6th and 7th lord, aspects the 3rd house where the retrograde 8th lord Jupiter is located. Saturn is associated with Mars. There is an exchange between the 3rd lord and the 8th lord.

In the Drekkana chart, RKA (MD) involves the lagna while Saturn, as 3rd lord, and Mars aspect the 3rd house.

Yogini dasha of Bhramari-Bhadrika (Mars-Mercury) operated from April 30, 1990 to November 20, 1990. Mars (MD) associates with Saturn to aspect the 3rd house. Mercury (AD) as the 11th lord (for elder sibling) is too close to Rahu and is

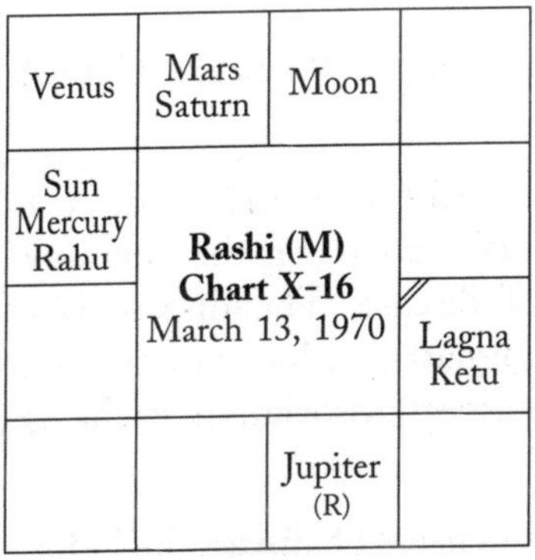

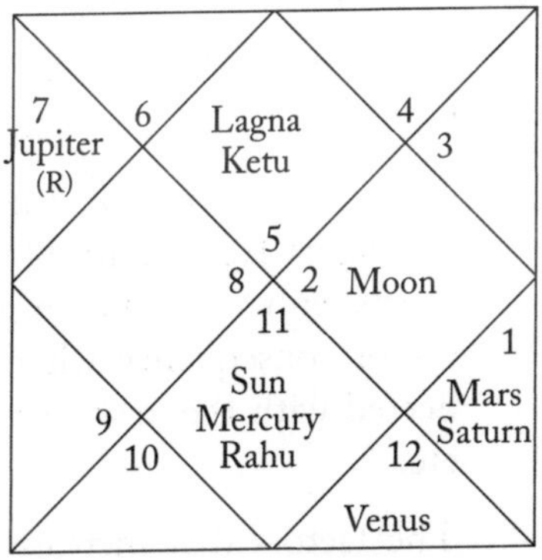

Lagna	14°56'	Mars	11°07'	Venus	10°34'
Sun	29°00'	Mercury	19°45'	Saturn	12°35'
Moon	12°30'	Jupiter (R)	11°48'	Rahu	18°25'

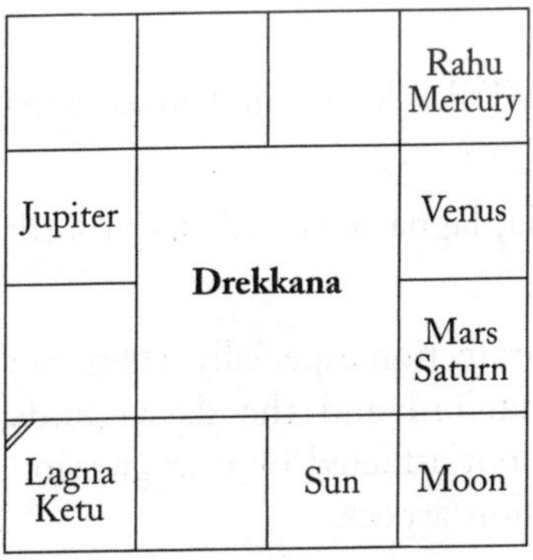

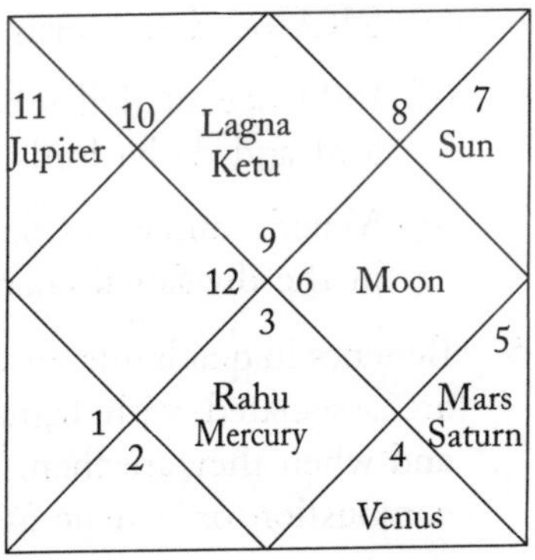

aspected by a retrograde 8th lord from the 3rd house. In the Drekkana it is again in RKA and aspects the lagna.

Note : Just as different dashas are used to time the same event for a native, so also the charts of different blood relations (parents, children, siblings) can be used to corroborate one's findings. It is important to consider the appropriate houses, appropriate significators and appropriate divisional charts for this purpose.

Conclusions

From the above narration it is logical to draw the following conclusions:

1. Disease usually manifests in the dasha of a planet adversely disposed toward a lagna.
2. When the dasha lords are under malefic influence, a relatively mild dasha may produce illness.
3. The relationship of the MD, AD and PD lords with the lagna/lagna lord of the rashi chart or the divisional charts enhances the impact of disease. The disease is of minor consequence when the lagna/lagna lord are not connected with the dasha lords by aspect, association, exchange, etc.
4. The factors that increase the intensity of disease include:
   (a) Malefic influence on dasha lords.
   (b) Malefic influence on lagna/lagna lord.
   (c) RKA on dasha lords.
   (d) Influence of Trika houses/Trika lords on lagna, lagna lord and dasha lords.
   (e) Malefic influences on lagna, lagna lord and dasha lords in the divisional charts.
5. Benefics in quadrants provide protection especially when they are associated with lagna/lagna lord and the dasha lords, and when they are themselves not afflicted by retrogression, combustion or malefic association/aspect.

6. When other factors are adverse, planets owning or occupying the 22nd Drekkana or the 64th Navamsha aggravate illness.
7. The results of the Vimshottari dasha must be confirmed by the use of another dasha. Yogini is one of the many subsidiary dashas that can be used. It will be seen here that many times similar dashas operate in the Vimshottari as well as the Yogini systems.
8. An important factor in the recovery of a patient is the subsequent dasha. When the subsequent dasha order is adverse, recovery does not follow. Improvement results when the subsequent dasha is more favourable.
9. The principle of interrelated destinies operates well in medical astrology. The event of an illness can be easily seen in the charts of parents, children and the siblings of a native.
10. A correct analysis of a horoscope demands a careful balancing of the benefic and malefic influences accompanied by their integration with the dasha system.
11. An important factor that has not been discussed here is the influence of planetary transits over various houses and dasha lords, both in the rashi and the divisional charts. When malefics like Mars, Saturn and RKA transit specific houses, their lords, as also the dasha lords, they produce malefic results. Jupiter's transit provides the healing touch and indicates recovery from illness.

Postscript

A. In old horoscopes cast more than fifty years ago in India, a lot of horoscopic details used to be given in coded language. An investigation into those details and our decoding of this language has led us to the conclusion that as expected there is more astrology in the *Parampara* (tradition) than in the books available. And even in the available books, there are only a single or two-planet combinations given without reference to the divisional charts. The obvious reason was to keep the subtle astrological principles a secret in order that these did not fall in unscrupulous hands. In the northern India, astrologers employed annual horoscopy or the 'Tajika' to substantiate their predictions and to time them more accurately.

In my book on annual horoscopy, *A Textbook of Varshaphala*, instances of indicating and timing illness have been described. Wherever birth data is accurate, the Tajika must be made use of to time the onset of disease. It is here that the astrologer is definitely very superior to the medical man in forewarning about an illness.

B. We have made use of two of the most popular dasha systems used in India. It may be pointed out that several other dasha systems give equally excellent results. In fact, in medical astrology, the use of additional dashas may ensure greater accuracy in prediction.

CHAPTER ELEVEN
MENTAL ILLNESS

ध्यायतो विषयान्पुंसः संगस्तेषूपजायते।
संगात्संजायते कामः कामात्क्रोधोऽभिजायते।।
क्रोधाद्भवति संमोहः संमोहात्स्मृतिविभ्रमः।
स्मृतिभ्रंशाद्बुद्धिनाशो बुद्धिनाशात्प्रणश्यति।।

Dwelling mentally on the objects of sense leads to attachment to them. From attachment arises desire and from desire anger. From anger springs forth lack of discrimination which leads to loss of memory. From loss of memory ensues the destruction of intelligence, and the destruction of intelligence results in decay.

—GITA II, 62, 63

The term 'mental illness' is a relatively vague term. It indicates certain variations in our day to day behaviour which would generally be considered abnormal under the circumstances. All of us experience phases of excitement, anger, aggression, melancholy and depression in response to different day to day situations. These variations in human behaviour are considered as normal reactions to fluctuations in our environment. These normal reactions thus have an explanation. These very reactions, when circumstantially abnormal, being extreme or unexpected or inexplicable for normal human behaviour, are termed as mental illness.

CLASSICAL COMBINATIONS FOR MENTAL ILLNESS

The classical astrological texts give certain combinations for mental illness or insanity. These combinations are often too vague and nonspecific. They cannot be applied to individual horoscopes in the literal sense. That in fact is true of combinations for any disease as given in the astrological texts. They, however, give certain clues about the causation of that disease. We shall quote here some of these combinations, and follow this with our understanding of mental illness and the relevant examples.

Some of the combinations for mental illness taken from the *Jataka Tattva* and other texts are as follows.

1. Jupiter in the ascendant and Mars in the seventh house, or vice versa.

   Note : (a) This (and some of the succeeding combinations!) appears vague. Jupiter is the planet of idealism; Mars indicates aggression. Too much emphasis on these could ruin the married life, as this combination involves the 7th house.

   (b) In the above yoga, substitution of Mars by Saturn has been said to have the same result though the nature of affliction would obviously change from aggressiveness toward depression.

2. Saturn in the lagna and Mars in the 5th or the 7th or the 9th house.

3. Saturn in the lagna, the Sun in the 12th house, and Mars or the Moon in a trine.

4. Saturn in the 12th house associated with a waning Moon.

   Note : Saturn's association with the Moon leads to a tendency towards negative thinking. The 12th house is an adverse house.

5. Association of Saturn and the lord of the second house with the Sun or Mars.

6. Birth in the Hora of Saturn or Mars, the Sun-Moon conjunction in the lagna or the 5th or the 9th, and Jupiter in a quadrant.

7. Mandi in the 7th house, afflicted by a malefic.

   Note : Same result may accrue from an afflicted Mandi in the 5th house.

8. Rahu and the Moon in the lagna, and malefics in the trines.

   Note : This combination goes by the name *'Pishaacha Grasta Yoga'*, i.e., a combination for being overtaken by the 'spirits'. It signifies phobias.

Mental Faculties: Astrological Basis

It will be seen from the above that the various combinations for mental disease are fairly generalised. No mention has been made of the time of onset of the ailment. In addition, there is generally no mention of the various divisional charts without which any combination would lose its specificity. We must thus look for the factors that govern our normal behaviour and, thereafter, proceed to detect abnormal behaviour from the nature and extent of affliction to such factors. The following points thus need attention for the assessment of the mental health of a native.

(a) *The Moon* : It is the significator of the mind. Its strength or weakness reflect the state of one's mind. It indicates our attachments, feelings, emotional reactions, mental compatibility with others, and such faculties as do not rely on mathematical logic. The Moon has no enemies.

(b) *Mercury* : It signifies the nervous system, academic discipline, rationality, logic and intellect, as also one's complexes. Its enemy is the Moon. Understandably, the mind (signified by the Moon) is opposed to reasoning and intellect (signified by Mercury).

(c) *Jupiter* : The best benefic Jupiter is the significator of maturity and wisdom. While Jupiter is neutral towards Mercury, the latter happens to be the enemy of Jupiter. Quite naturally the strict limits of logic can only restrain the exercise of wisdom.

Note : When the Moon, Mercury and Jupiter are strong and well placed, the native has a sound mind, a healthy reasoning and a mature wisdom. When these three planets are afflicted, weak or ill placed, there is a vulnerability to mental illness, nervousness, intellectual confusion, and inability to take wise decisions and to implement them.

(d) *The fifth house* : The fifth house is the house of fascination, thinking, logic and wisdom. For a sound mental health, the 5th house and the fifth lord must be unafflicted and under benefic influence.

(e) *The lagna and the sign Mesha* : Mesha happens to be the first house equivalent to the head of the Kalapurusha. The lagna is the first house or the head of the native. Both should be unafflicted for a sound mental health.

(f) *Malefic and benefic yogas* : Besides the above factors, certain malefic and benefic yogas in the horoscope may promote the occurrence of a mental illness, or favourably compensate for it. The following are especially important:

(i) *The Kemadruma yoga,* i.e., the Moon without a planet on either side of it. This is an adverse yoga. The Moon needs support in order to ensure a sound mind. When there is no planet in the 2nd or the 12th from the Moon, an inherent weakness is indicated in the chart.

(ii) *The Gajakesari yoga,* i.e., the presence of Jupiter in a quadrant from the Moon. This is a very potent benefic yoga. Planets in mutual quadrants influence each other. Jupiter in a quadrant from the Moon causes strengthening of the Moon.

(iii) *The Chandradhi yoga.* This consists of the presence of benefics in the 6th, 7th and 8th from the Moon. Benefics in these houses promote, and the malefics obstruct and hinder, the functioning of the Moon.

Afflictions to the Moon

Most of the mental disorders manifest when the Moon is afflicted. These vary from simple mental aberrations to gross neuro-psychotic disorders. The Moon suffers affliction when it is weak, placed in adverse (6, 8 or 12) houses, and under the aspect or association of malefics.

(a) *Affliction by the Sun* : Quick temper, quarrelsome, self-aggrandisement.

(b) *By Mars* : Quick temper, aggressive, violent.

(c) *By Saturn* : Acute depression; maniac depressive psychosis.

(d) *By Rahu* : Cunning in thought, schizophrenia, phobias, maniacal suicidal tendencies.

(e) *By Ketu* : Maniacal /suicidal tendencies, phobias, irrational suspicion of others.

Note : (i) Affliction to Mercury and Jupiter causes abnormalities in behaviour in a similar manner. For example, placement of Mercury in the 6th house aspected by Saturn leads to some sort of mental derangement. Jupiter-Saturn or Jupiter-Mars opposition have already been pointed out.

(ii) How close these planets are in degrees must be examined.

MENTAL ILLNESS : Sozme Examples

Chart XI-1

This chart belongs to a lady suffering from schizophrenia characterised by episodes of aggression, with occasional depression and suicidal tendencies. The Moon is located in the 12th house in association with a retrograde 8th lord, and aspected by the 6th lord Saturn. Mercury is placed in the 6th house aspected by the 12th lord as well as the retrograde 8th lord. Jupiter itself is the retrograde eighth lord, as also the 5th lord, aspected by Saturn. The 5th house of intelligence and thinking is grossly afflicted by the association in it of the Sun and Rahu, and the aspect of Saturn.

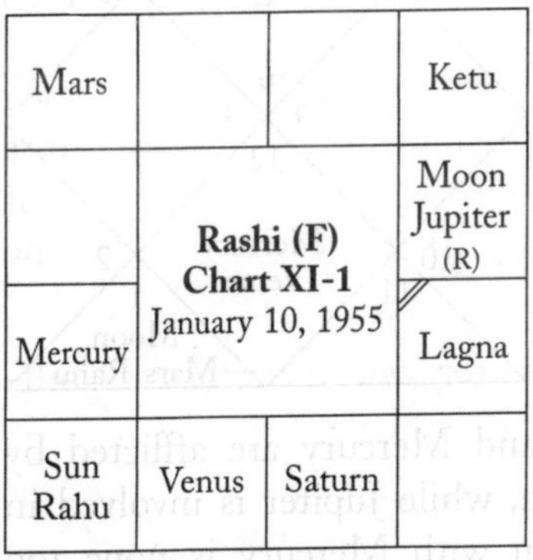

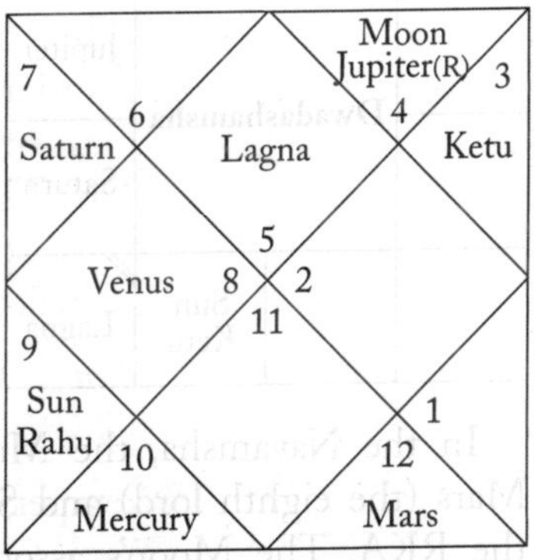

Lagna	03°11'	Mars	03°29'	Venus	10°29'
Sun	26°22'	Mercury	06°12'	Saturn	25°55'
Moon	23°54'	Jupiter(R)	02°22'	Rahu	11°41'

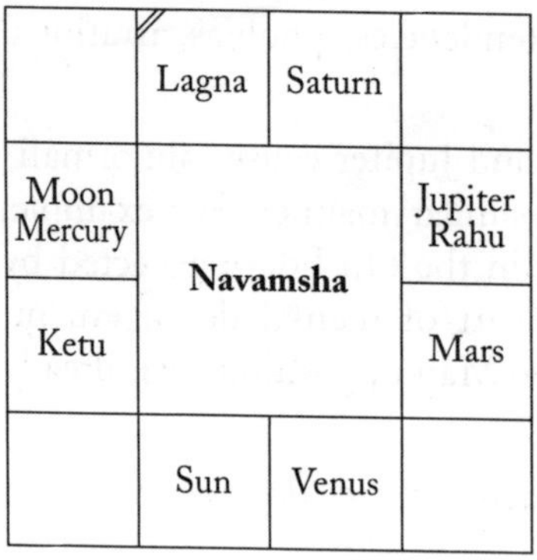

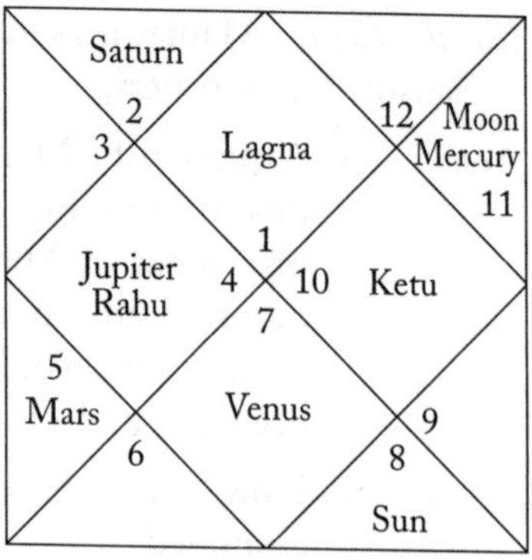

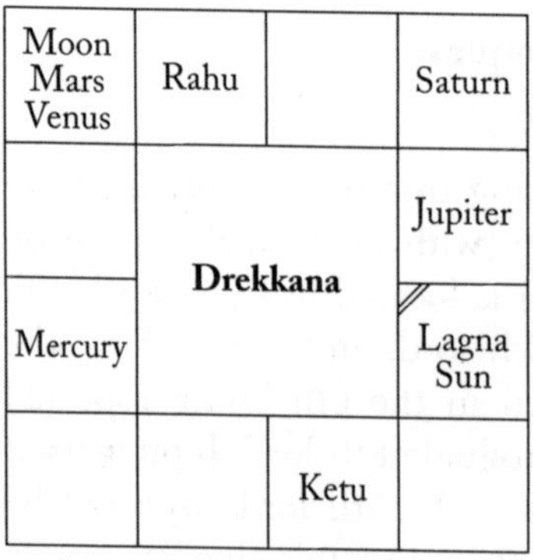

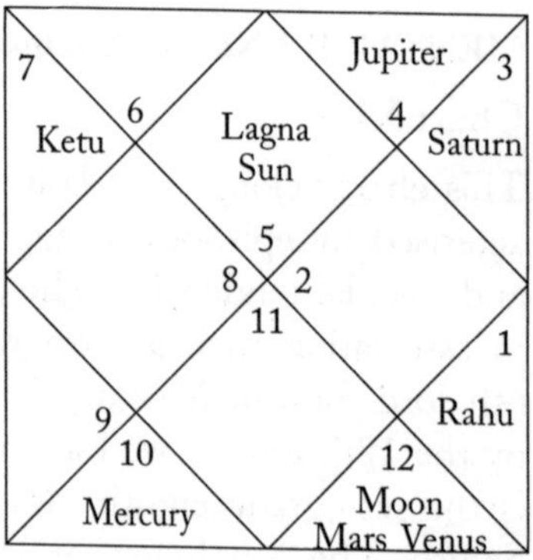

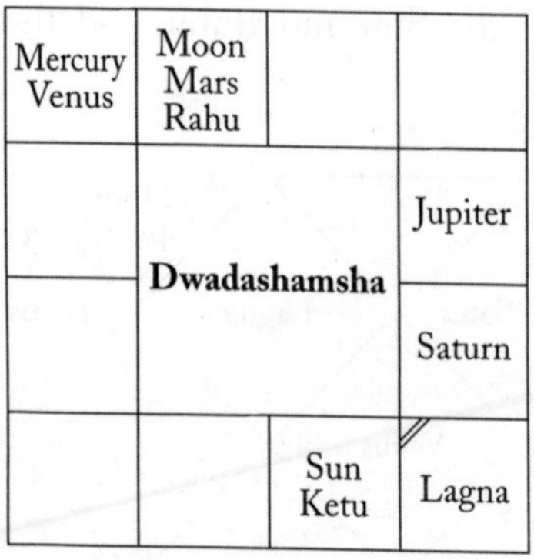

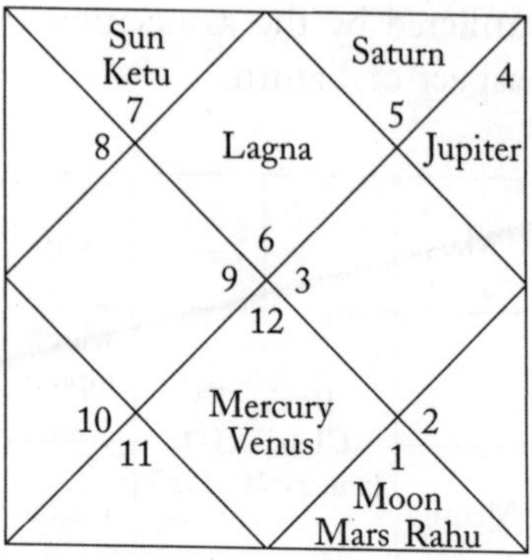

In the Navamsha, the Moon and Mercury are afflicted by Mars (the eighth lord) and Saturn, while Jupiter is involved in the RKA. The Moon's association with Mercury is none too good as Mercury is the 6th lord. The eighth lord occupies the 5th house, and the 5th lord goes into the 8th house aspected by Mars and Saturn.

In the Drekkana chart, the Moon is in the 8th house associated with Mars and aspected by the 6th lord Saturn. Mercury occupies the 6th and Jupiter the 12th house. Saturn also aspects the 5th house.

In the Dwadashamsha chart, the Moon is associated with the eighth lord Mars, and with Rahu, in the 8th house. The 5th lord goes into the 12th house. Jupiter is exalted but aspected by the 8th lord Mars. The 5th house receives some relief as does Mercury because of the aspect of an exalted Jupiter.

Vimshottari dasha

The symptoms first became manifest in Venus-Rahu (December 24, 1976 to December 25, 1979). In Venus-Ketu (August 24, 1988 to October 24, 1989) they became worse. In the MD of the Sun (commencing from October 24, 1989) they have become too severe.

Venus is a malefic lord, suffering from a Papakartari and aspected by a retrograde eighth lord Jupiter. Rahu, Ketu and the Sun influence the 5th house. Ketu is afflicted by the aspect of the Sun, as also of Mars from the eighth house.

Yogini dasha

At the time of commencement of the illness, the Yogini dasha was Sankata - Bhramari (Rahu-Mars). Rahu's affliction has already been mentioned. Mars is afflicted in the 8th house of rashi, Drekkana and Dwadashamsha charts, and is the 8th lord of the Navamsha chart located in the 5th house.

From 1989, the MD of Bhramari (Mars) started and continued till almost the end of 1992. Symptoms aggravated during this period. The next major period, of Bhadrika, too promises little relief as its lord, Mercury, is also under affliction.

Chart XI-2

Here, the Moon, Mercury and Jupiter are afflicted respectively by Gulika, RKA and Saturn's aspect. Gulika in the 5th house is adverse for normal mental balance. The 5th lord is retrograde in the 6th house.

In the Navamsha, the Moon is the 8th lord aspecting the lagna. RKA involves the 5th house which is also aspected by Mars. Jupiter and Mercury, in adverse houses, are afflicted by the Sun

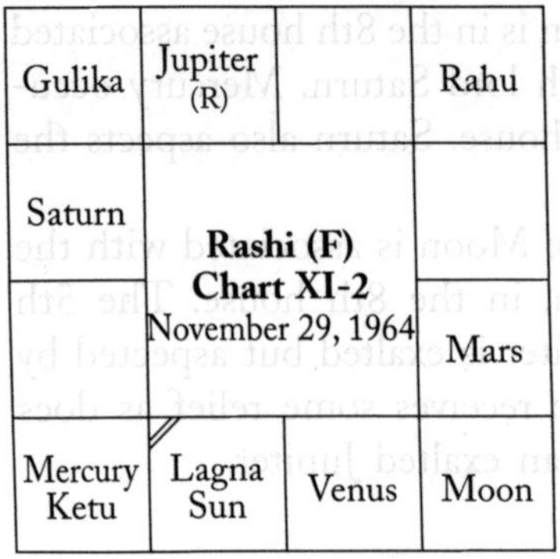

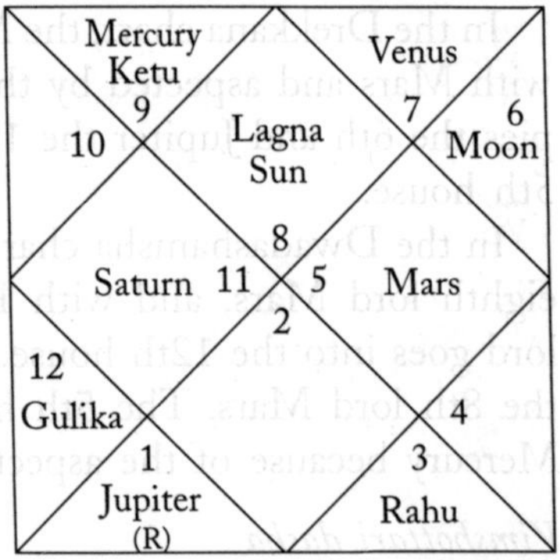

Lagna	19°32'	Mars	17°58'	Venus	11°33'
Sun	13°29'	Mercury	04°47'	Saturn	05°37'
Moon	16°55'	Jupiter (R)	25°38'	Rahu	00°22'

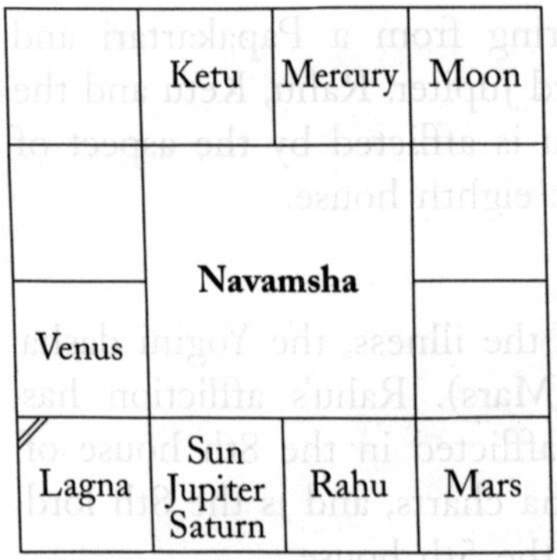

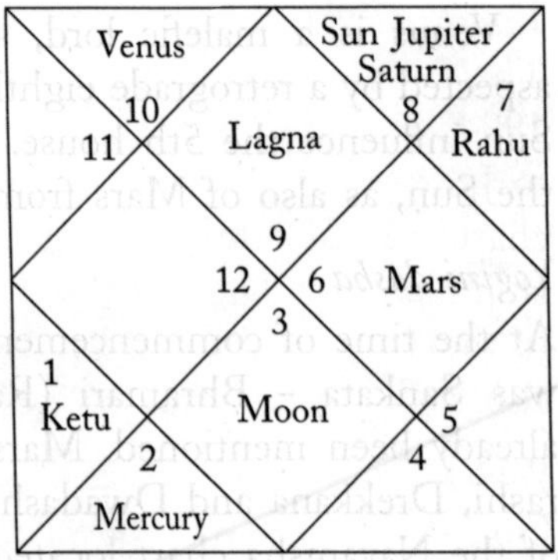

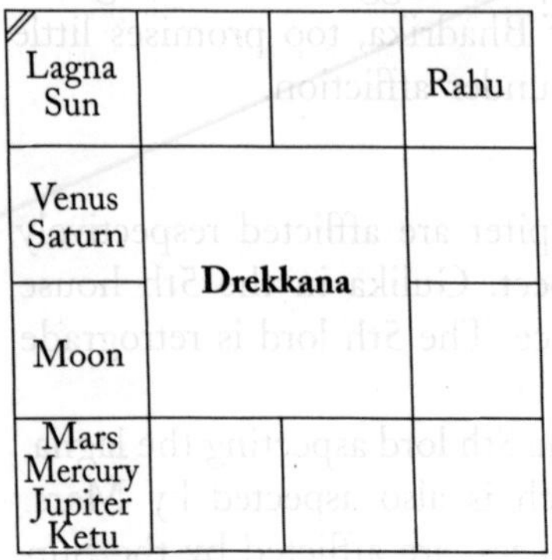

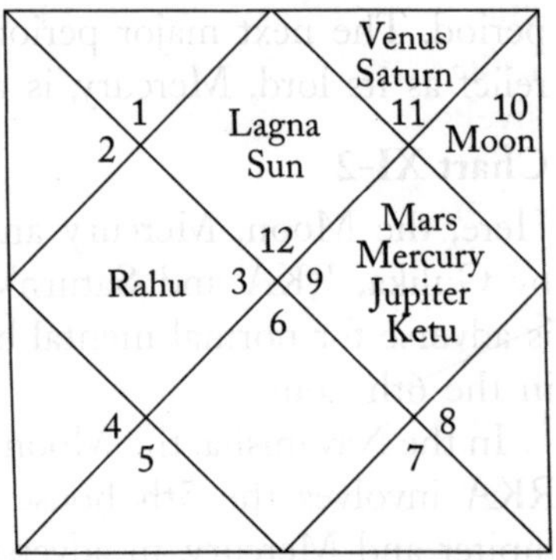

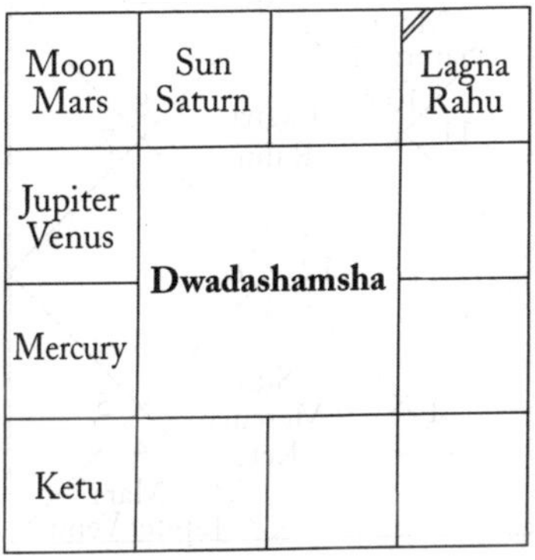

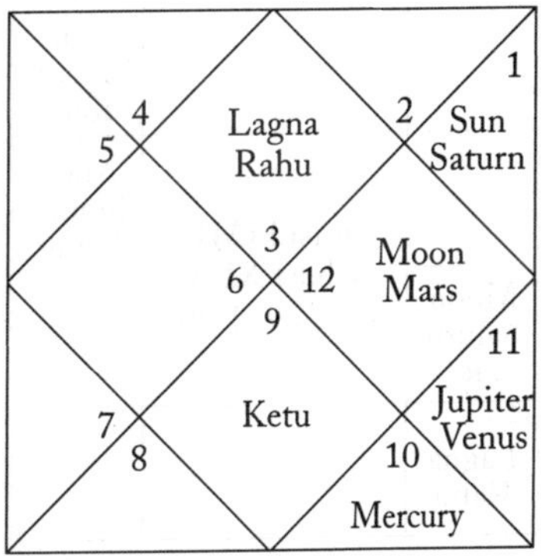

and Saturn. Varying afflictions affect the Moon, Mercury, Jupiter and the 5th house in the Drekkana and the Dwadashamsha.

The native is an alcoholic, takes drugs, is violent and aggressive, and holds her mother responsible for her predicament.

Vimshottari dasha

The MD of Rahu lasts from September 1976 to September 1994. The troubles arose soon after the end of Rahu-Rahu (up to June 4, 1979). Rahu is located in the 8th house in the rashi chart, involves the 5th house in its axis in the Navamsha, and is afflicted by Mars in the Drekkana, and by Mars and Saturn in the Dwadashamsha. The subsequent major period of Jupiter also suffers affliction.

Yogini dasha

From 1978 onwards, the major periods of Bhadrika (Mercury), Ulka (Saturn) and Siddha (Venus) operate. Mercury, Saturn and Venus are all afflicted in the rashi as well as the divisional charts and also own adverse houses. With successive dashas showing little improvement, the mental state of the native has progressively deteriorated.

Chart XI-3

This child was born with mental retardation. The Moon and Jupiter are placed in the 2/8 axis (generally held adverse) and afflicted by a retrograde Saturn, Mars, and the 6th lord. Jupiter is also the lagna lord. The Moon is too close to Saturn. The 5th lord Mars is debilitated in the 8th house, associated with the 6th lord and aspected by Saturn.

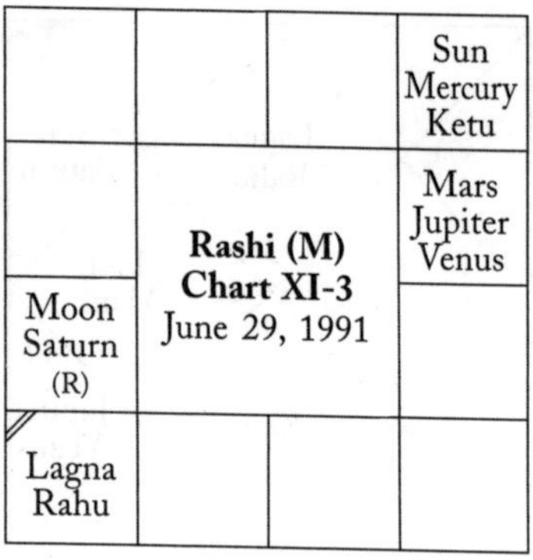

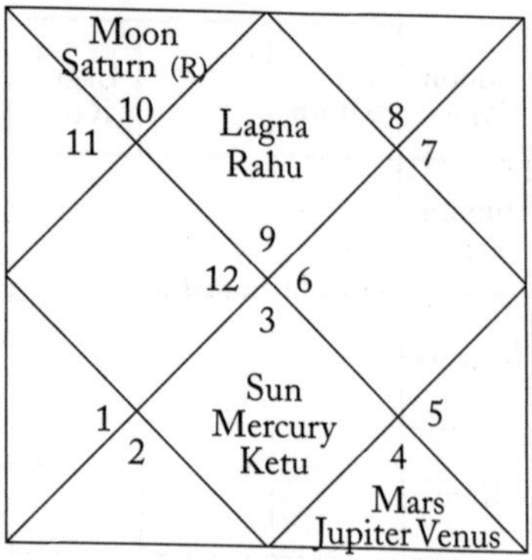

Lagna	23°44'	Mars	26°33'	Venus	27°55'
Sun	13°37'	Mercury	27°46'	Saturn (R)	11°42'
Moon	10°33'	Jupiter	20°21'	Rahu	25°11'

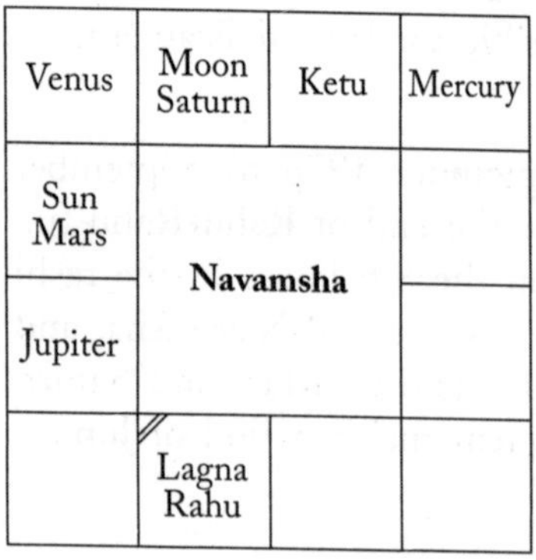

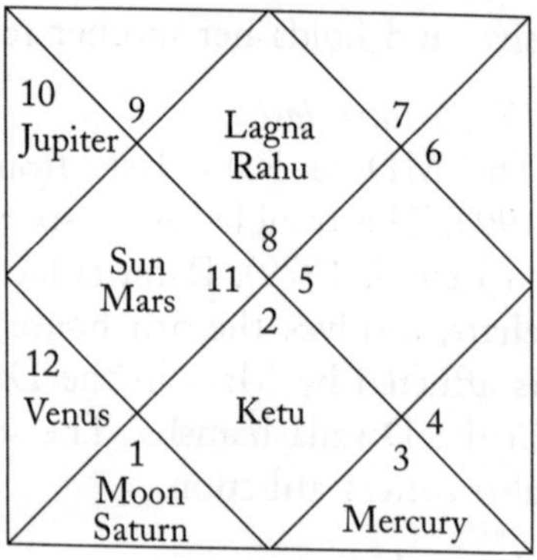

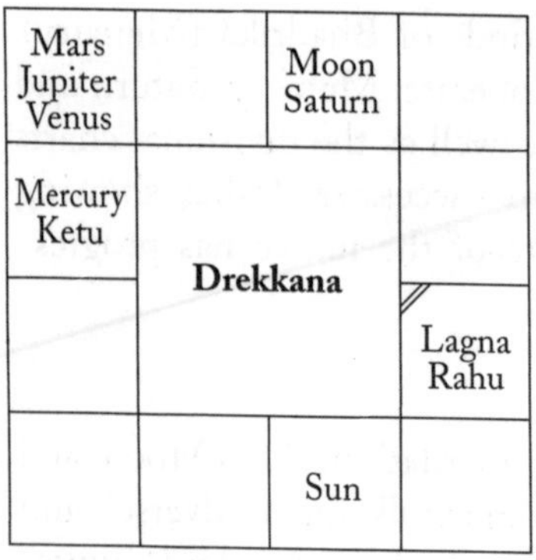

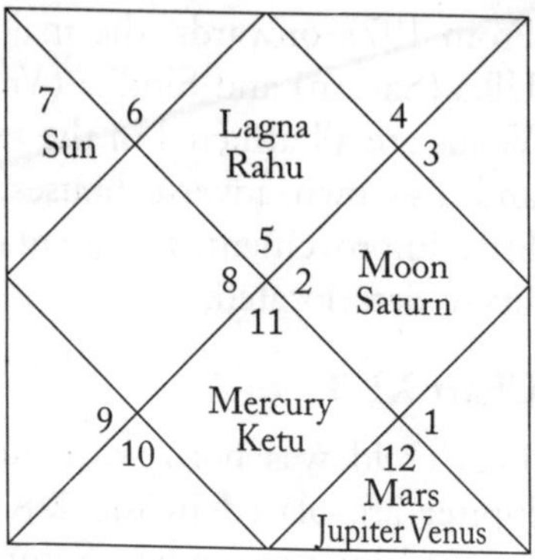

The Moon, Mercury and Jupiter are under the influence of Saturn in the Navamsha. Mercury is in the 8th house. Jupiter is also the lord of the 5th house and debilitated.

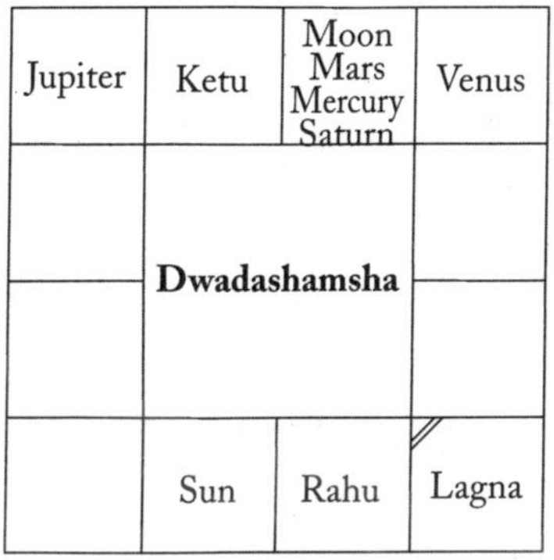

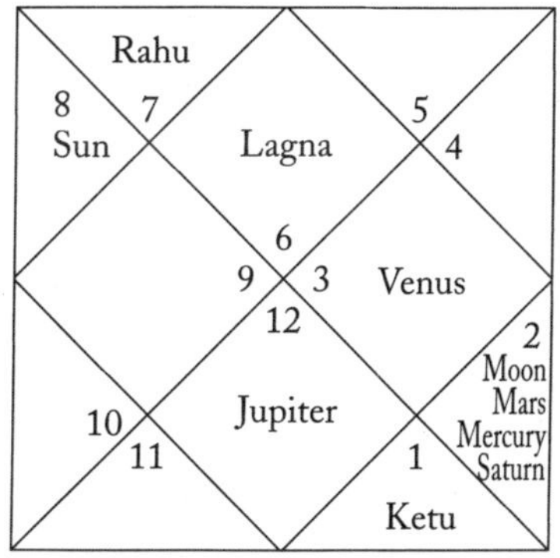

In the Drekkana chart, Mercury, Jupiter as well as the Moon and the 5th lord are afflicted. Jupiter escapes affliction in the Dwadashamsha.

The *Vimshottari dasha* at the time of birth was Moon-Moon, involving the 8th house lordship. The *Yogini dasha* was Mangala-Pingala (Moon-Sun). The Sun is in RKA in the 7th house and associated with Mercury, a malefic lord. The Sun is under affliction in the remaining divisional charts, and is also debilitated in the Drekkana.

Chart XI-4

This is another child born mentally retarded. The Moon is afflicted in the 12th house by the aspect of 8th lord Saturn.

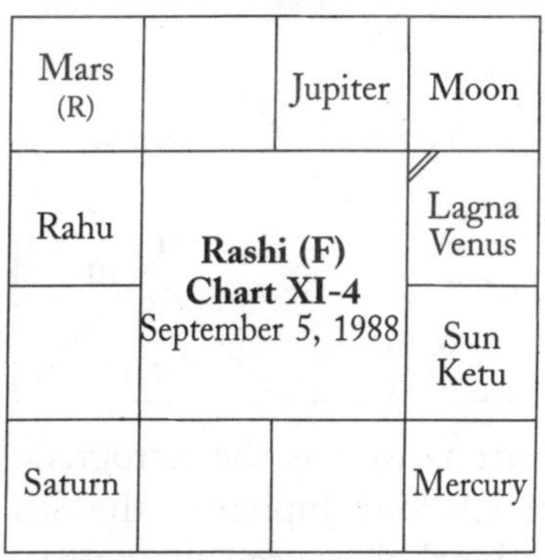

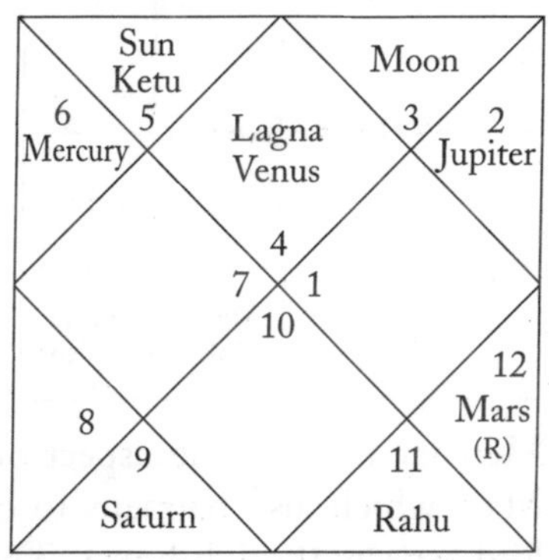

Lagna	25°08'	Mars (R)	17°09'	Venus	03°38'
Sun	18°54'	Mercury	13°23'	Saturn	02°18'
Moon	10°02'	Jupiter	11°49'	Rahu	20°24'

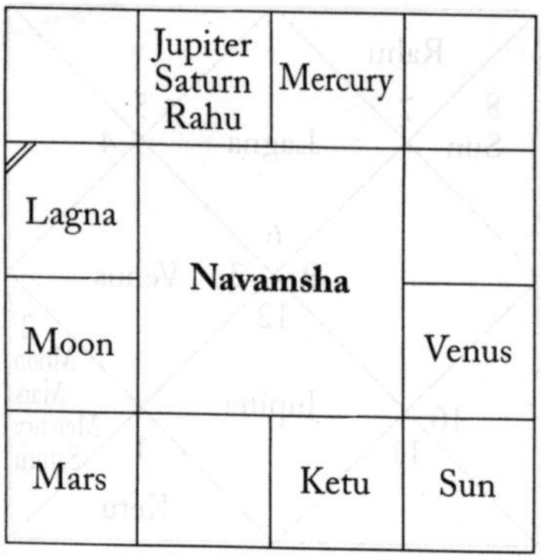

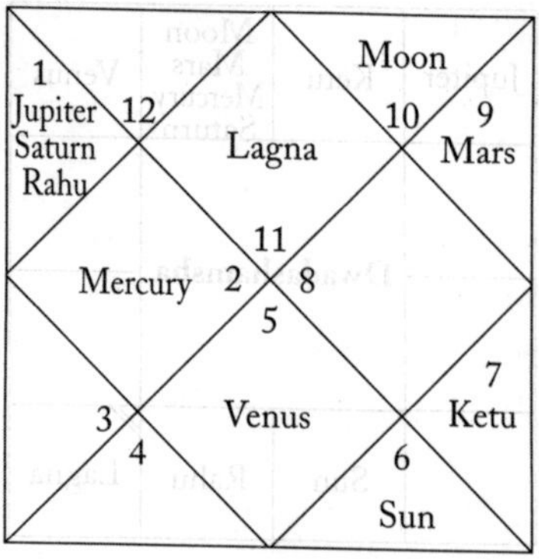

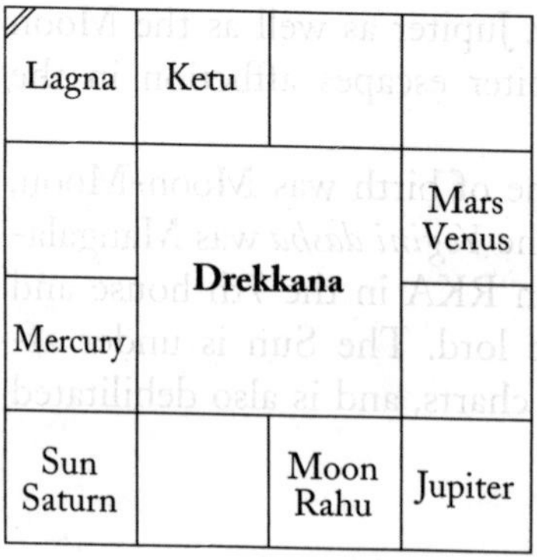

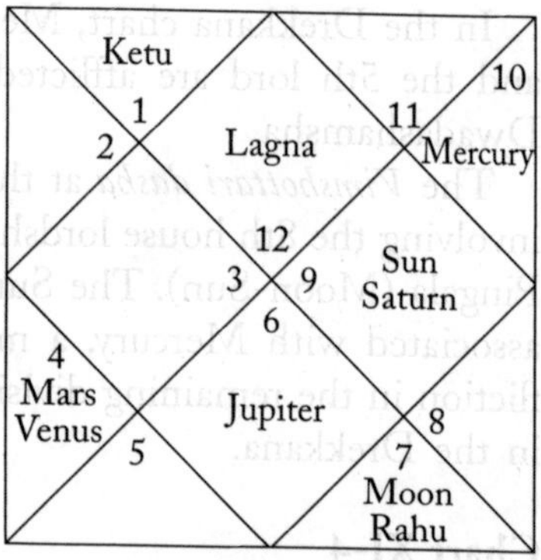

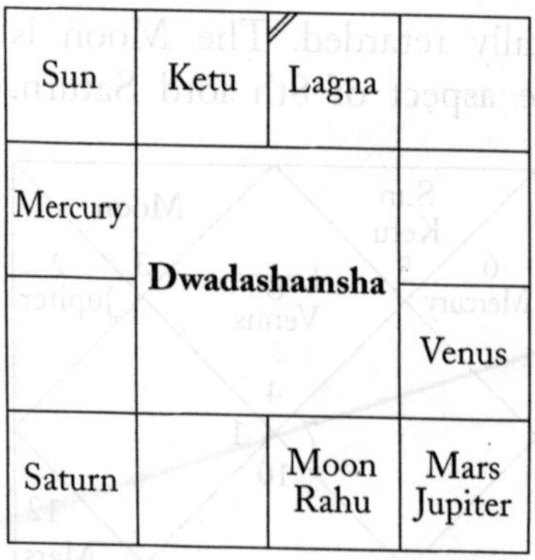

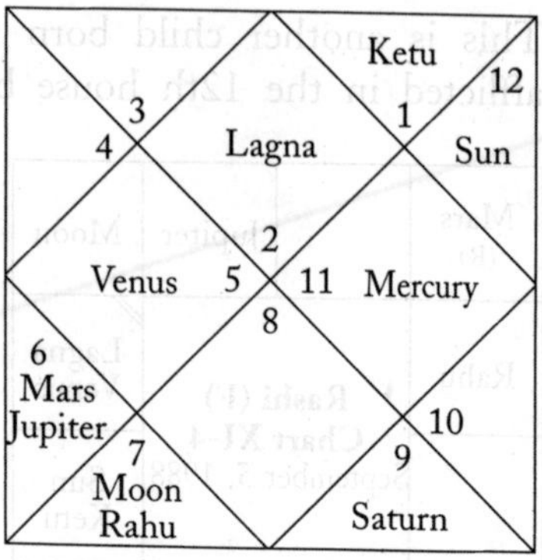

Mercury receives the aspect of Saturn as well as the retrograde Mars which also happens to be the 5th lord. Jupiter as the 6th lord aspects the 5th house. The divisional charts too show varying affliction to these.

The *Vimshottari dasha* operative at birth was Rahu-Jupiter. Rahu is in the 8th house aspected by the Sun and Saturn. Jupiter, the

6th lord, aspects the 5th house. In the Navamsha, both Jupiter and Rahu are conjunct and afflicted by a debilitated Saturn.

In the Drekkana, Rahu is associated with the 5th lord, the Moon, and aspected by a debilitated Mars. Jupiter is aspected by Saturn. In the Dwadashamsha, Moon and Rahu occupy the 6th house while Jupiter, as the 8th lord in the 5th house, is under the influence of Mars, Saturn and the Sun.

The *Yogini dasha* at the time of birth was Mangala-Bhramari (Moon-Mars). The Moon is afflicted in all the charts by lordship and by association or aspect. Mars is the retrograde 5th lord, again variously afflicted in the divisional charts.

CHAPTER TWELVE

DISEASE OF THE EYE

योो मां पश्यति सर्वत्र सर्वं च मयि पश्यति।
तस्याहं न प्रणश्यामि स च मे न प्रणश्यति।।

The one who sees Me everywhere, and sees all in Me,
I am not lost to him nor is he lost to Me.

—GITA, VI - 30

Numerous combinations for eye disease and blindness have been described in the classical astrological literature. These combinations again are too general and cannot be subjected to a literal application. In addition, they have to be integrated with the dasha scheme in order to decipher the time when eye disease might manifest.

CLASSICAL COMBINATIONS

It may be relevant to point out here that wherever combinations for blindness have been indicated, they may only mean some defective vision or even normal vision if there is adequate compensation by the aspect or association of benefics. Similarly, combinations which have been described to cause minor ailment may result in blindness if there is sufficient additional affliction.

A. Poor Vision/ Eye disease

The following combinations may adversely affect the vision or lead to some eye disease not necessarily leading to blindness.

1. Presence of the Sun in the lagna.

   Note : The Sun in the lagna is considered bad for eyes:

   (a) In Mesha lagna, it leads to inflammation of the eyes (influence of Mars through its sign Mesha!);

   (b) In Simha lagna, it leads to night blindness;

(c) In Karka, it results in cataract; and

(d) In Tula, it results in blindness.

2. Weak Moon aspected by Saturn, unaspected by Jupiter.
3. The Sun in the second house.
4. Two malefics in the second house.
5. The Moon in the second house aspected by malefics.

   Note : The Sun and the Moon together in 2nd house are said to cause night blindness.
6. The Moon as the sixth lord located in the sign of a retrograde planet.

   Note : (a) This can happen only in the case of Kumbha lagna.

   (b) Any sixth lord located in the sign of a retrograde planet is also considered adverse by some.
7. The Moon posited in the 6th house without the aspect or association of benefics.
8. Venus as the 6th lord in the lagna, and a retrograde benefic in the 6th or the 8th or the 12th house.
9. The Sun, Venus and Mars located together in any house.
10. The 2nd lord and the 12th lord together in the 6th or the 8th or the 12th from Venus.

B. Blindness

As has already been indicated, blindness from these combinations should only be expected if there is sufficient affliction in all the divisional charts, and the dasha periods also indicate it.

1. The Moon in the 2nd house from the Sun, afflicted by the association or aspect of malefics.
2. Debilitated Moon in the 6th or the 12th house associated with or aspected by malefics.
3. Combust Mars in the lagna.
4. The Sun and the Moon together in a quadrant, in the eighth Navamsha of a watery sign.
5. The Moon in the lagna, in Karka or Mesha or Vrisha Navamsha, or in the first half of Dhanu Navamsha.

6. The Moon in the lagna in Vrisha 19° or in Meena 20°.
7. The lord of the lagna in the sign of a malefic, in the eight house.
8. Mars located in the sixth house from the Moon.
9. The Sun, the Moon, Mars and Saturn posited in any order in the houses 2, 6, 8 and 12.

   Note : Malefics in the 6/12 axis damage the left eye; those in the 2/8 axis damage the right eye.
10. The Sun in the lagna in RKA, with malefics posited in the trines.
11. The Sun and the Moon in houses 6 and 8; or Mars and Saturn in houses 6 and 8.
12. The Sun and the Moon together in the 12th house afflicted by malefics.
13. The Moon and Venus together in the second house afflicted by malefics.
14. The lagna lord, the second lord and the Sun posited together.

    Note : (a) When posited together in the 2nd house there is blindness since birth.

    (b) The Sun and the 2nd lord together associating with the 4th lord cause blindness to mother; when they associate with the third lord, they cause blindness to sibling; and when associating with the ninth lord they lead to blindness to father.
15. The second lord associated with Venus and the lagna lord, and placed in the Amsha (Navamsha), the MoolaTrikaona or the exaltation sign of Venus.

C. Blindness since birth

1. The Sun, Venus and the lagna lord together in the Trika houses.
2. The Sun, the Moon, Venus, Mars and Saturn posited together in any sign.
3. Saturn debilitated and combust, and birth taking place at the time of eclipse (perhaps solar eclipse!).
4. The Sun in RKA, with Mars and Saturn in a trine.
5. The lagna lord, the 2nd lord, the Sun and Venus together in any of the Trika houses.

6. The lagna lord, the 2nd lord, the 12th lord and Venus together in any of the Trika houses.

D. Blindness in one eye

1. Mars or the Moon in the lagna aspected by Venus or Jupiter.
2. The Moon in the 7th house in Simha, aspected by Mars.

   Note : This is possible for Kumbha lagna.
3. The Sun in Karka in the 7th house, aspected by Mars.

   Note : Possible for Makara lagna.
4. The Moon and the Sun in the 12th and the 6th houses: The native is one-eyed as also is his wife!

E. Injury to the eye

1. Mars in the 12th and Saturn in the 2nd cause injury to the left and the right eye respectively.
2. The 2nd lord, the 12th lord and Venus debilitated in Navamsha and afflicted therein by malefics.
3. Lords of the 2nd, the 6th and the 10th associating with Venus in the lagna indicate loss of eyes through the wrath of the ruler.

Many of the above combinations have been taken from the *Jataka Tattva*. It is again stressed here that one should only pick up the principles underlying these dicta and never pronounce predictions without a judicious balancing of all the malefic and benefic factors. It has been observed, however, that these combinations never fail, if the dasha-periods and transits are adverse.

Astrological Principles Underlying Eye Disease

The following factors must be considered.

1. *The luminaries* : The Sun and the Moon represent the right eye and the left eye respectively.
2. *Venus* : Venus is the significator for eyes as well as for vision. Unafflicted Venus located in the lagna gives rise to beautiful eyes and face. Venus associated with Saturn gives rise to small eyes. Venus also represents the lens of the eye.

Note : Those doing optical business have a prominent Venus connected with their houses of profession and profit.

3. *The Second house/Second lord* : The second house is concerned with vision. A strong and powerful 2nd lord, or a benefic influence on the 2nd house leads to beautiful and healthy eyes. When the 2nd lord is placed in the 6th or the 8th or the 12th house, it causes some eye defect.
4. *The Twelfth house* : The 2nd house is particularly indicative of the right eye and the 12th house of the left eye. The Moon in the 12th house damages the left eye. The Sun, which signifies the right eye, located in the 12th house (also the house of loss!) damages the right eye.

Eye Disease : Some Examples

Chart XII-1

The native suffered injury to his left eye while he was quite young. This lead to a near total loss of vision as well as a corneal opacity.

All the planets and houses that are concerned with eyes and vision are afflicted. The Moon is located in the 6th house with the 6th lord as well as Ketu. The Sun is in the 8th house. Venus in the 7th house is aspected by a retrograde Saturn. The second house receives the aspect of the Sun from the 8th house. The 12th house is involved in the RKA and receives the aspects of Mars and the Moon from the 6th house. Venus, however, also receives the benefic aspect of Jupiter.

In the Navamsha, the Moon is in the 8th house aspected by Mars, whereas the Sun is in RKA aspected by Saturn. Venus is located in the 6th house, and the 2nd house is occupied by Mars.

In the Drekkana chart, the Moon is in the 6th house and the Sun in the 8th house. Venus in the 7th receives the aspect of the 8th lord Saturn. The 12th lord, Mercury, is aspected by Mars.

In the Dwadashamsha, the 2nd house has Rahu aspected by Saturn and Mars; the twelfth house has Saturn. The Sun is afflicted in the 7th house but receives the aspect of Jupiter, which is not totally beneficial as Jupiter is the 6th lord also.

It will thus be seen that affliction to the luminaries, Venus, as also to the 2/8 and 6/12 axes is important in causing eye disease.

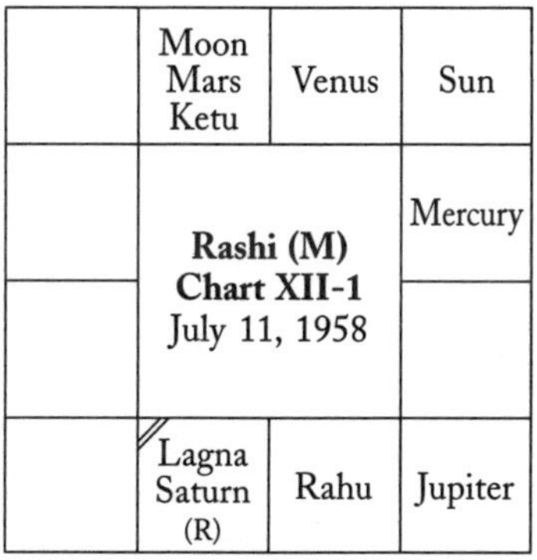

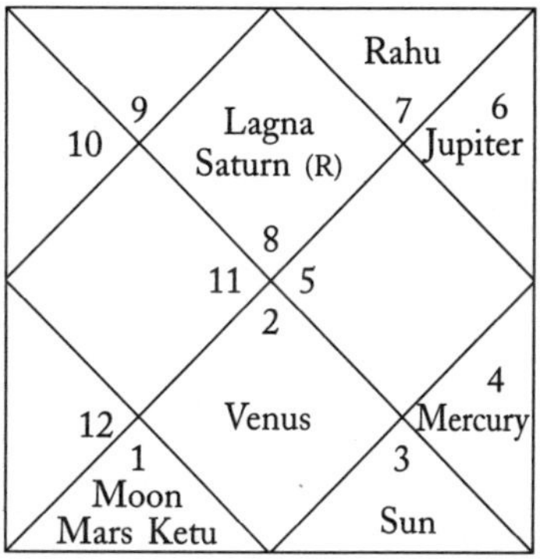

Lagna	29°52'	Mars	00°23'	Venus	23°54'
Sun	25°23'	Mercury	17°35'	Saturn (R)	27°14'
Moon	22°36'	Jupiter	29°13'	Rahu	04°26'

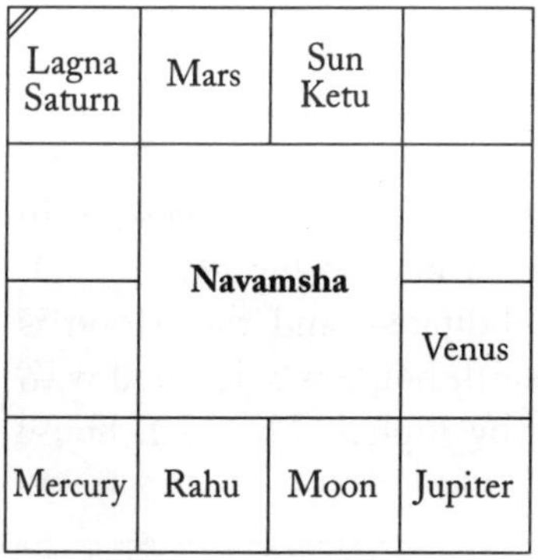

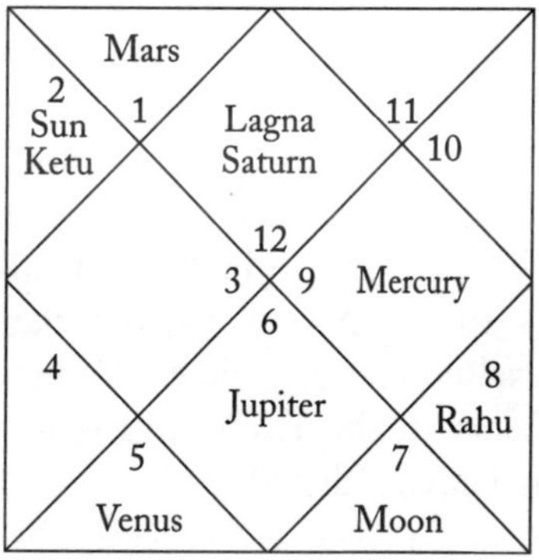

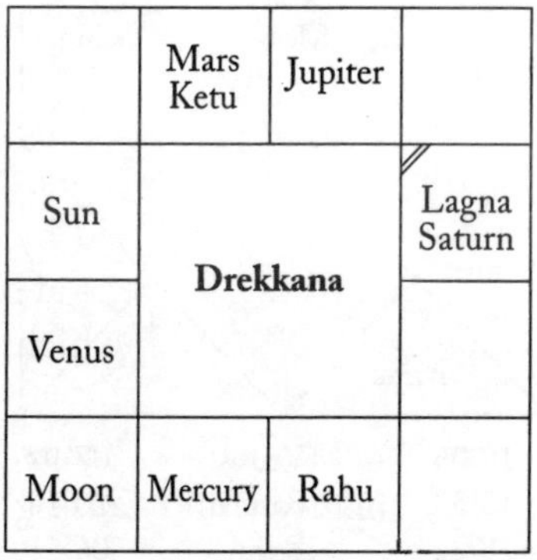

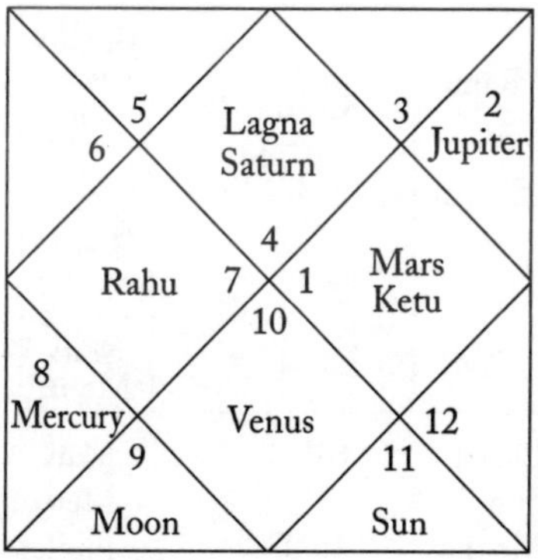

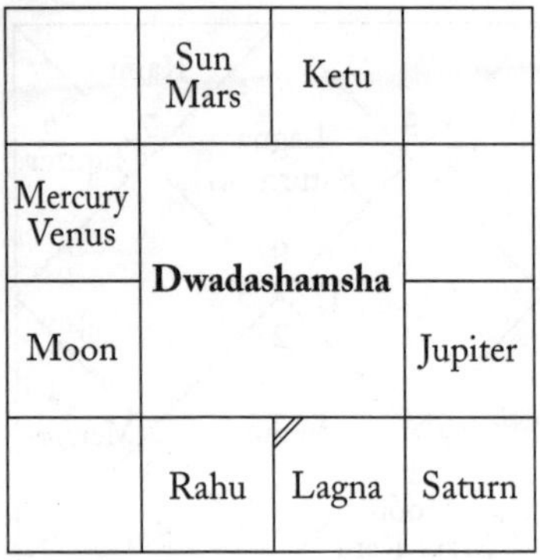

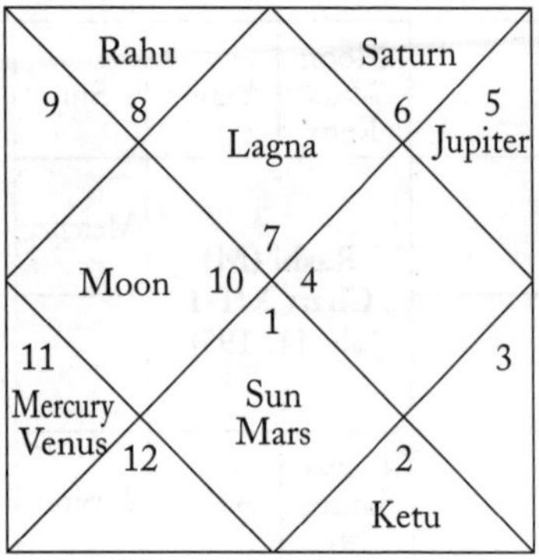

Chart XII-2

This chart belongs to a native who developed retinal detachment in his left eye in August 1993. On November 2, 1993 he had surgical treatment for it but got no relief and in fact his condition deteriorated. He had another surgery on January 27, 1994 and has been improving since.

The Moon occupies the lagna in association with the 8th lord Mars. The Sun is the 12th lord associated with a retrograde lagna lord, and aspected by a retrograde 6th lord, Saturn. Venus lies in the 12th house in RKA as also with a benefic Jupiter.

In the Navamsha, the Sun is debilitated, and the Moon is exalted and unafflicted. Venus in the 6th house is associated with Mars in the RKA, and is aspected by Jupiter. The 12th house is badly afflicted.

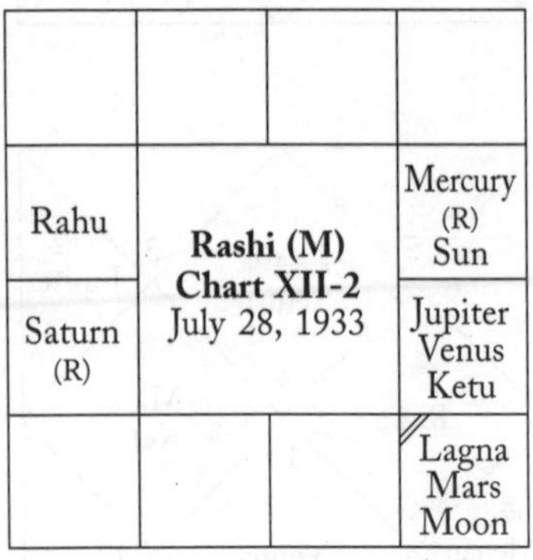

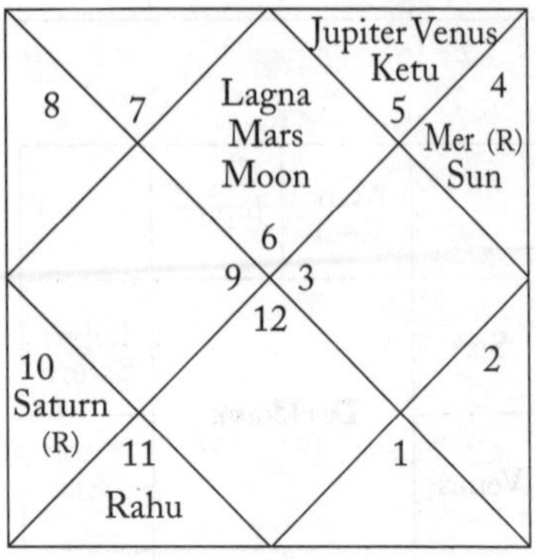

Lagna	02°18'	Mars	19°06'	Venus	07°39'
Sun	11°40'	Mercury (R)	15°33'	Saturn (R)	20°44'
Moon	16°07'	Jupiter	28°22'	Rahu	06°51'

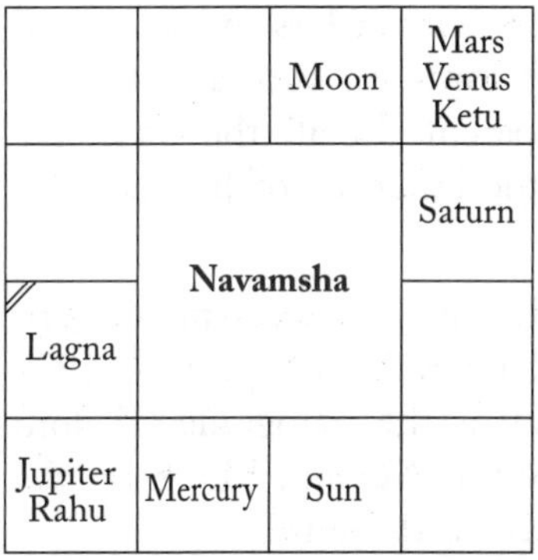

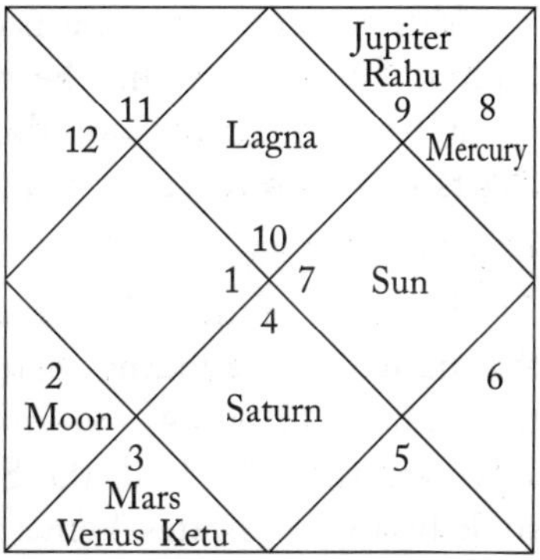

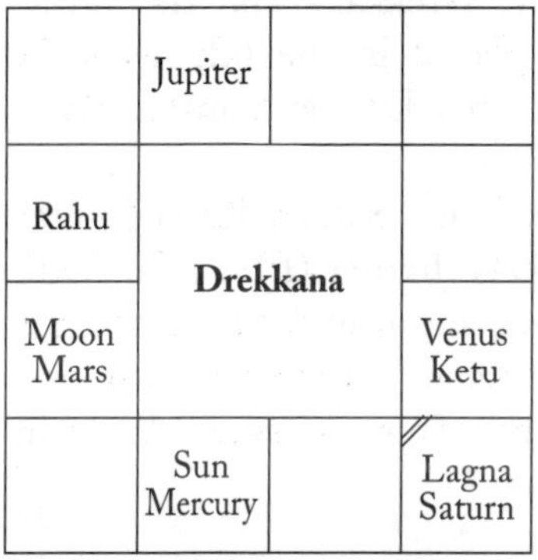

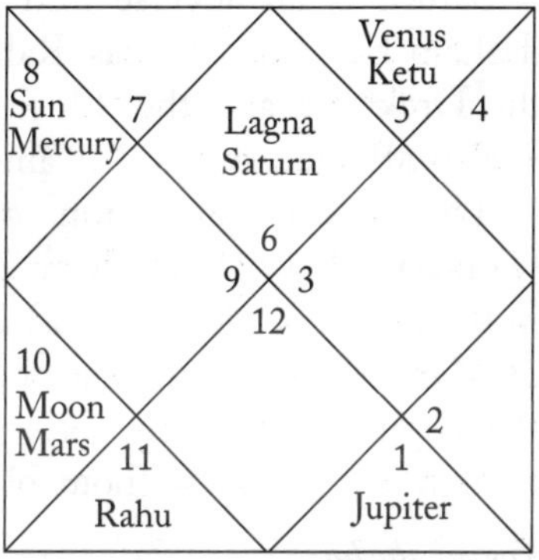

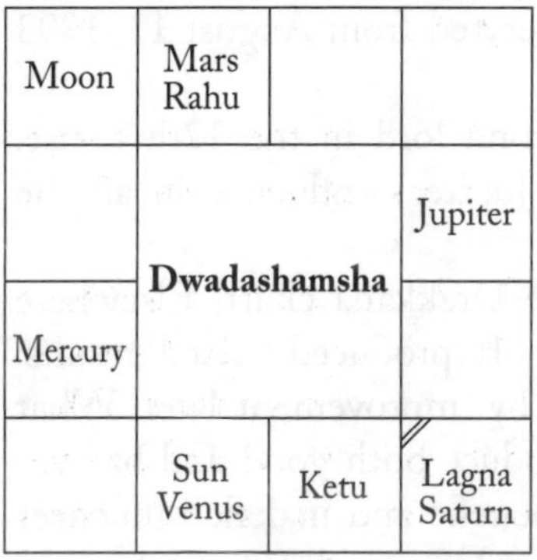

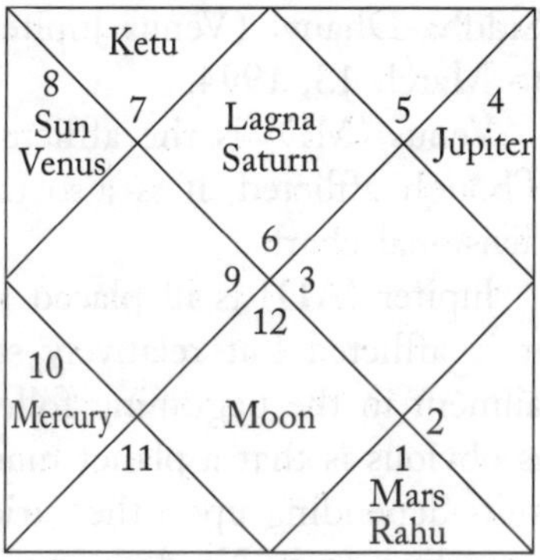

In the Drekkana, the Moon is afflicted by the 8th lord Mars, and the Sun by the 6th lord Saturn. Venus in the 12th house, in the RKA, is aspected by Mars; a benefic Jupiter, however, also aspects Venus.

In the Dwadashamsha, the Moon, the Sun as well as Venus, are all aspected by the 6th lord Saturn. The Venus and the Sun in addition receive the aspects of the 8th lord Mars and an exalted Jupiter. The second and the twelfth lords are both afflicted.

Mixed influences are thus apparent. In all the divisional charts considered, Venus is under the influence of Jupiter.

Vimshottari dasha

At the time of his ailment and the first unsuccessful surgery, the native was running Saturn-Rahu-Rahu (August 8, 1993 to January 12, 1994). Saturn (MD) is the retrograde 6th lord aspecting the 12th lord, the Sun. Rahu (AD and PD) from the sixth house implicates Venus and the 12th house.

Saturn is an adverse lord for the Drekkana and the Dwadashamsha also, whereas Rahu is placed in the 6th house in the Drekkana and the 8th house in the Dwadashamsha. Rahu is also afflicted in the Navamsha.

The second operation occurred in Saturn-Rahu-Jupiter (January 12, 1994 to May 29, 1994). Jupiter (PD) is in RKA in the rashi and the Navamsha charts, and is under the influence of Mars in the Navamsha, the Drekkana and the Dwadashamsha. Jupiter is relatively better by strength, position and lordship though not totally without blemish.

Yogini dasha

Siddha-Dhanya (Venus-Jupiter) operated from August 13, 1993 to March 13, 1994.

Venus (MD) is the afflicted second lord in the 12th house. Though afflicted, it is also under Jupiter's influence in all the divisional charts.

Jupiter (AD) is ill placed in the Drekkana chart. Elsewhere it is afflicted but relatively strong. It produced mixed results: ailment in the beginning followed by improvement later. What is obvious is that a planet must produce both good and bad results depending upon the various benefic and malefic influences operating on it. No dasha period can be considered purely good or purely bad.

The reader is also referred to Chart VI-5 in the chapter on Balarishta. This chart shows gross affliction to the 6th house resulting in an incurable, and eventually fatal, eye ailment. The adverse dasha sequence operated early in life to cause the tragic end.

CHAPTER THIRTEEN

EAR AILMENTS AND DEFECTIVE SPEECH

वागेव विश्वा भुवनानि जज्ञे वाच इत्।
स सर्व्वममृतं यच्च मर्त्यमिति श्रुतिः।।

From the Word have originated all worlds.
The Word has produced the imperishable and the perishable regions.

—VAKYAPADIYA

Hearing is an important function of the body. Ancient astrological literature gives several combinations for detecting ear disease in a horoscopic chart. In fact the various combinations have been given for deafness, although deafness is not the only disease that affects the ears. There could be a variety of ailments affecting the ears or the hearing mechanism. We shall first refer to the classical combinations that are supposed to cause deafness.

CLASSICAL COMBINATIONS FOR DEAFNESS

As is customary with the various combinations given in the classical literature, they are quite general and not applicable in the literal sense. Their underlying principles have to be grasped in order to apply them to individual horoscopes. Besides, although it is deafness that is supposed to result from these combinations it is important to see in the individual charts any benefic influences which neutralise affliction. It is the balance between benefic and malefic influences which decides the final outcome at a time indicated by the appropriate dashas. The classical combinations for deafness are as follows.

1. Mercury in the 6th or the 8th or the 12th house aspected by Saturn.

2. Saturn aspecting the 6th house as well as Mercury, which happens to be the 6th lord.

   Note : This can happen in case of Mesha and Makara lagnas, with Saturn in houses 4 or 9 or 12.

3. Mercury in the 4th house from Saturn, and the 6th lord in one of the Trika houses.

4. Mercury and Venus conjoined in the 12th house lead to defective hearing in the left ear.

5. Malefics located in the 3rd or the 11th or the 5th or the 9th house, unaspected by benefics.

   Note : Malefics in the 3/9 axis would afflict the right ear and those in the 5/11 axis would damage the left ear.

6. Debilitated Venus associated with Rahu.

7. Mercury and the 6th lord in one of the Trika houses aspected by Saturn.

8. Mercury and the 6th lord in the 4th house, with Saturn occupying the lagna.

9. Conjunction of the Sun and Mercury in houses 3, 6 or 11.

10. Venus in the Vrisha or Dhanu lagna, and a malefic Moon aspecting Venus.

11. Birth taking place at night time, with Venus in the fifth house and Mercury occupying the 6th house.

12. Jupiter occupying Dhanu, with Mercury and Venus in the Hudda of Saturn.

    Note : The Hudda is a special feature of the Vedic system of annual horoscopy. For a detailed understanding of the Hudda, the reader is referred to *A Textbook of Varshaphala* by the author.

13. The Moon, Mars and Mercury together in the RKA in the 3rd or the 11th house.

    Note : This combination indicates severe mastoiditis (internal ear disease).

14. Mercury associated with the Sun in the 3rd, 6th or the 11th house, opposed by Mars and Saturn.

Note : This combination leads to internal ear disease where surgical intervention becomes necessary.

Astrological Principles

Ear disease must be judged from the following:

(a) *Mercury*: Mercury deals with hearing as well as communications of any sort. A strong Mercury under benefic influences indicates a strong and healthy hearing mechanism. Affliction indicate the reverse.

(b) *The third house* : The third is the house in the horoscope concerned with hearing. Benefic influences on the 3rd house/3rd lord ensure a healthy hearing system.

(c) *The eleventh house* : The 3rd house and the 3rd lord indicate the right ear (besides the faculty of hearing). The 11th house and the 11th lord indicate the left ear.

Benefic and malefic influences on Mercury, the 3rd house/3rd lord, and the 11th house/11th lord indicate the state of health of the ears.

Ear Disease: Example

Chart XIII-1

This chart belongs to a girl who became virtually deaf right in her childhood. The left ear has very slight hearing left in it; the

Jupiter (R)	Moon Ketu	Mars	Lagna
	Rashi (F) **Chart XIII-1** September 22, 1975		Saturn
			Venus
		Rahu	Sun Mercury

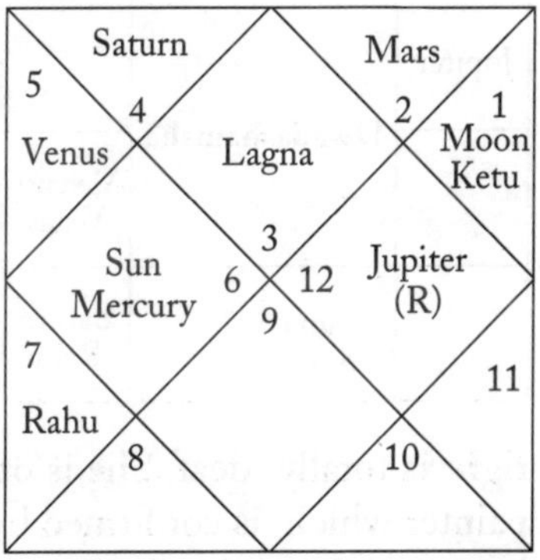

Lagna	13°57'	Mars	27°39'	Venus	02°19'
Sun	05°36'	Mercury	29°57'	Saturn (R)	07°03'
Moon	00°22'	Jupiter (R)	28°48'	Rahu	29°40'

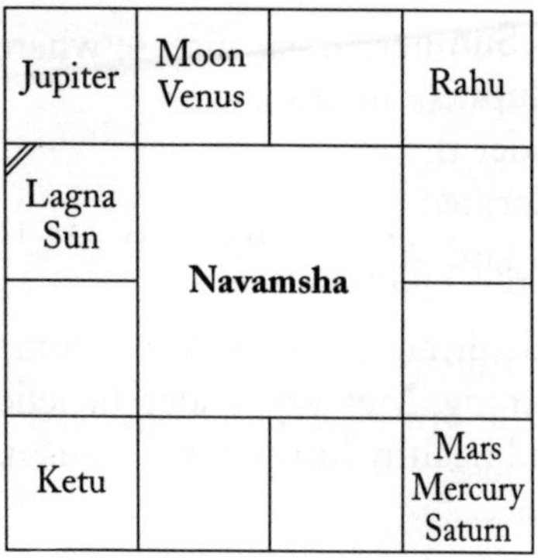

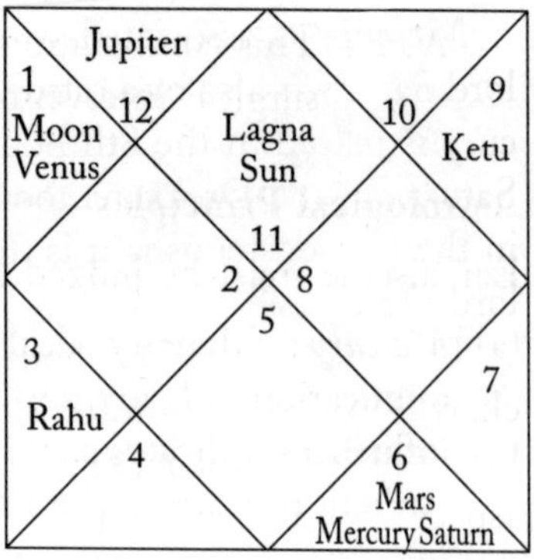

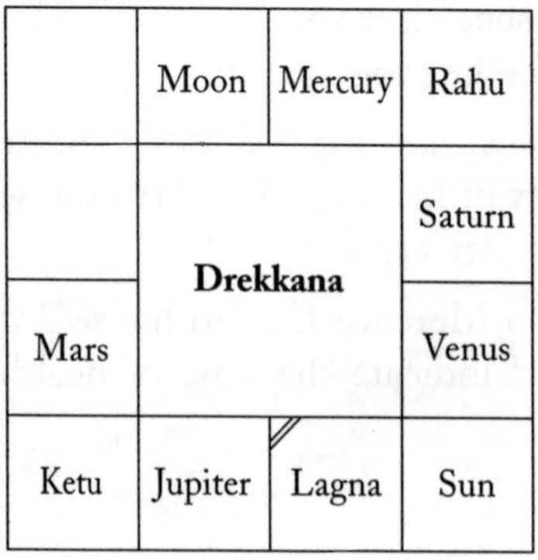

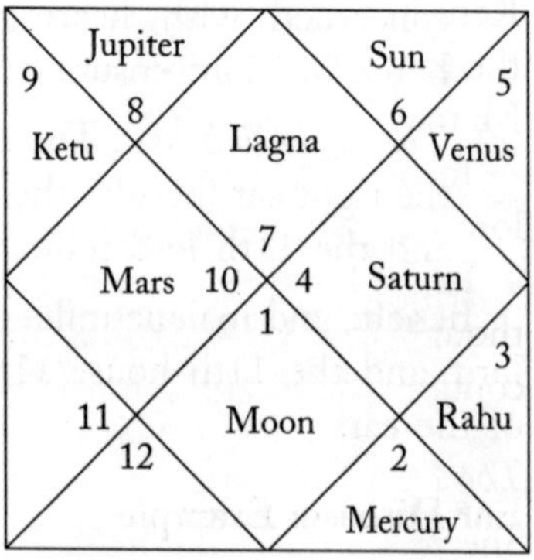

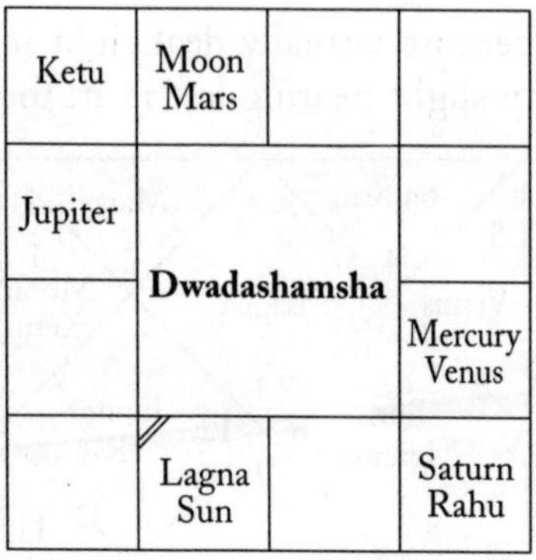

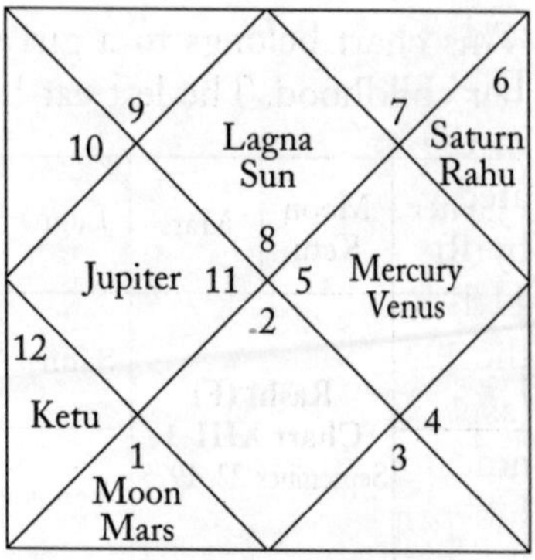

right is totally deaf. She is otherwise highly talented and a keen painter which is confirmed by the presence of Venus in the third house in the rashi chart, and Venus and the Moon in the 3rd house in the Navamsha chart.

Mercury is associated with the Sun and aspected by the 8th lord Saturn as also by a retrograde Jupiter. In the Navamsha, Mercury is placed in the 8th house under the influence of Mars and Saturn. In the Drekkana too it is located in the 8th house, while in the Dwadashamsha it is the 8th lord associated with a malefic lord Venus.

The 3rd and the 11th houses are afflicted variously. In the rashi chart, Mars, the 6th lord, aspects the 3rd house where the 12th lord Venus is situated. The 11th house is involved in the RKA, aspected by Saturn, which is also the eighth lord.

In the Navamsha, the 6th lord Moon in the 3rd house and Ketu in the 11th house are both aspected by Mars. Mars is also the lord of the 3rd house, associated with Saturn and the 8th lord Mercury, in the 8th house.

In the Drekkana, there is Ketu in the 3rd house while the 8th lord Venus occupies the 11th house aspected by Mars.

In the Dwadashamsha, the 3rd house receives no malefic aspect though the 3rd lord is associated with Rahu. The 11th house contains Rahu and Saturn.

The Dasha Scheme

She was born in the Vimshottari dasha of Ketu-Ketu. It will be seen that the RKA involves the 11th house in the rashi, Navamsha and the Dwadashamsha, while it involves the 3rd house in the Drekkana. Next AD is that of Venus, occupying the 3rd house in the rashi and Navamsha, 11th in the Drekkana, and associated with the 11th lord in the Dwadashamsha. This is followed by the Sun (lord of the 3rd house), the Moon (occupant of the 11th house, Mars (the lord of the 11th house), Rahu (involving the 11th house in RKA), Jupiter (aspecting the 3rd lord), Saturn (aspecting the 3rd lord and 11th house), and Mercury (the significator for hearing, associated with the 3rd lord). Thus all the sub-periods are related to the hearing mechanism in one way or the other. Naturally that will hold true for the MD's also. There is thus little hope for improvement of her defect.

The Yogini dasha at birth was Bhramari-Bhramari (Mars-Mars). Mars is the 11th lord aspecting the 3rd house from the 12th house. As in case of Vimshottari dasha, the various dasha lords in the Yogini dasha scheme will also be related to either the 3rd house/3rd lord or the 11th house/11th lord.

Classical Combinations for Defective Speech

Some combinations indicating dumbness as mentioned in astrological classics are being listed below.

1. Mercury as the 6th lord in a speechless sign, aspected by malefics.

   Note : (a) Mercury is the significator of speech as it is for hearing.

   (b) Speechless signs are Karka, Vrishchika and Meena.

2. Mercury as the 6th lord in the lagna, under the influence of malefics.
3. Mercury in the 9th house and Venus in the 10th house.

   Note : This combination is supposed to cause stammering.

4. Malefics in Karka, Vrischika and Meena; the Moon in Rashyanta in Vrisha aspected by malefics.

   Note : (a) A planet is in Rashyanta when it is at 29° or beyond in a sign.

   (b) When benefics aspect the Moon in the above combinations the speech comes later (after 5 years of age).

5. Lord of the 2nd house with Jupiter, in the 8th house.

   Note : (a) When the 2nd lord and Jupiter are in the 8th house with the 4th lord, the mother of the native is dumb.

   (b) The 2nd lord and Jupiter in the 8th house associated with the 9th lord result in a dumb father.

6. Full Moon associated with Mars, in the lagna.

   Note : Strong Mars, Mercury and the Moon associated with each other or aspecting each other result in a fast speech.

Children born deaf and dumb

This section of the chapter is based on a research paper by Shunny Nigam*. He has applied simple principles of astrology to the rashi chart only, without going into the divisional charts.

* See *The Astrological Magazine*, December 1993 and April 1994 issues.

It will be appreciated that children who are born deaf have problems of expression. They cannot speak unless special attention is paid to this aspect. Very often the deafness in a child is not detected early enough to ensure proper speech therapy at an appropriate early age. It is interesting as well as useful to be able to detect defects of hearing, with consequent defects of speech, in a newborn.

The following factors are of importance.

1. *Affliction to the 3rd house or the 3rd lord.* The 3rd house is the house for the organ of hearing as well as the faculty or hearing. For a child to be born deaf (and consequently dumb!), the 3rd house or the 3rd lord must show affliction.
2. *Affliction to the Moon.* Affliction to the Moon in a chart indicates Balarishta. A child who is born with a defect obviously suffers from a Balarishta. The Moon in such cases is likely to be ill placed or otherwise afflicted.
3. *Afflicted 8th house/8th lord.* The eighth house represents incurable or chronic or lingering illness. An affliction to the 8th house or the 8th lord in the birth chart confirms the presence of such an ailment. The 8th lord may have association with the 3rd house or the 3rd lord.
4. *Importance of the Rahu-Ketu axis.* The RKA tends to be adjacent to the 3rd house or the 3rd lord. That is, the RKA involves the 3rd house/3rd lord or lies in the 2nd or 12th from them. This is as if the RKA casts its shadow over the 3rd house/ 3rd lord. Affliction by the RKA is an important factor in the causation of disease.
5. *The dasha scheme.* The MD/AD/PD at birth are generally adverse, and related to the 3rd house or the 3rd lord in most cases.

Children born deaf and dumb : Examples

The above principles will be applied to the bare rashi charts.

Chart XIII-2

Here the 3rd house is occupied by the Sun aspected by a retrograde Jupiter. The Moon is in the 8th house, hence under affliction.

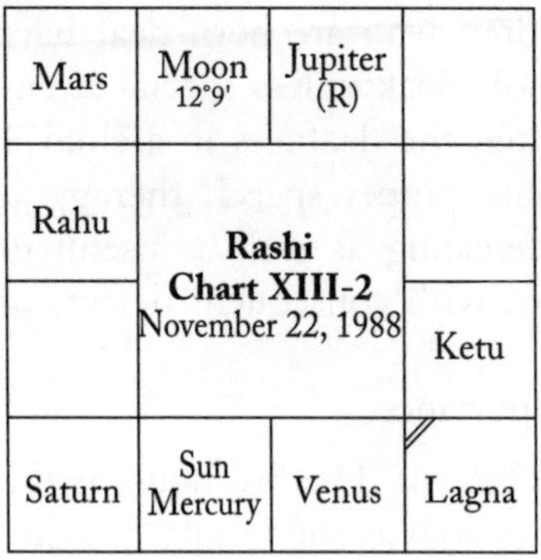

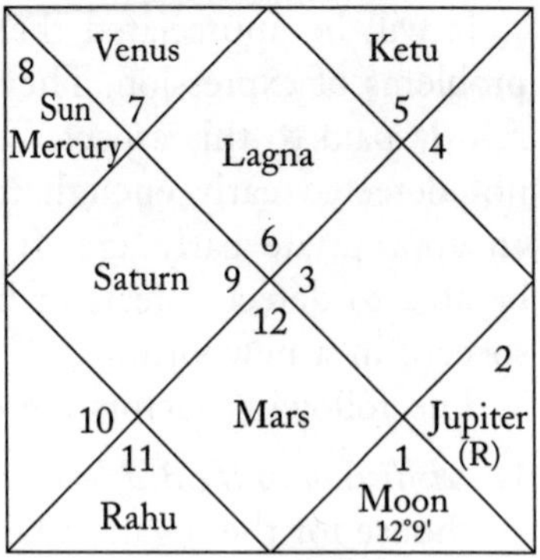

The 8th lord is well placed but aspects the lagna along with the 6th lord Saturn. The RKA lies adjacent to the 3rd lord Mars.

The Vimshottari dasha operating at the time of birth was Ketu-Merc-Sun. Mercury and the Sun are located in the 3rd house. Ketu being part of the RKA lies adjacent to the 3rd lord Mars.

The Yogini dasha at birth was Bhramari-Pingala (Mars-Sun). Mars is the 3rd lord and the Sun occupies the 3rd house.

Chart XIII-3

The 3rd house is afflicted by Ketu while the 3rd lord, which is also the 8th lord, is debilitated. RKA falls on the 3rd house. The Moon is in the 12th house with the Sun and retrograde 2nd lord (a maraka) Venus ensuring a Balarishta.

The Vimshottari dasha at birth was Ketu-Mars-Ketu. Ketu (MD and PD) is located in the 3rd house while Mars is the debilitated 3rd lord.

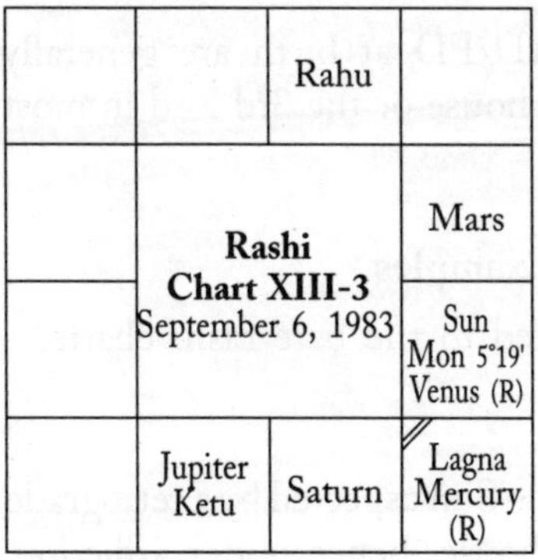

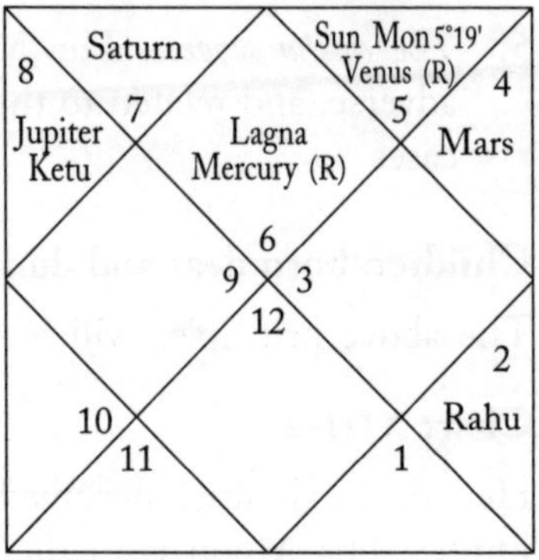

The Yogini dasha at birth was Bhadrika-Siddha (Mercury-Venus). Mercury (MD) is the retrograde lagna lord in the lagna whose dasha at birth indicates a congenital illness. Mercury is also the significator for hearing. Venus (AD) is the malefic 2nd lord, retrograde, in the 12th house associated with the 12th lord, confirming the presence of a congenital ailment.

CHAPTER FOURTEEN

HEART DISEASE

साधवो हृदयं मह्यं साधूनां हृदयं त्वहम् ।
मदन्यत्ते न जानन्ति नाहं तेभ्यो मनागपि ।।

The saintly ones are My heart, and I am theirs. They know none other than Me and I know none other than them.

—SHRIMAD BHAGAVATA 9:4/68

Heart disease is one of the commonest afflictions of the modern day man. Mental tensions, professional competitiveness, rich diet, lack of exercise, sedentary habits, smoking, etc., all lead to proneness to this malady in the modern times. Advances in medical science have increased the life span of people, and many infective and other diseases are already under control. Increasing longevity renders more and more people susceptible to heart disease. It may, however, be added that while heart disease takes a heavy toll of human lives each year, rapid advances in its management have been the cause of more and more people surviving this disease.

The above description holds true for the most common type of heart disease known as the ischaemic heart disease (IHD) or the coronary artery disease (CAD). In this the blood supply to a part of the cardiac muscle is impaired because of obstruction to the blood vessels which supply it. The treatment for this disease is either (a) purely medical, in which case it is hoped that during the treatment new blood vessels will form in the heart muscle over a period of time and restore blood supply to the affected area; or (b) medical, combined with surgical, wherein the obstruction to the affected blood vessels is either bypassed or removed through surgical or associated procedures.

In addition to the CAD, the heart may suffer from a variety of other ailments. Of these, the congenital heart disease (CHD) is of particular significance. The CHD may take several forms most of which tend to require surgical correction. Again this surgical correction may provide a complete cure or only a partial relief.

Another important cardiac disease is a genetic disorder known as cardiomyopathy wherein the heart becomes larger in size but ineffective in function. No satisfactory medical or surgical curative treatment is generally available for this.

Astrologically, it may be possible to ascertain the susceptibility to develop heart disease from the analysis of a chart. By considering the dasha scheme, it becomes possible to determine the timing as well as the course of illness.

ASTROLOGICAL PRINCIPLES

The following factors signify the heart and its surroundings.

1. *The Sun* : The Sun is the significator for heart. When several malefic influences operate upon the Sun, heart disease may be indicated in the presence of other adverse influences and appropriate dasha periods.
2. *The sign Simha*: Simha indicates the heart of the Kalapurusha. Its affliction is an additional negative influence on the state of health of the heart.
3. *The fifth house*. The fifth house indicates the heart of the native just as Simha, the fifth sign of the natural zodiac, indicates the heart of the Kalapurusha. Affliction of the fifth house and the fifth lord is important in causing heart ailments.
4. *The fourth house*. The fourth house indicates the chest of the native. Complications of heart disease involving the chest, and indications of surgical treatment of heart disease (which of necessity involves opening up the chest), may be taken from the fourth house.

Indicators of Cardiac Illness

In a given horoscope, the following points must be examined to determine cardiac illness:

1. *Affliction of the Sun.* This is by far the most important factor in causing cardiac illness. The Sun may suffer affliction as given below:
   (a) Association or aspect of Mars, Saturn and RKA
   (b) Debilitation
   (c) Paapakartari, i.e., being surrounded on either side by malefics
   (d) Relationship with the 6th, the 8th or the 12th houses or lords
2. *Affliction of Simha.* By malefic association or aspect.
3. *Affliction to the fifth house.* By association or aspect of natural malefics or the lords of Trika houses. Here it is important to consider the fifth house:
   (a) from the lagna;
   (b) from the Sun;
   (c) from the MD and AD lords.
4. *Affliction to the fifth lord.* Affliction by natural malefics, by lords of the Trika houses or by retrograde planets.
5. *The fourth house.* Affliction to the fourth house from the lagna or the Sun indicates chest complications or surgical treatment of heart disease. Predominance of benefic influence here, as on the Sun and the 5th house/5th lord, indicates conservative treatment and recovery.
6. *The dasha scheme.* In the presence of sufficient affliction, the dashas of planets associating with the Sun, the 5th house, the 5th lord, etc., lead to cardiac illness. The AD of a retrograde planet in the 5th house, in the MD of a malefic is of particular importance.

HEART DISEASE : Examples

The above mentioned principles are now being applied to actual horoscopes.

Chart XIV-1

This lady suffers from cardiomyopathy, a progressive crippling genetic disorder of the heart muscle, from which she can have little chance of cure.

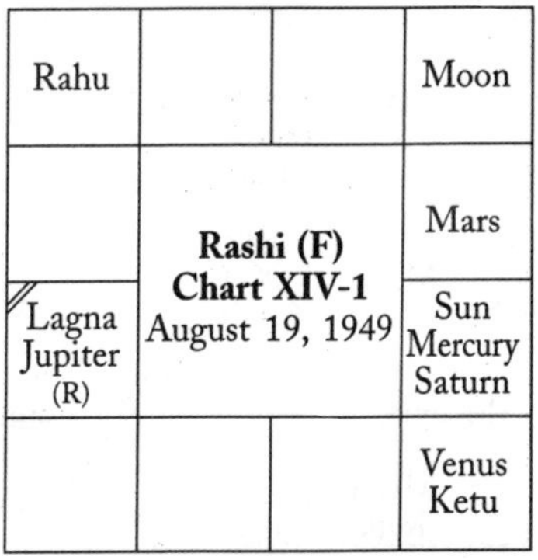

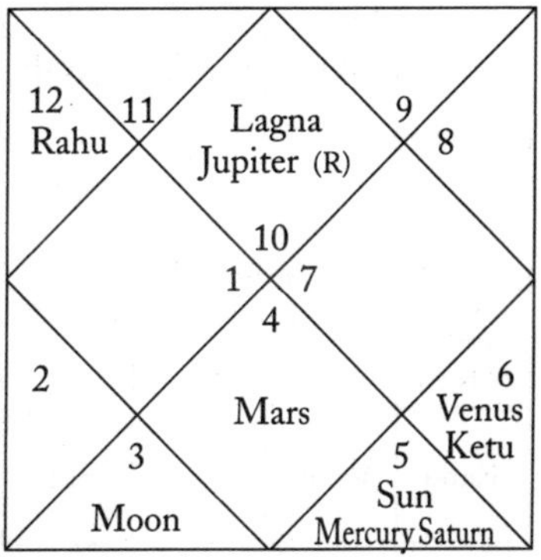

Lagna	00°44'	Mars	24°52'	Venus	05°36'
Sun	02°59'	Mercury	23°42'	Saturn	14°41'
Moon	02°06'	Jupiter (R)	00°35'	Rahu	24°37'

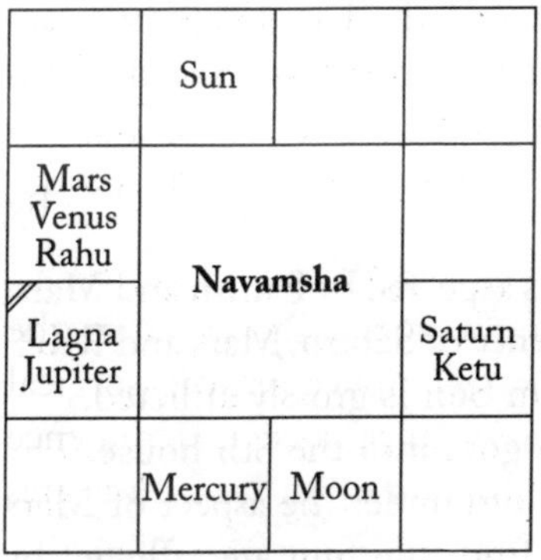

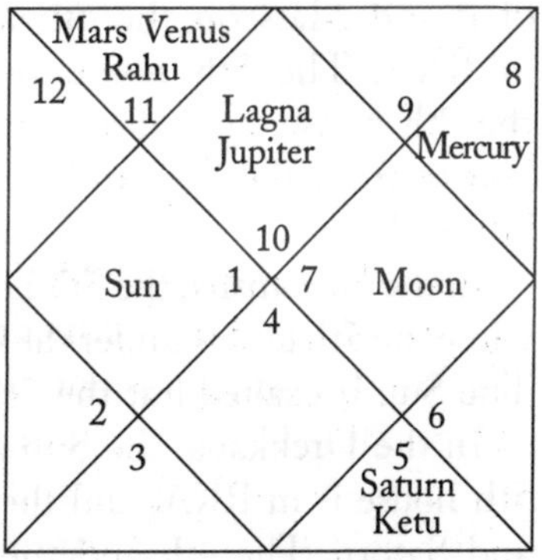

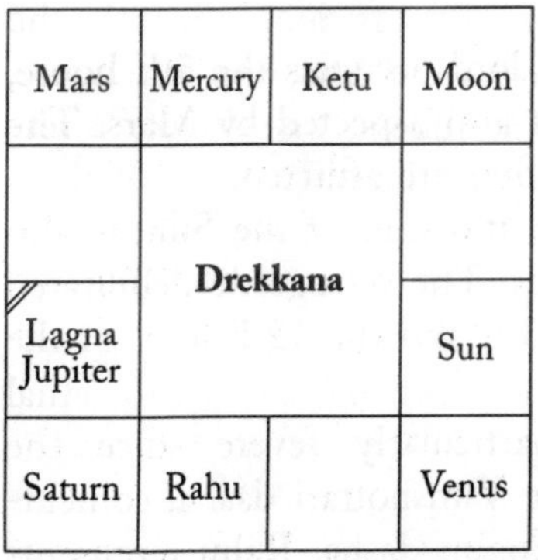

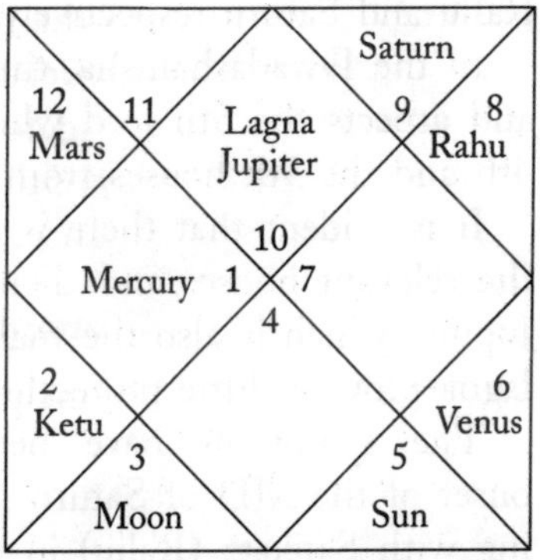

The lagna is occupied by a debilitated retrograde Jupiter, and the lagna lord is located in the 8th house in association with the 6th lord and a hostile 8th lord. A debilitated Mars aspects the

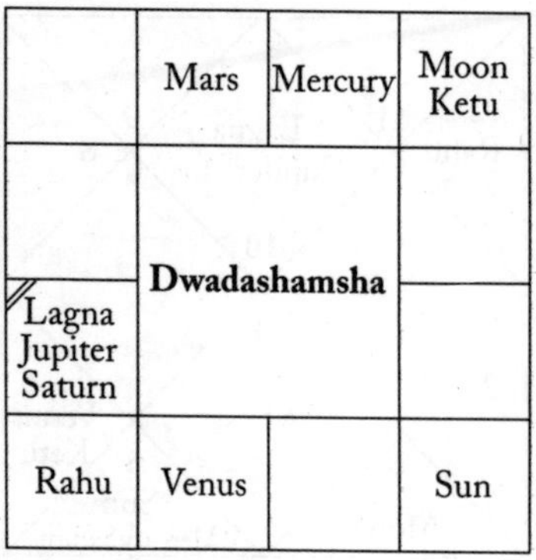

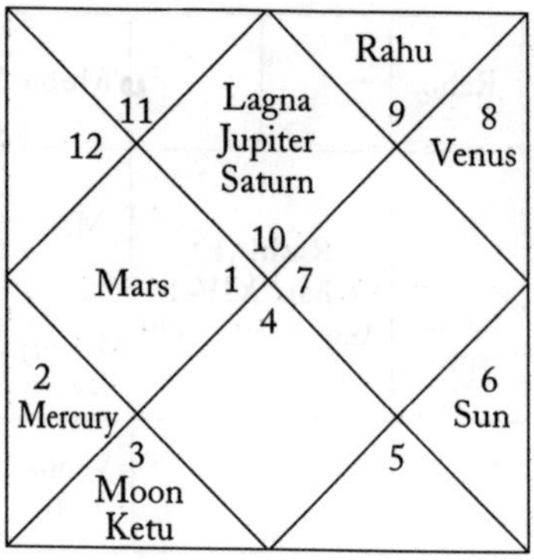

lagna from the 7th house. There is thus an inherent weakness in the chart in respect of health.

The Sun is located in the 8th house, with Saturn on one side of it and Mars on the other. The fifth lord is debilitated and in RKA. The 5th house receives the aspect of Saturn from the 8th house, and of a retrograde Jupiter. The fourth and 5th houses from the Sun are unafflicted though their lords are debilitated.

In the Navamsha, the 5th house is aspected by Saturn and Mars, while the 5th lord is under the influence of Saturn, Mars and RKA. The Sun is exalted but the 5th from Sun is grossly afflicted.

In the Drekkana, the Sun again goes into the 8th house. The 5th house is in RKA, and the 5th lord under the aspect of Mars and Saturn. The 4th and the 5th from the Sun are afflicted by Rahu and Saturn respectively.

In the Dwadashamsha, the 6th lord occupies the 5th house, and aspects the 5th lord which is also aspected by Mars. The 4th and the 5th houses from the Sun are afflicted.

It is evident that there is gross affliction of the Sun as also the relevant houses and their lords. The retrograde debilitated Jupiter, which is also the malefic 3rd and the 12th lord, in the lagna provides little protection.

The symptoms have been particularly severe since the onset of the MD of Saturn in the Vimshottari dasha, coinciding with Sankata (Rahu) in the Yogini dasha. Rahu represents Saturn only. Saturn as the lagna lord is grossly afflicted in the 8th house.

Chart XIV-2

The native suffers from coronary artery disease which has been controlled by balloon angioplasty, a relatively mild substitute for coronary bypass surgery.

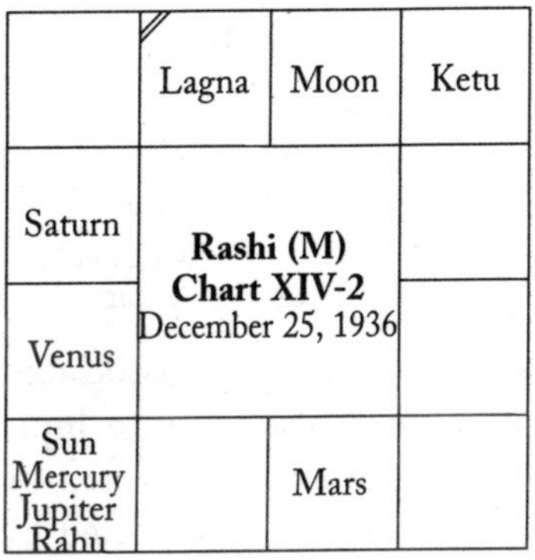

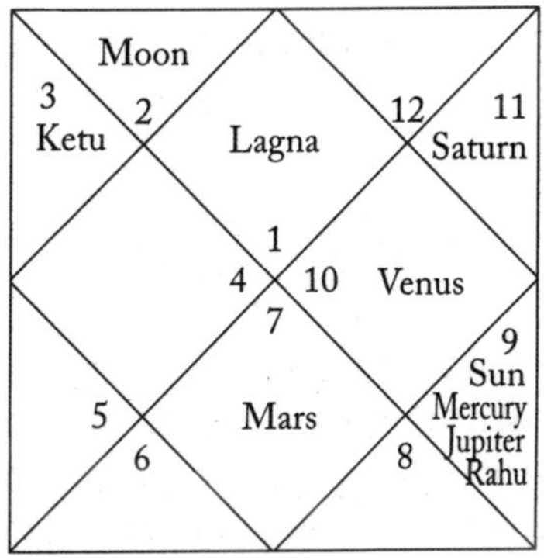

Lagna	01°53'	Mars	00°39'	Venus	23°17'
Sun	10°23'	Mercury	29°15'	Saturn	23°56'
Moon	01°47'	Jupiter	12°15'	Rahu	01°28'

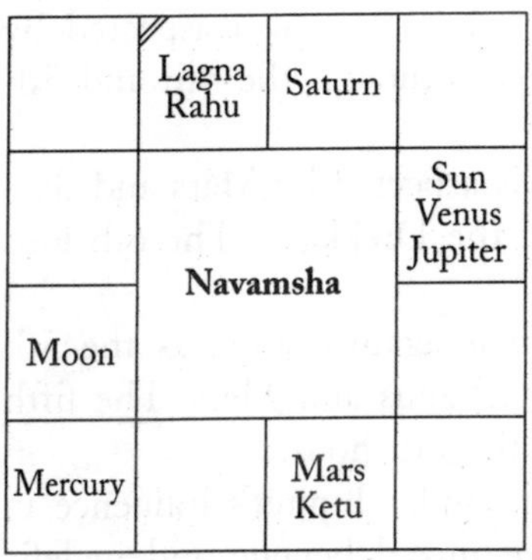

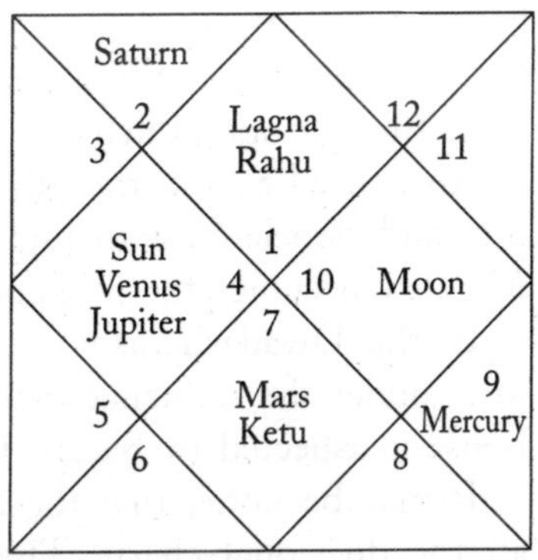

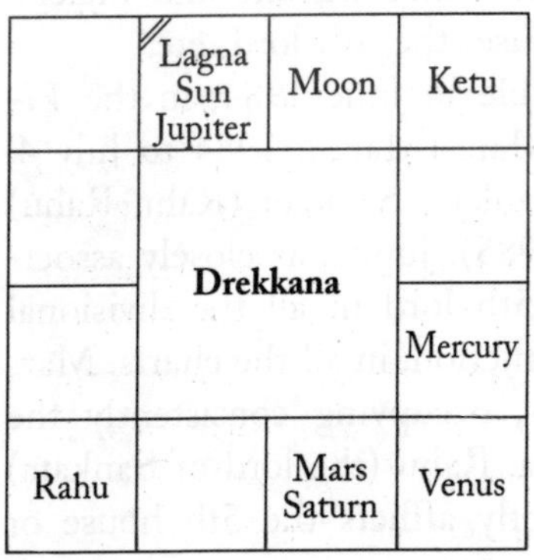

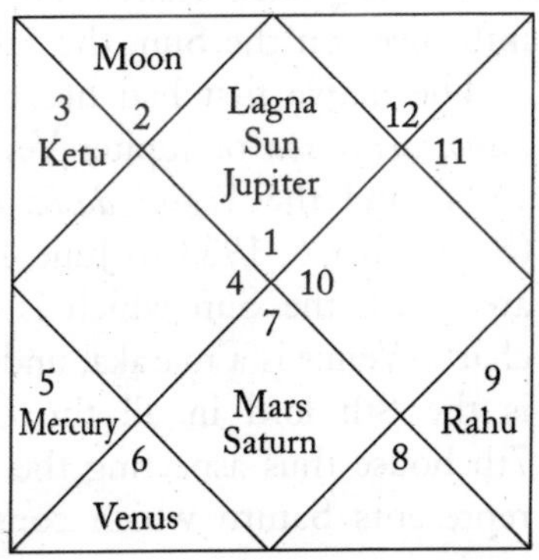

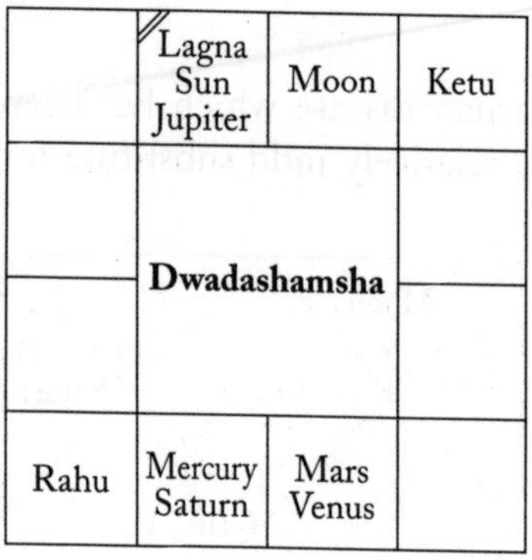

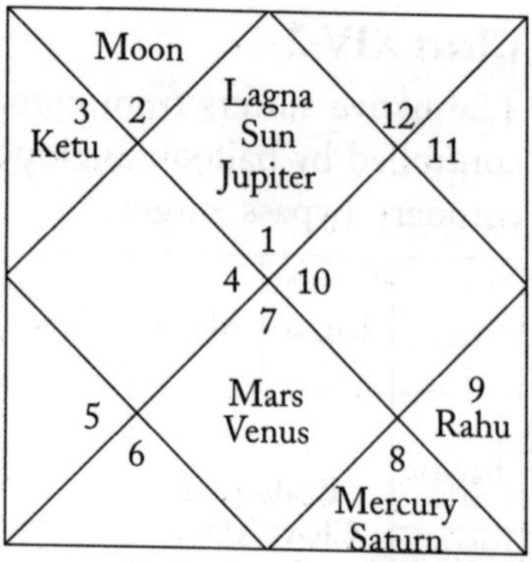

The Sun, which also happens to be the 5th lord, is associated with the 6th lord Mercury, and Rahu, but is also close to Jupiter. The 5th house, coinciding with sign Simha, is aspected by Saturn as well as Jupiter. The 5th from the Sun is aspected by Saturn, Mars and Jupiter. The fourth from the lagna as well as the Sun is unafflicted.

In the Navamsha, the Sun is associated with two natural benefics and aspected by a third, while it is also aspected by Saturn. The 5th house is unafflicted although the 4th and 5th from the Sun are afflicted.

An exalted Sun as the 5th lord is aspected by Mars and Saturn, and associated with Jupiter in the Drekkana. The 6th lord Mercury occupies the 5th house.

In the Dwadashamsha, the Sun is again exalted as the 5th lord, under the influence of Jupiter, Venus and Mars. The fifth house is aspected by Saturn from the 8th house.

It may be noted that the Sun is under Jupiter's influence in all the divisional charts. There are mixed benefic and malefic influences on the Sun, the 5th house, the 5th lord, etc.

The native first had heart trouble in June 1984, in the *Vimshottari dasha* of Jupiter-Venus-Mars (May 8, 1984 to July 4, 1984) and the *Yogini dasha* of Sankata-Sankata (Rahu-Rahu) (September 6, 1983 to June 16, 1985). Jupiter is closely associated with the Sun which is the 5th lord in all the divisional charts. Venus is a maraka, under affliction, in all the charts. Mars is the 8th lord in all the charts, occupying consistently the 7th house thus aspecting the lagna. Rahu (the lord of Sankata) represents Saturn which consistently afflicts the 5th house or the Sun in all charts. Rahu involves the 5th lord, the Sun, in the RKA.

In Feb 1992, the native underwent balloon angioplasty for his ailment. The Vimshottari dasha of Saturn-Saturn-Saturn (September 7, 1991 to February 28, 1992) operated at that time, coinciding with the Yogini dasha of Mangala-Ulka (Moon Saturn) from February 6, 1992 to April 6, 1992. The role of Saturn has been mentioned earlier. The Moon happens to be the lord of the 4th house. It is exalted in the rashi, Drekkana and the Dwadashamsha charts, and under the malefic influence of Mars in all the charts. It is aspected by the Sun in the Navamsha.

The second angioplasty was necessitated in September 1992 in the Vimshottari dasha of Saturn-Saturn-Ketu (August 2, 1992 to October 5, 1995). Ketu aspects the Sun in the rashi chart. The corresponding Yogini dasha was Pingala-Pingala (Sun-Sun) which is self explanatory.

It will be seen that the Sun, the 5th lord, as well as the sign Simha and the 5th house from the Sun, all have mixed benefic and malefic influences. While the afflictions did cause a cardiac ailment, the benefic influences have had their say, and angioplasty alone has kept things under control.

Chart XIV-3

This patient had coronary bypass surgery in September 1989.

The Sun is associated with the lagna lord, the 8th lord and Rahu. The fifth house from the Sun and lagna is aspected by

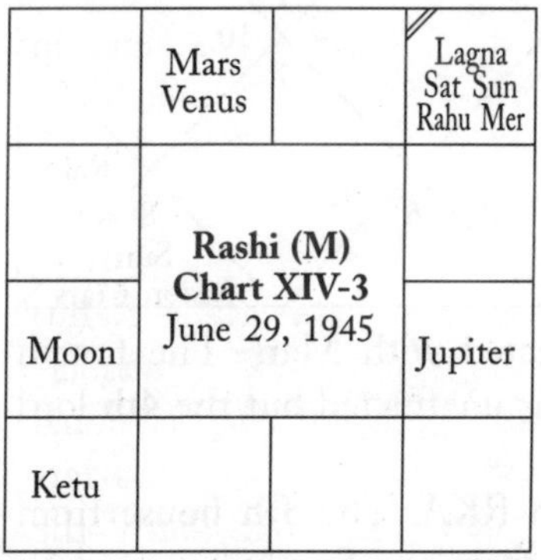

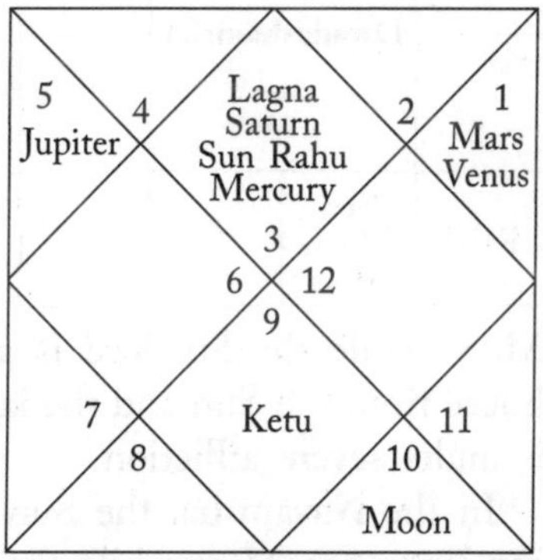

Lagna	25°54'	Mars	19°46'	Venus	28°17'
Sun	13°54'	Mercury	28°38'	Saturn	20°17'
Moon	26°11'	Jupiter	27°19'	Rahu	16°14'

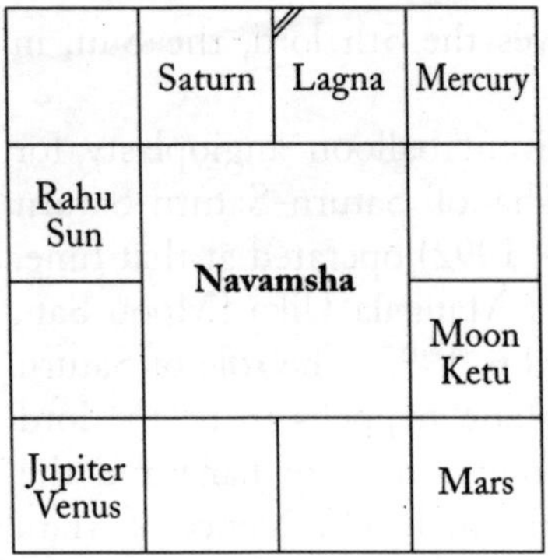

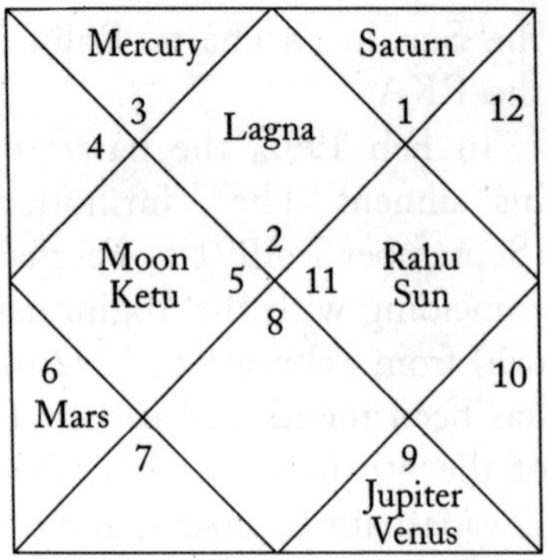

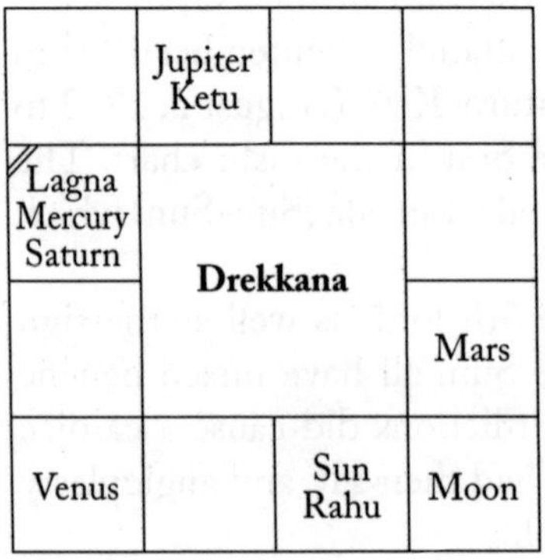

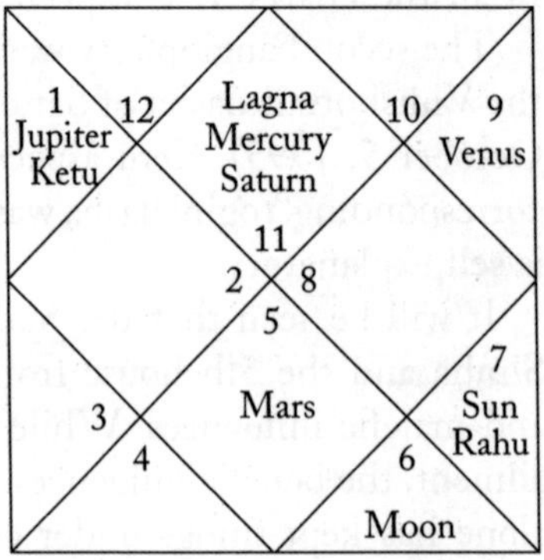

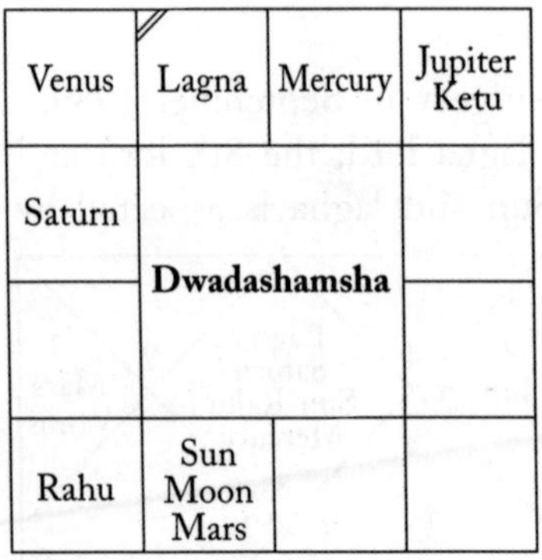

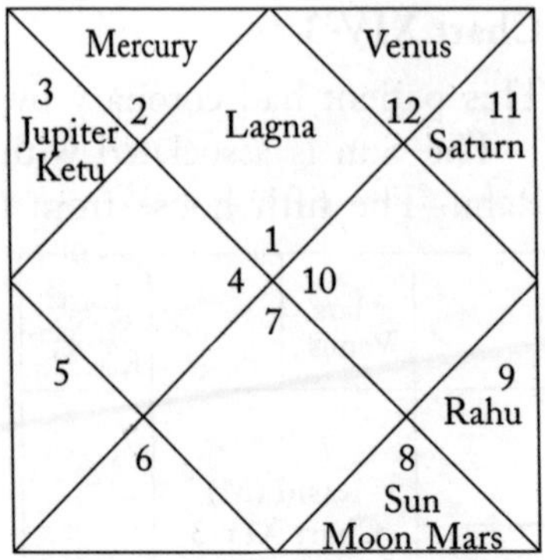

Mars, while the 5th lord is associated with Mars. The fourth house from the Sun and the lagna is unafflicted but the 4th lord is under severe affliction.

In the Navamsha, the Sun is in RKA. The 5th house from the lagna has Mars while the 5th from the Sun is aspected by the 6th lord, the 8th lord and Saturn. The fourth from the lagna is also afflicted.

In the Drekkana, the Sun is debilitated and afflicted by RKA. The fifth lord is afflicted by Saturn and Mars. The 5th from the Sun also has the affliction of Saturn and Mars. The fourth house and the 4th lord are unafflicted.

The Dwadashamsha shows the 5th house , the 5th lord, and the Sun under affliction. The 4th house from the Sun and the 4th lord from the lagna are afflicted; the 4th lord is debilitated also.

Vimshottari dasha

The native had coronary bypass in Saturn-Mercury-Rahu which operated from July 1, 1989 to November 26, 1989.

Saturn (MD) as the 8th lord afflicts the Sun and the lagna and the 4th lord Mercury (AD) in association with Rahu (PD).

In the Navamsha, Saturn aspects the 5th lord Mercury, while Rahu afflicts the Sun and the 4th house.

In the Drekkana, Saturn is associated with the AD and the 5th lord Mercury, while Rahu associates with the Sun.

In the Dwadashamsha, Saturn afflicts the 5th lord, the Sun, and is itself afflicted by the 8th lord Mars. Mercury is the 6th lord in mutual aspect with the 5th lord. Mars afflicts Mercury. Rahu in the 9th house is aspected by Jupiter.

The sign Simha is afflicted in all the divisional charts although Jupiter variously protects it, except in the Dwadashamsha. Jupiter also provides protection to the dasha lords in various ways.

Yogini dasha

Bhramari-Sankata (Mars-Rahu) operated from July 5, 1989 to May 25, 1990.

Mars (MD) is the 6th lord associated with the 5th lord Venus and aspecting the 5th house from the Sun and the lagna. In the Navamsha, Mars is located in the 5th house.

In the Drekkana, it is located in Simha and aspects the 5th lord Mercury, as also the lagna.

In the Dwadashamsha, it is the 8th lord associating with the 4th and the 5th lords, and itself aspected by Saturn, and the 6th lord Mercury.

Rahu (AD) has been discussed under Vimshottari dasha.

Note : It will be seen here too that whereas the malefic influences indicate illness as well as surgery, the benefic influences provide relief.

Chart XIV-4

This is another case of coronary bypass performed in October 1986.

The Sun is debilitated in the lagna and associated with the 6th

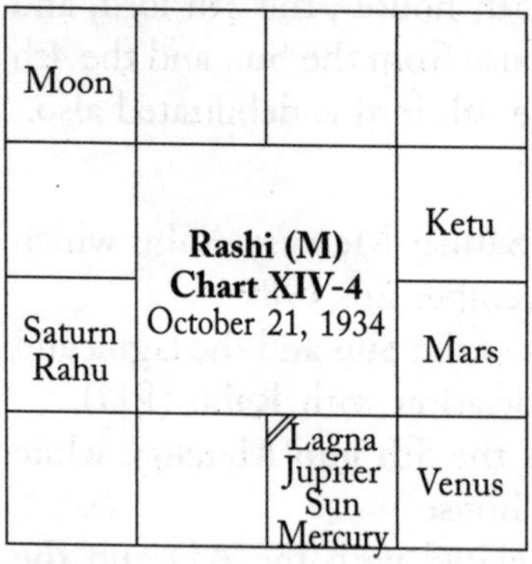

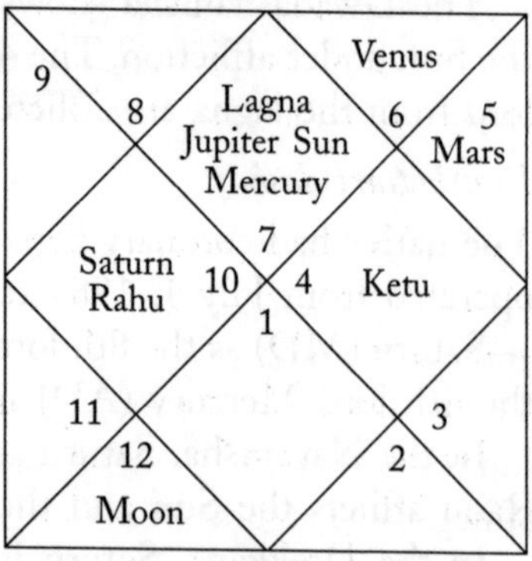

Lagna	03°34'	Mars	08°43'	Venus	26°41'
Sun	04°00'	Mercury	25°43'	Saturn	28°35'
Moon	13°24'	Jupiter	09°11'	Rahu	13°07'

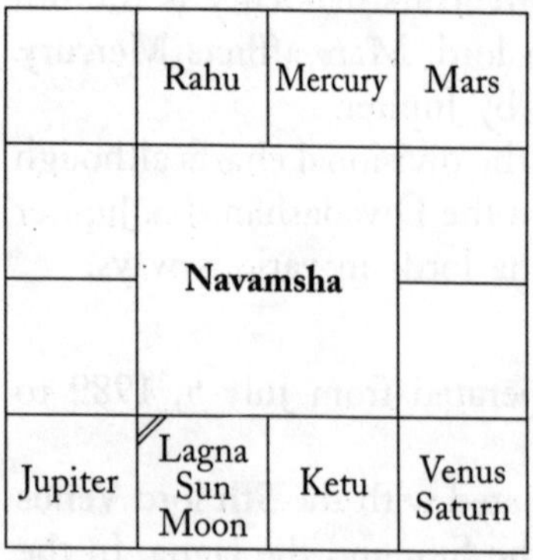

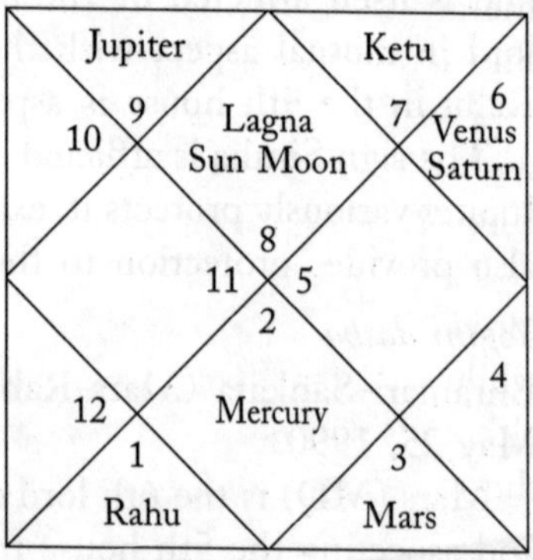

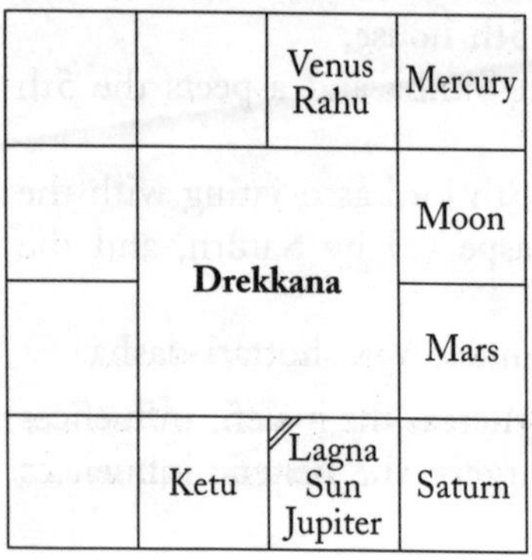

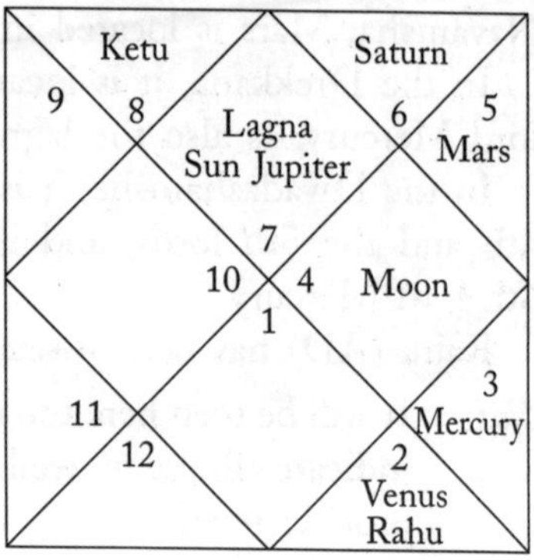

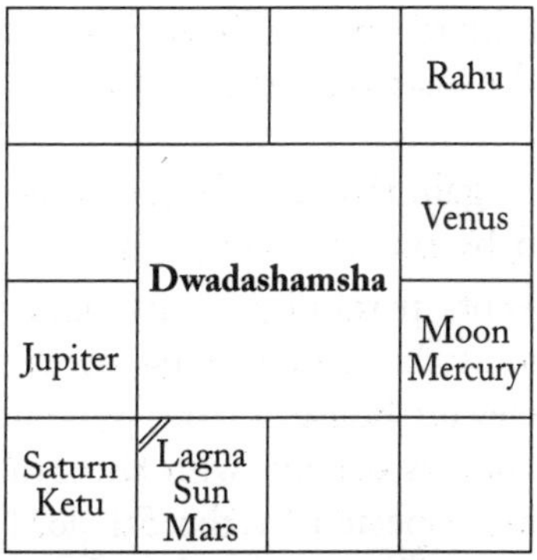

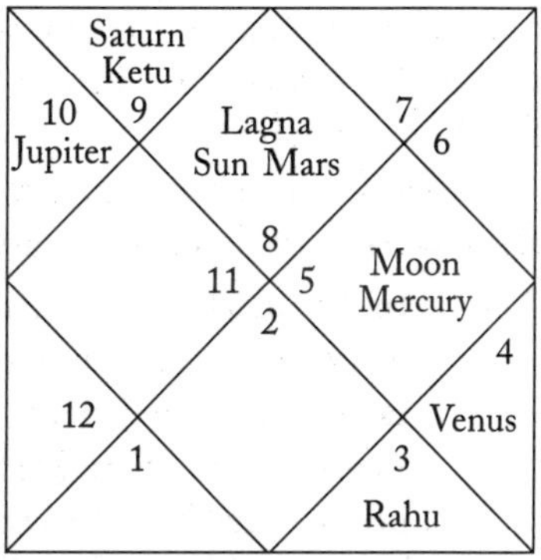

and the 12th lords, Jupiter and Mercury, and aspected by Saturn. The fifth from the lagna and the Sun is aspected by Mars (and Jupiter) while the 5th lord is in the RKA. The fourth house is afflicted by Saturn and Rahu.

In the Navamsha, the Sun is afflicted by the 8th lord Mercury, and by Saturn. The 5th lord is under the aspect of the 6th lord Mars from the 8th house. The fifth house from the Sun receives the aspect of Saturn. The fourth house from the lagna and the Sun is unafflicted, but the 4th lord is aspected by Mars.

The Sun is debilitated in the lagna in the Drekkana, associated with the 6th lord Jupiter. The fifth house is aspected by Mars. The 4th house is not afflicted.

The Dwadashamsha shows the Sun associated with the 6th lord Mars. The 5th lord is debilitated. The 4th lord is in RKA while the 4th house receives the aspects of Saturn and Mars, although it is also aspected by benefics Mercury and the Moon; the former is, however, the 8th lord also.

Vimshottari dasha

Sun-Saturn-Venus operated from August 28, 1986 to October 25, 1986.

The Sun (MD) is debilitated in the lagna, joined by the 6th lord, and aspected by an afflicted 5th lord Saturn (AD). Venus (PD) is the 8th lord of rashi chart. The PD of Venus is followed by that of the Sun.

In the Navamsha, the Sun in the lagna is aspected by the 8th lord; Saturn is the afflicted 4th lord aspecting the 5th house. Venus is the 12th lord, afflicted by Saturn and Mars, and aspecting the 5th house.

In the Drekkana, the Sun is debilitated and afflicted. Saturn is the 5th lord in the 12th house. Venus is the 8th lord in the 8th house, in RKA.

In the Dwadashamsha, the Sun is again afflicted. Saturn is the afflicted 4th lord. Venus is aspected by the 5th lord Jupiter.

Note : In the dasha of a planet, events pertaining to its significatorship can happen without the planet being necessarily concerned with the relevant house. In the present example, the Sun (MD) is not associated with the 5th house anywhere (except being aspected by the 5th lord in the rashi chart), still the heart disease precipitated and its relevant treatment instituted.

Yogini dasha

Sankata-Sankata (Rahu-Rahu) operated from January 12, 1985 to October 22, 1986.

Rahu (MD and AD) represents Saturn. In the rashi chart, Rahu associates with the 5th lord. In the remaining divisional charts, it is placed in adverse houses.

Note : Once again, the role of natural benefics in bringing about relief is obvious. The natural benefics, however, would prove harmful in their own dasha periods when they own adverse houses. This will be obvious from the next case.

Chart XIV-5

The native underwent coronary bypass on July 25, 1990. The operation, however, did not prove successful and the patient has

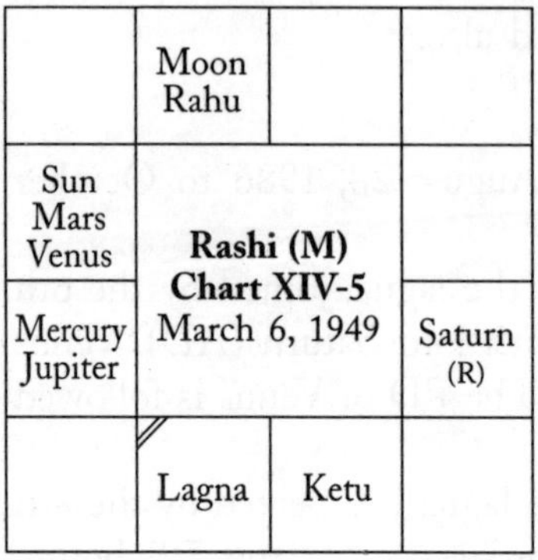

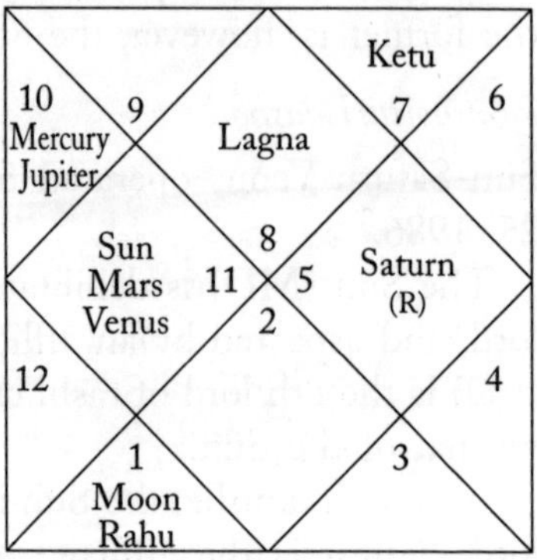

Lagna	19°32'	Mars	24°15'	Venus	11°06'
Sun	21°46'	Mercury	25°24'	Saturn (R)	08°41'
Moon	26°23'	Jupiter	01°05'	Rahu	03°13'

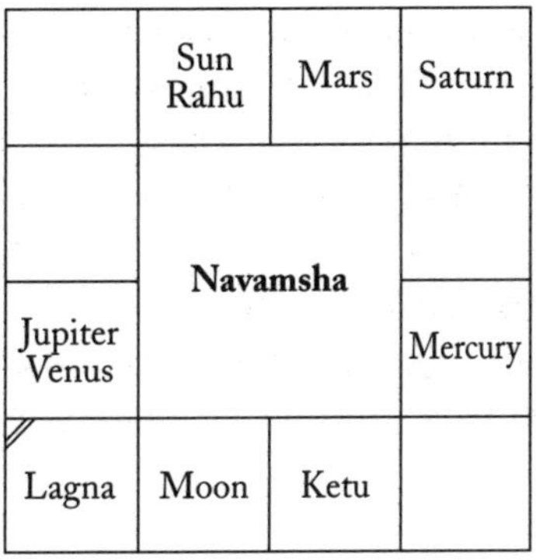

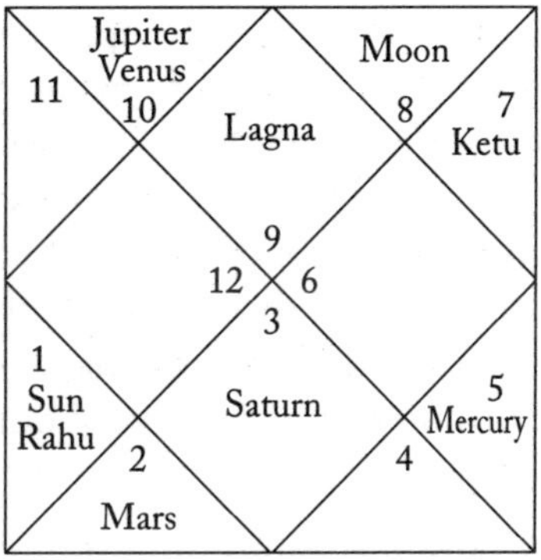

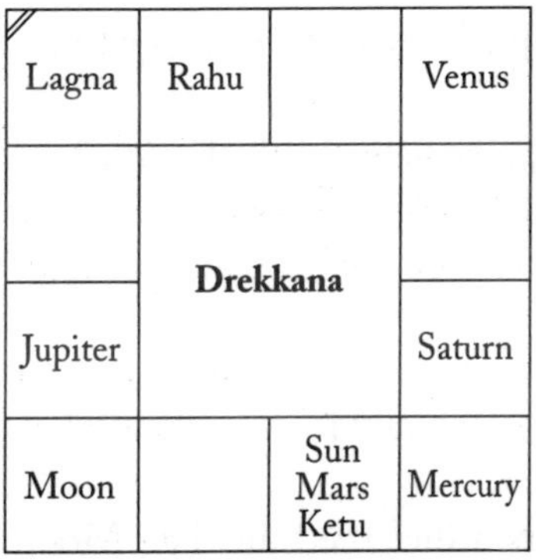

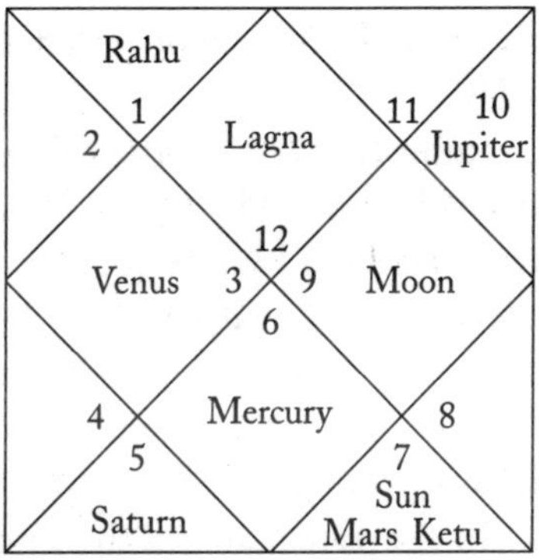

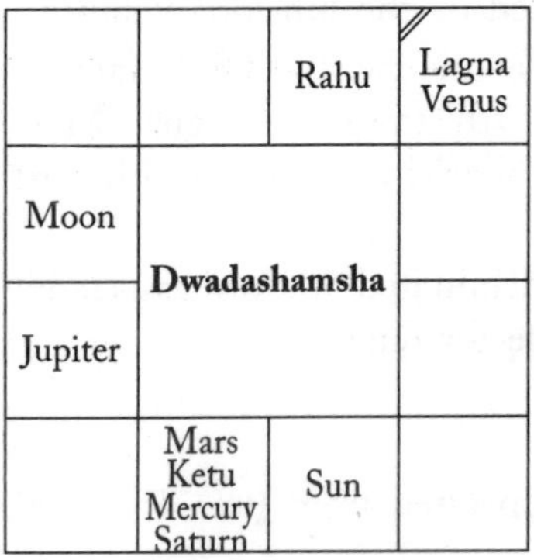

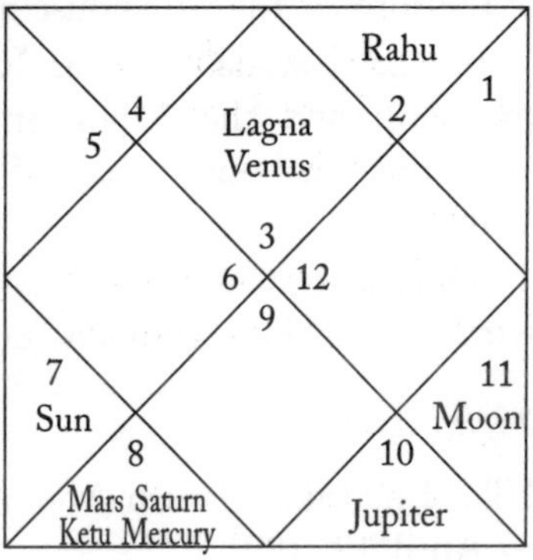

had no relief of symptoms.

The Sun is afflicted in the 4th house by the 6th lord Mars and by a retrograde Saturn. The fourth from the lagna and the 4th from the Sun are afflicted. Malefics afflict the sign Simha. The 5th lord Jupiter is debilitated and associated with the 8th lord Mercury.

In the Navamsha, the Sun is in the RKA in the 5th house,

while the 5th lord occupies the adverse 6th and is aspected by a debilitated 8th lord from the 12th house. The 5th from the Sun, coinciding with Simha, is aspected by Saturn and Mars.

The Drekkana chart shows a debilitated Sun in the 8th house, in the RKA and afflicted by Saturn and Mars, and no benefic aspect. The 5th from the Sun is afflicted by Saturn.

In the Dwadashamsha, the Sun is again debilitated, in the 5th house. The 5th lord from the Sun is afflicted by Mars and Ketu.

Vimshottari dasha

Rahu-Mars-Moon operated from July 12, 1990 to August 13, 1990.

Rahu (MD) is in the 6th house, associated with the 6th lord from the Sun. Mars (AD) is the 6th lord afflicting the Sun, and itself afflicted by a retrograde Saturn. The Moon (PD) occupies the 6th house with Rahu.

In the Navamsha, Rahu in the 5th house afflicts the Sun; Mars is the 5th lord in the 6th house; the Moon is the eighth lord aspecting the 5th lord.

In the Drekkana, Rahu and Mars afflict the Sun. The Moon is the lord of the 5th house aspected by the 8th lord Venus.

In the Dwadashamsha, Rahu is in the twelfth, Mars in the sixth and the Moon in the 9th from the lagna. Mars from the 6th house aspects Rahu, the Moon and the 5th lord Venus.

The subsequent MD of Jupiter, debilitated 5th lord associated with the 8th lord, provides no hope for relief.

Yogini dasha

Ulka-Bhadrika (Saturn-Mercury) operated from June 13, 1990 to April 13, 1991.

Saturn (MD), retrograde in Simha, afflicts the Sun. Mercury (AD) is the 8th lord afflicting the debilitated 5th lord.

In the Navamsha, Saturn aspects the 5th house from the Sun and Mercury lies in the 5th from the Sun. Mercury is afflicted by both Saturn and Mars.

In the Drekkana, Saturn from the 6th house aspects the Sun as well as the 5th from the Sun. Saturn is the lord of the 5th from the Sun. Mercury is aspected by a benefic, though debilitated, Jupiter.

In the Dwadashamsha, Saturn is again the lord of the 5th from the Sun, afflicted by Mars and the RKA. Mercury is also afflicted by Mars, Saturn and RKA.

The subsequent MD in the Yogini dasha, viz., Siddha, does not promise much relief as its lord Venus is also afflicted.

Note : Venus, the next MD lord in Yogini dasha, suffers triple affliction from the Sun, Mars and retrograde Saturn. No relief thus can be expected from it.

The reader is also referred to chart VIII-6, a case of congenital heart disease where a retrograde Jupiter as the lagna lord occupies the lagna in the rashi chart. The Sun is afflicted in the 8th house by the 6th lord as well as by Saturn. The 5th from the Sun has Ketu while the 5th from the lagna is aspected by Saturn and Mars. The fourth house from the Sun is also afflicted.

The Sun is afflicted in the Navamsha, the Drekkana and the Dwadashamsha also. The 5th house and/or the 5th lord, in these divisional charts, show varying afflictions.

The native was born in an adverse dasha, including that of a retrograde lagna lord placed in the lagna, in the Vimshottari system. However, benefic influences on the lagna/lagna lord in the divisional charts lead to relief, albeit partial, after surgery.

CHAPTER FIFTEEN

MISCELLANEOUS DISEASES

कृष्ण त्वदीयपदपङ्कजपञ्जरान्ते
अद्यैव मे विशतु मानसराजहंसः।
प्राणप्रयाणसमये कफवातपित्तैः
कण्ठावरोधनविधौ स्मरणं कुतस्ते।।

Lord Krishna! May the swan of my mind enter
the cage of Your lotus feet today itself.
For how shall I remember You when on death-bed
the Vaata, Pitta and Kapha strangle my throat?

—VAIRAGYASHATAKA

Medical astrology is a relatively poorly developed branch of astrology today. No research worth the name has been conducted in this direction. The medical people are too busy in their own affairs while the astrologers seem to have little inclination towards understanding the elements of medical science. Some older astrologers do understand the principles of what is considered today as Ayurveda. But they care little about Allopathy which has to be recognised as the most prevalent and the most effective system of diagnosis and treatment of disease today.

It is, therefore, appropriate to accept at the outset that astrological combinations for most of the ailments are not well understood in our present state of knowledge of astrology. An attempt will be made here to explain things within our limits of understanding. Final conclusions must wait till adequate research is carried out in this direction.

Certain diseases are being picked up here at random. Translating the names of some of these from the classical astrological texts is a problem, though an attempt is being made in this direction also. Combinations for various diseases are being primarily picked up from the *Jataka Tattva*, though other texts as well as our own research, albeit scanty, are also utilised.

1. DIABETES MELLITUS

This is a disease of glucose metabolism in the body. The body tends to derive energy from glucose. In cases of diabetes, there is excess glucose in the blood and body tissues, but it cannot be utilised. So the body starves despite there being plenty of glucose around ('starvation in the midst of plenty'). The cause of this is the deficiency of a hormone called insulin. This hormone is produced by the pancreas gland and helps the body to utilise the glucose. With deficiency of insulin, the glucose level in the body increases and produces complications which virtually affect all parts of the body.

Combinations for Diabetes

The following astrological combinations have been described for diabetes.

1. Jupiter debilitated, or located in houses 6, 8 or 12.
2. Saturn and Rahu afflicting Jupiter by association or aspect.
3. Combust Jupiter in RKA.
4. Venus in the 6th house aspected by Jupiter from the 12th house.
5. Lord of the 5th house in conjunction with the 6th, 8th or 12th lords.
6. Jupiter retrograde, afflicted, in a Trika house.

Comments

The liver which metabolises glucose, and the pancreas which produces insulin are located in the upper part of the abdomen. This area falls under the jurisdiction of the fifth house. Jupiter is the significator for the liver as well as for a part of the pancreas. Venus is the significator for the remainder of the pancreas. Venus also rules over the hormonal system of the body. Jupiter, Venus and the 5th house thus come into play in cases of diabetes. It must be admitted, however, that combinations for liver disease must be somewhat similar although Venus should not come into play there.

Diabetes : Examples

Chart XV-1

This lady developed diabetes mellitus which was detected in 1982.

Jupiter is placed in the 6th house and aspected by the debilitated 8th lord Mars. Venus is associated with the debilitated 12th lord, the Sun, and aspected by the 6th lord Saturn and the 8th lord Mars. The 5th house and the 5th lord are afflicted by RKA and Mars.

In the Navamsha, the 5th house has Jupiter and Mars together; Venus in the 11th house is aspected by Mars and Saturn.

In the Drekkana, the 5th lord Mercury joins the 8th lord Jupiter; both are aspected by Mars and Saturn. Venus is associated with the Sun and aspected by Mars (as well as Jupiter).

Saturn as the 8th lord afflicts Jupiter, the 6th lord, in the Dwadashamsha, and both aspect the 5th house. Mars aspects both Jupiter and a debilitated Venus from the 8th house.

Vimshottari dasha

The disease was detected in Saturn-Moon (from December 13, 1981 to July 13, 1983).

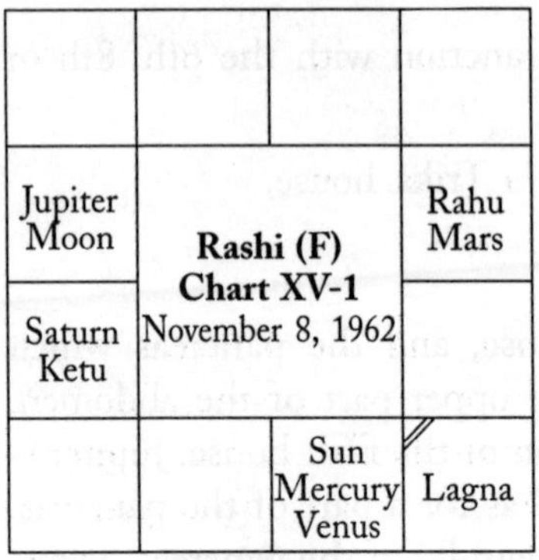

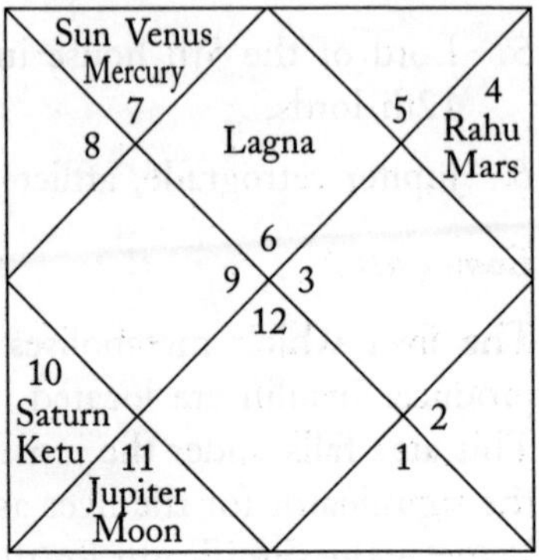

Lagna	25°39'	Mars	19°39'	Venus	29°54'
Sun	21°43'	Mercury	11°14'	Saturn	12°09'
Moon	26°31'	Jupiter	09°39'	Rahu	09°42'

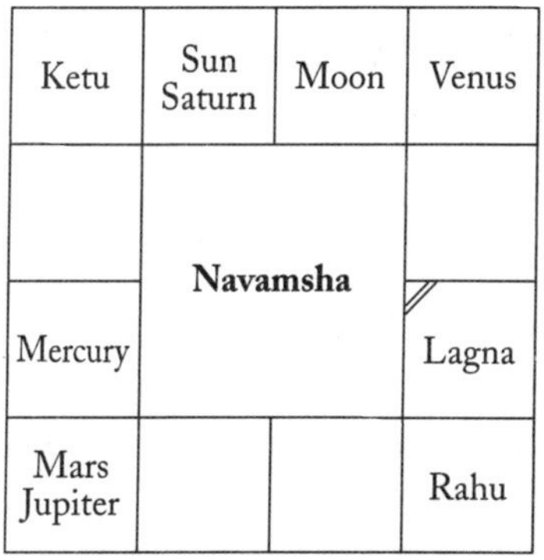

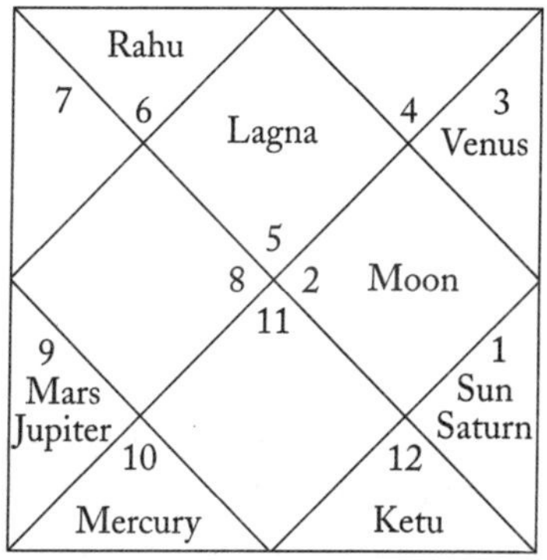

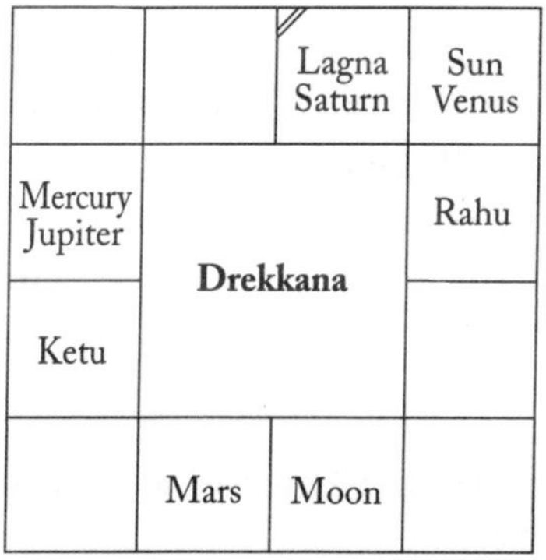

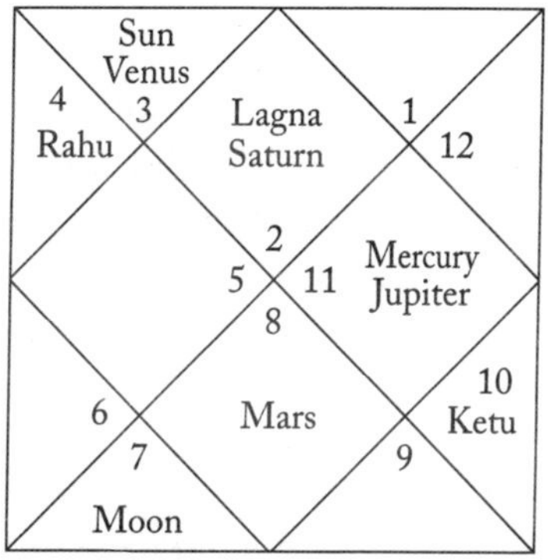

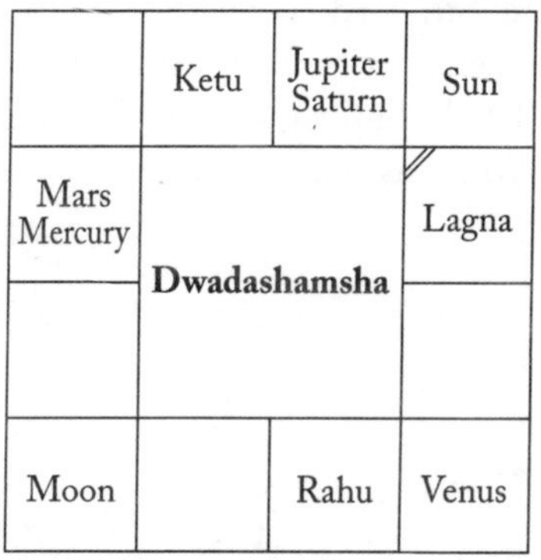

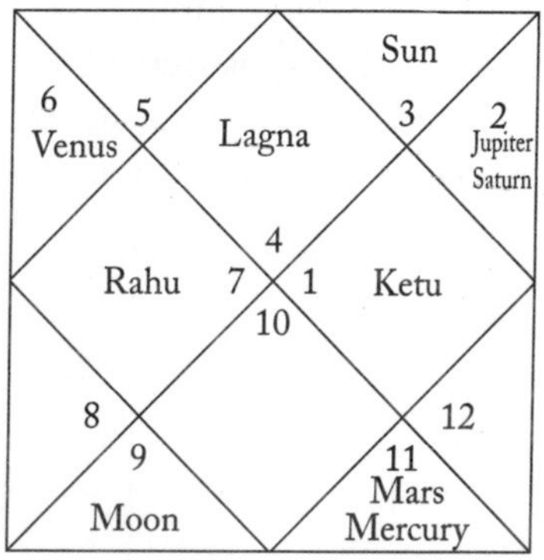

Saturn (MD) is the afflicted 5th lord. The Moon (AD) is located in the 6th house. Both MD and AD lords are aspected by a debilitated 8th lord.

Saturn is the debilitated and afflicted 6th lord and the Moon the 12th lord in the Navamsha.

An afflicted Saturn aspects the 5th lord in the Drekkana; the

Moon here is located in the 6th house and aspected by the 8th lord Jupiter.

In the Dwadashamsha, Saturn as the 8th lord, in association with the 6th lord, aspects the 5th house, and is in mutual aspect with the 5th lord Mars. The Moon, as the lagna lord, is located in the 6th house.

Yogini dasha

Siddha-Ulka (Venus-Saturn) operated from September 24, 1981 to November 24, 1982.

The role of Saturn (AD) has already been mentioned.

Venus (MD) is afflicted in all the divisional charts, and gets related to the 5th house or the 5th lord except in the Drekkana.

Note : There is a link of the 8th lord with the 5th house or 5th lord in all the charts. Does it indicate an inherited disease? The eighth house rules over inheritance. The mother of the native suffered from diabetes.

Chart XV-2

Diabetes was detected in this case in 1951. The native developed blindness as a complication of diabetes.

A retrograde Jupiter, as also the 6th lord, is placed in the lagna in RKA, aspected by Saturn. Venus is the 8th lord, and is afflicted by Saturn, Mars and the RKA. Saturn as the 5th lord is debilitated and also afflicted by Mars as well as RKA.

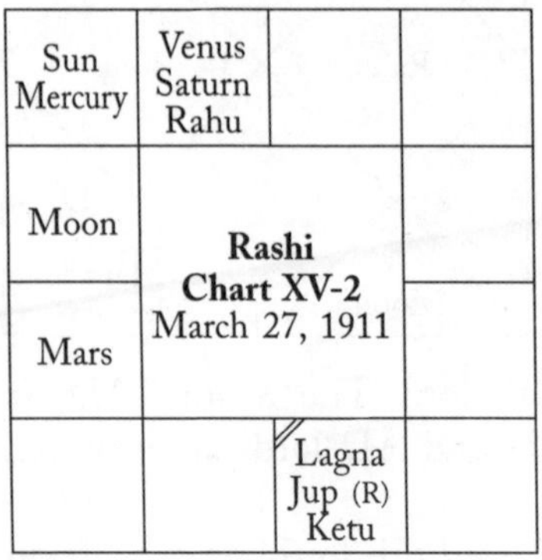

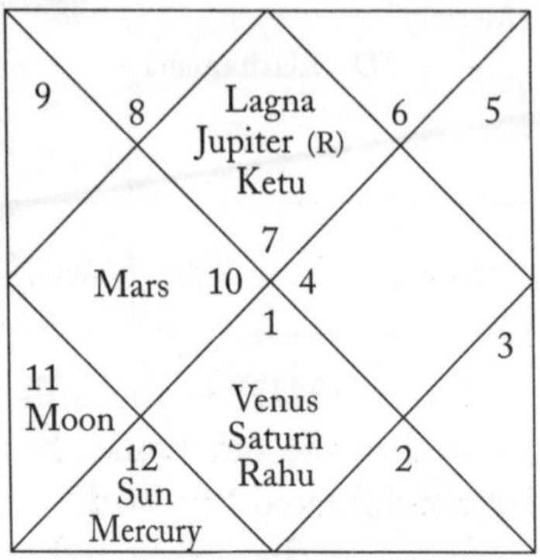

Lagna	04°58'	Mars	17°27'	Venus	11°48'
Sun	13°11'	Mercury	20°25'	Saturn	12°49'
Moon	05°53'	Jupiter (R)	20°53'	Rahu	17°33'

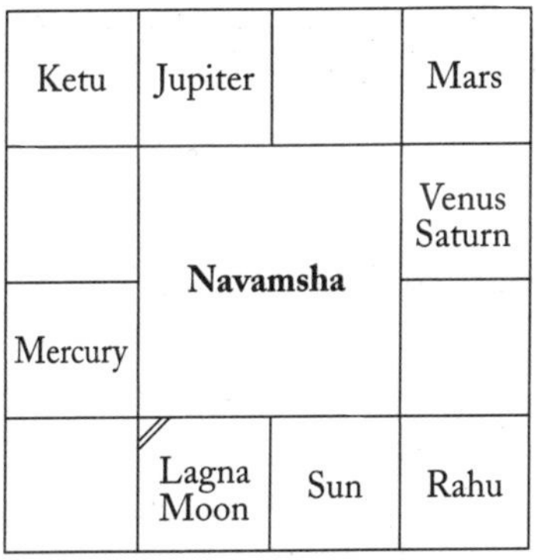

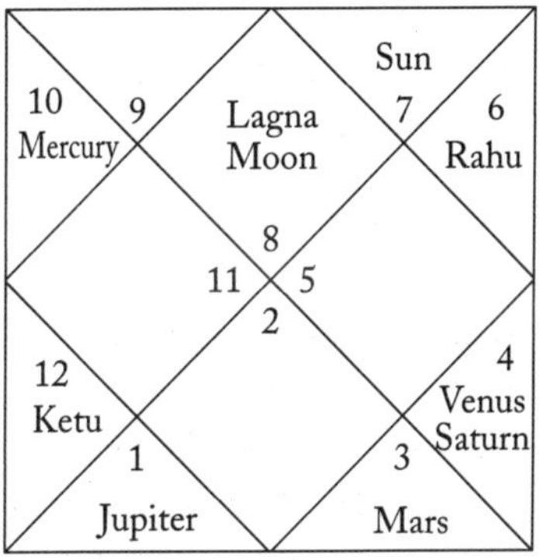

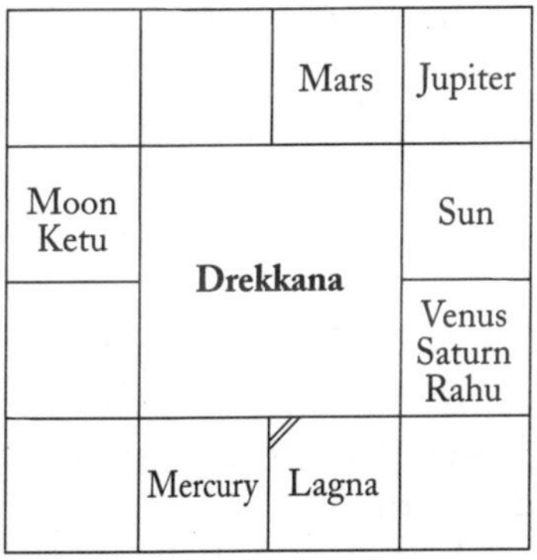

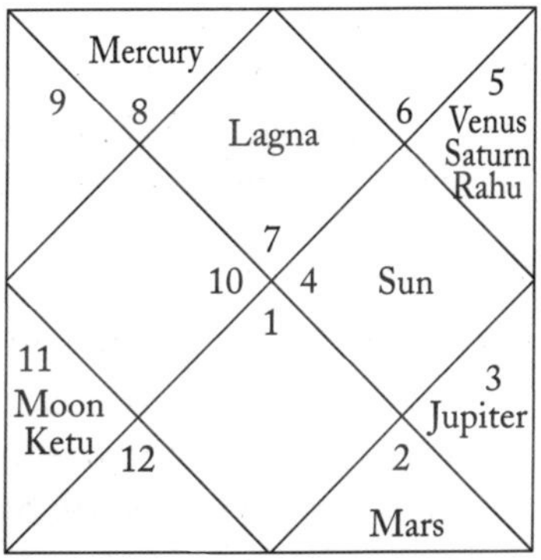

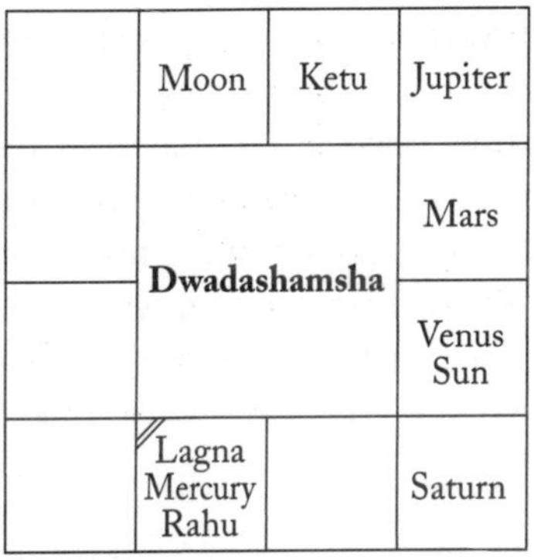

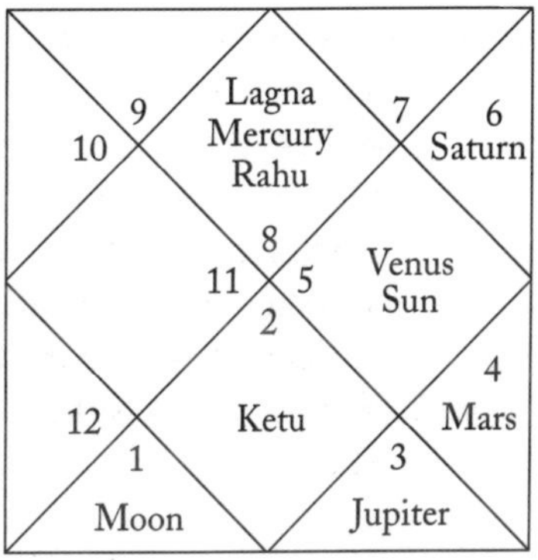

In the Navamsha, both Jupiter and Venus are afflicted by Saturn. RKA falls along the 5th house.

In the Drekkana, the 5th house, the 5th lord as well as Venus are all afflicted by RKA, aspect of Mars, association of Saturn, etc. Jupiter as the 6th lord aspects the 5th house.

In the Dwadashamsha, Jupiter, the 5th lord, is in the 8th house. Venus is with the Sun. The 5th house and 5th lord are aspected by Saturn.

Vimshottari dasha

Saturn-Mercury operated from August 28, 1948 to May 7, 1951; Saturn-Ketu from May 7, 1951 to June 16, 1952.

Saturn (MD) has been already shown to be afflicted and related to the 5th house by aspect or lordship.

Mercury (AD) is the debilitated 12th lord in the 6th house associated with a malefic. It is under the influence of Saturn and/or Mars in the Navamsha and Drekkana, and of Saturn and RKA in the Dwadashamsha.

The subsequent AD lord Ketu afflicts the 5th lord Saturn and occupies the 5th house in the Navamsha and the Drekkana.

Yogini dasha

Bhramari (Mars) operates from May 9, 1950 to May 9, 1954.

Mars (MD) aspects the 5th lord Saturn in the rashi chart. It is located in the 8th house in the Navamsha and the Drekkana; in the latter it aspects the 5th lord Saturn.

In the Dwadashamsha, it is the debilitated 6th lord.

Note : In a chronic disease like diabetes, it is not possible to exactly find out the time when the disease starts. The use of PD, therefore, is not always possible. It may also be relevant only to consider the MD in cases of the Yoginis of shorter duration. The dasha sequence may, however, be taken note of. In the above instance, for example, Bhramari is followed by Bhadrika (Mercury), Ulka (Saturn), then Siddha (Venus), etc., ensuring no complete relief.

2. APPENDICITIS

This is a common ailment which normally requires operative treatment. Unless the treatment is delayed, surgical intervention generally leads to quick recovery. A disease that could be potentially fatal responds to a simple surgical procedure performed well in time.

Astrological factors

We do not get any references to combinations for appendicitis. On the basis of our observations, the following may be considered.

1. *Venus.* Venus is the significator for appendix. Its affliction is a pre-requisite to the presence of appendicitis. The extent of malefic influence (by the Sun, Mars, Saturn, RKA) indicates the extent of severity of disease.
2. *The 6th house/6th lord.* The sixth house indicates the site of appendix. Its affliction is another important factor.
3. *K.N. Rao's view.* According to Mr K.N. Rao, appendicitis is generally characterised by the affliction of Vrisha, Mithuna and Venus.

Chart XV-3

Shows affliction to Vrisha, Mithuna, the 6th house, the 6th lord, as well as Venus.

In the Navamsha, Venus is placed in the 6th house aspected by the Sun and the 6th lord Jupiter.

In the Drekkana, Venus in the RKA is afflicted by the 6th lord Jupiter, the 8th lord Saturn and by Mars.

In the Dwadashamsha, Venus is in the 12th house aspected by the 6th lord Jupiter.

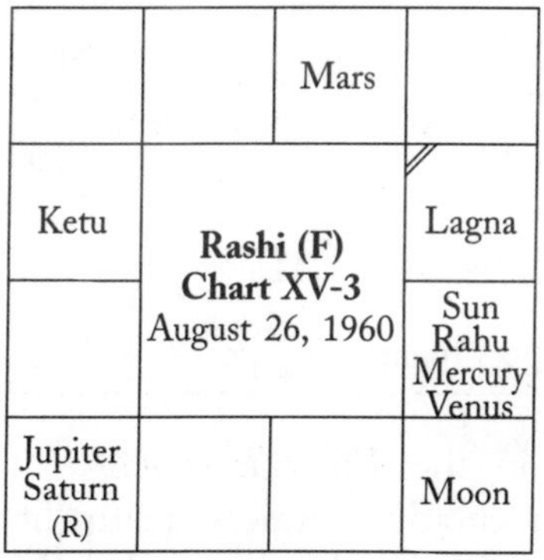

Rashi (F)
Chart XV-3
August 26, 1960

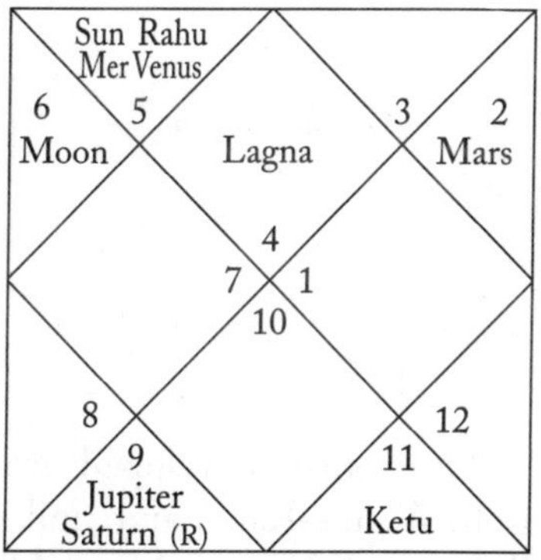

Lagna	01°55'	Mars	21°49'	Venus	26°57'
Sun	09°21'	Mercury	04°14'	Saturn (R)	18°52'
Moon	20°19'	Jupiter	00°31'	Rahu	22°18'

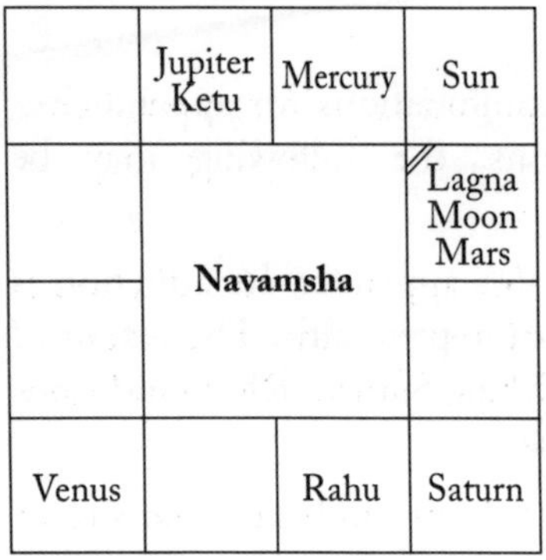

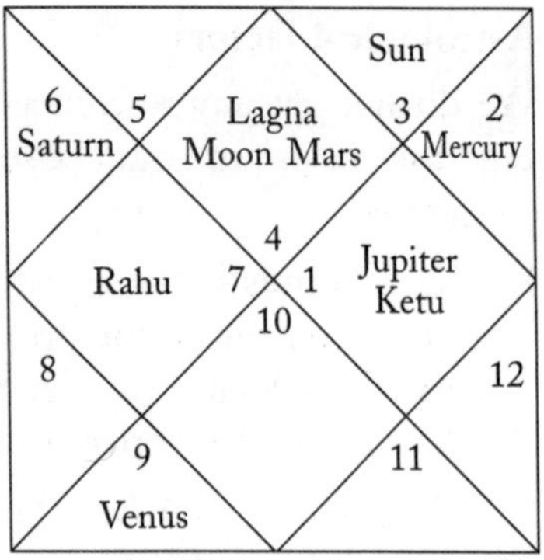

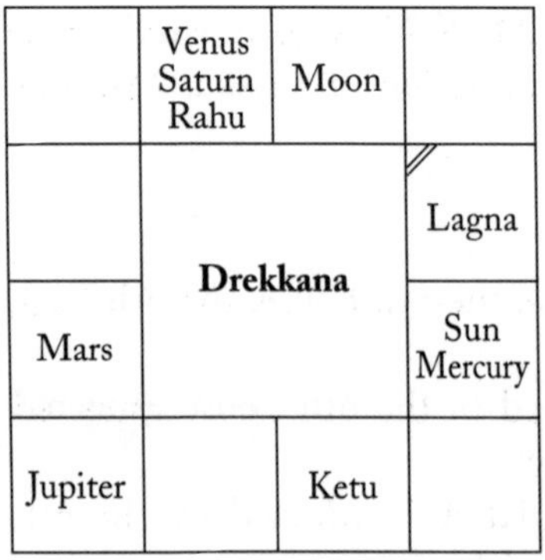

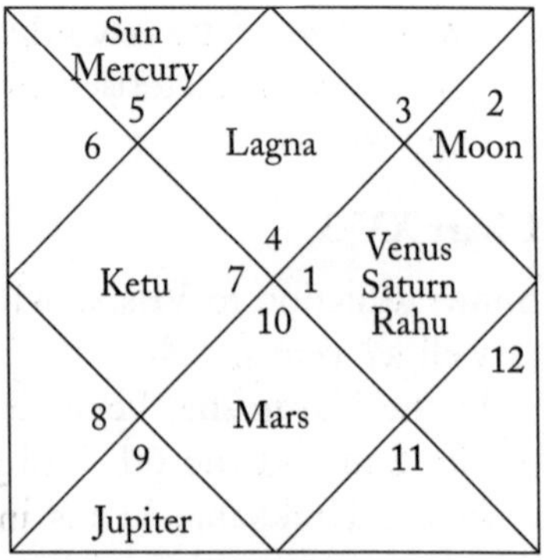

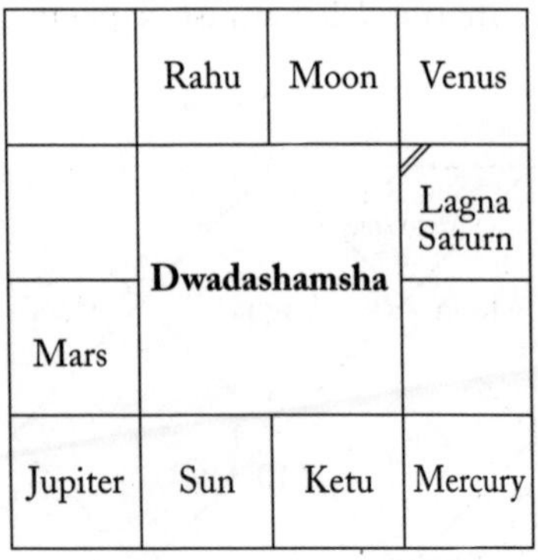

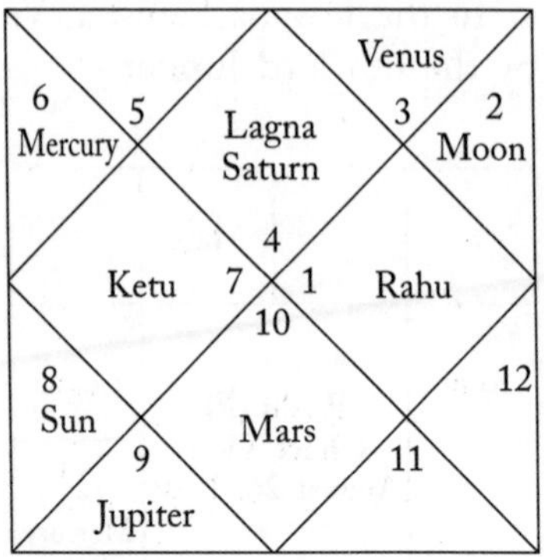

The native developed trouble in the *Vimshottari dasha* of Rahu-Venus-Rahu and underwent curative surgical treatment. Rahu and Venus (MD, AD and PD lords) are under the influence of the 6th lord Jupiter, the retrograde 8th lord Saturn, and also Mars.

The corresponding *Yogini dasha* was Ulka-Bhadrika (Saturn-Mercury). Saturn is the 8th lord in all the divisional charts. It is retrograde in the 6th house in rashi chart, afflicting the 6th lord Jupiter. Mercury is also associated with Venus and in RKA aspected by Mars and Jupiter.

It may be appropriate here to refer again to Chart X-3 where appendectomy was carried out in the Vimshottari dasha of Venus-Rahu-Saturn (comparable to Rahu-Venus-Rahu in the above example). Vrisha, Mithuna and the 6th lord are afflicted here. Venus is a malefic lord for the rashi chart and is grossly afflicted in the Navamsha.

3. PRONENESS TO INJURY

The following combinations indicate physical injury to the native.

1. Presence of malefics in the quadrants.

   Note : Malefics in the quadrants have been repeatedly referred to as adverse for health. Their propensity to do evil is neutralised by the location of benefics in the quadrants.

2. Presence of the 4th lord in the 6th house, or the 6th lord in the 4th house, or an exchange between the 4th and 6th lords.

   Note : The fourth house is concerned with the native's residence, vehicles, etc. The 6th is the house of accidents.

3. The Moon under the influence (i.e., aspect or association) of Mars.
4. Association or aspect of Mars on the 4th house.
5. The Sun in the 10th house aspected by Mars from the 4th house. This combination leads to vehicular accident.
6. The Sun and Saturn in the ascendant in RKA. This combination leads to fall from a tree.
7. Mars in the 4th house with the Sun or Saturn in the 7th house.

   Note : This combination leads to injury from fire. Mars-Sun combination causes fire accidents.

8. Mars and Saturn in the lagna and the Moon in the 8th house.
9. Ketu and the 4th lord in the 6th house.
10. Saturn, Mars and Rahu together in the 8th house.

    Note : Combinations 8, 9 and 10 lead to injury or death from a weapon.
11. Rahu or Ketu in the 6th or the 8th or the 12th house, with a quadrant or a trine lord: Very prone to injuries.
12. The fourth lord associated with a malefic and located in a quadrant.
13. The 4th lord and the lagna lord conjoined in the 4th and aspected by the 10th lord.
14. Saturn in the 4th house, the Moon in the 7th house and Mars in the 10th house.

    Note : The preceding three combinations (Nos. 12, 13 and 14) cause injury or death by drowning.

Chart XV-4

This has a retrograde eighth lord Saturn located in the 6th house, aspecting the retrograde 4th lord, and itself aspected by the 6th lord Mars.

Mars also aspects the Sun, the lord of the 3rd house and the significator for bones. Additionally it is in the RKA. Jupiter is itself afflicted but aspects the lagna from the 5th house.

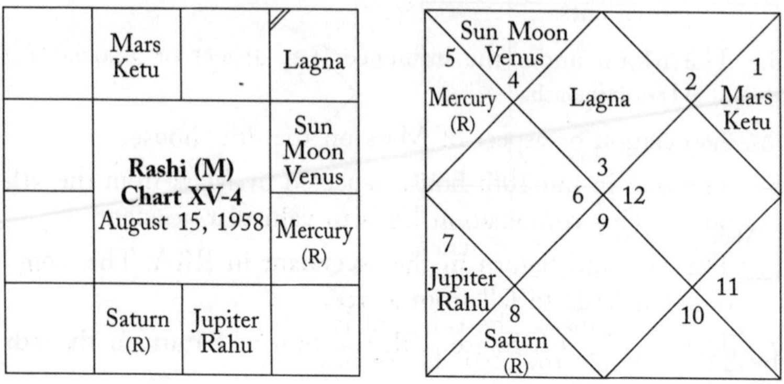

Lagna	24°25'	Mars	21°41'	Venus	05°18'
Sun	28°18'	Mercury(R)	13°13'	Saturn (R)	25°53'
Moon	24°04'	Jupiter	02°53'	Rahu	01°02'

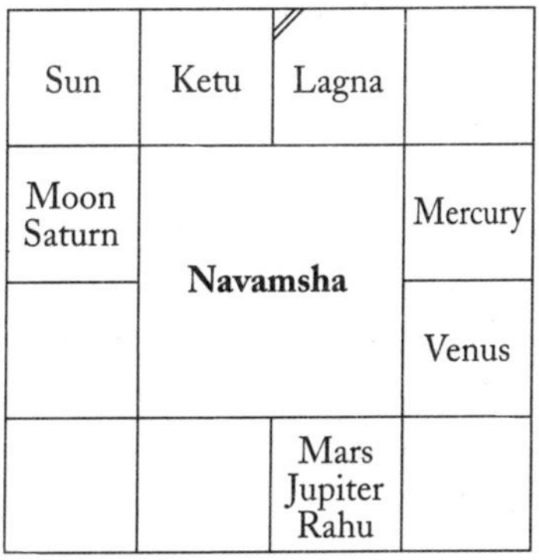

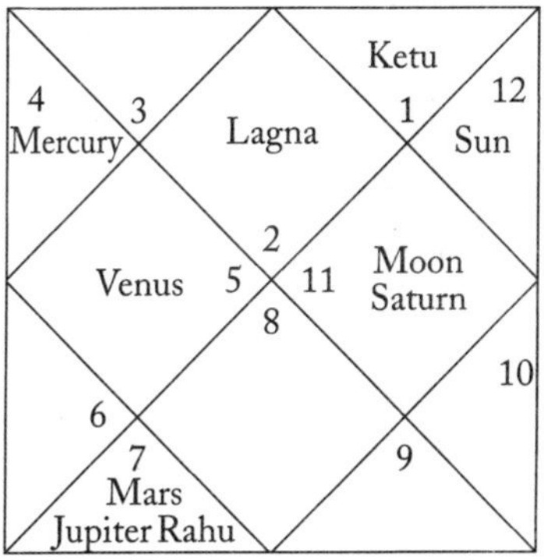

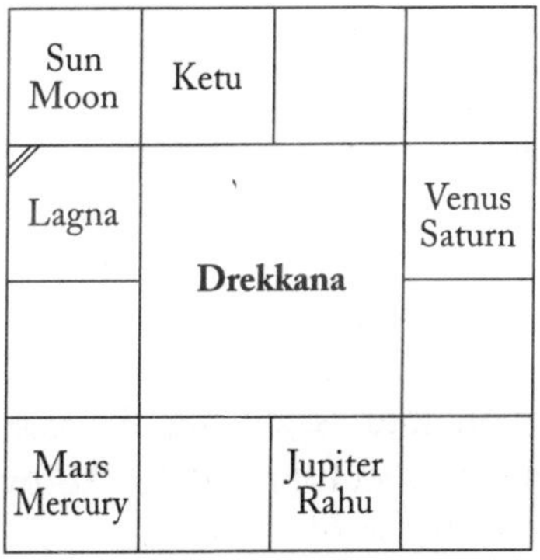

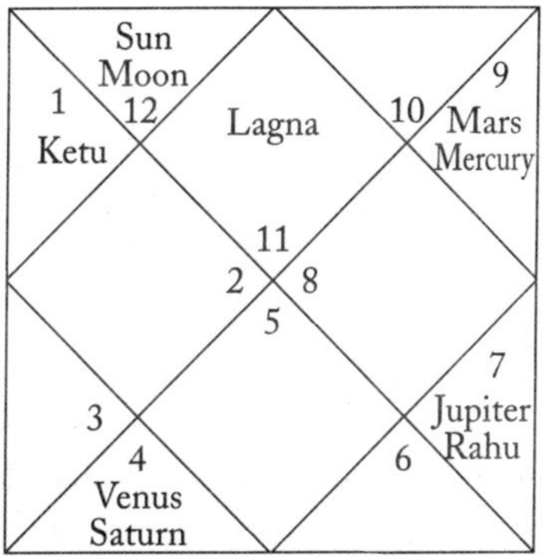

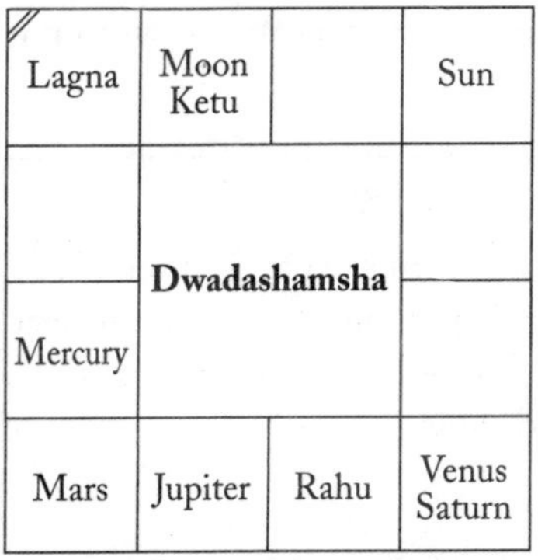

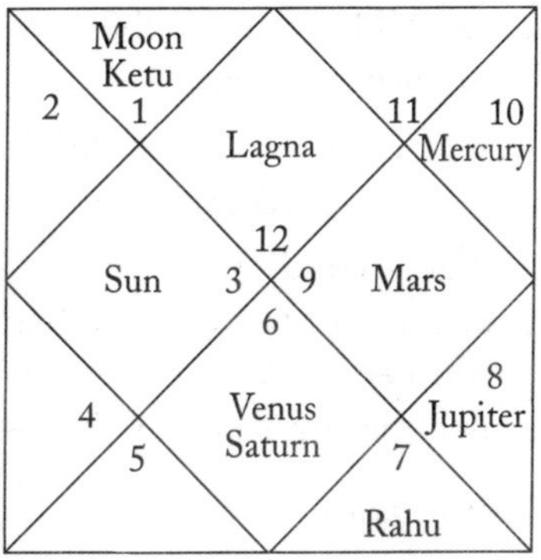

In the Navamsha, the 6th lord is in the 4th house aspected by Saturn, while the sixth house has Mars, Rahu and the 8th lord Jupiter.

In the Drekkana, the 4th lord goes into the 6th house in association with Saturn, and is aspected by Mars.

The Dwadashamsha chart shows the 6th lord, the Sun, in the 4th house aspected by Mars as well as Saturn.

Jupiter aspects the lagna in the Drekkana and the Dwadashamsha.

The native had a vehicular accident leading to a fracture of his left femur (thigh bone) for which he was operated upon on April 24, 1992. After initial recovery, he got a refracture of the same bone on November 2, 1992 and had to be re-operated on November 11, 1992. He has been making gradual recovery since.

Vimshottari dasha

Venus-Ketu-Sun (April 20, 1992 to May 11, 1992) operated during his initial injury and surgical treatment.

Venus (MD), Ketu (AD) and the Sun (PD) are all under the influence of the 6th lord Mars.

In the Navamsha, Venus is the 6th lord in the 4th house whereas Ketu, under the influence of the 8th lord as well as Mars, aspects the 6th house.

In the Drekkana, Venus as the 4th lord occupying the 6th house is aspected by Mars. The Sun is also aspected by Mars. Ketu receives the aspect of Saturn from the 6th house.

In the Dwadashamsha, Venus is the 8th lord associated with Saturn. The Sun as the 6th lord in the 4th house is aspected by Saturn and Mars.

Note : Involvement of the 3rd lord, the Sun, indicates accident in movement; Venus indicates vehicle.

The second injury occurred during Venus-Ketu-Jupiter (September 14, 1992 to November 10, 1992), while the operation was performed in Venus-Ketu-Saturn. Jupiter and Saturn are both under the influence of the 6th lord Mars.

Yogini dasha

Dhanya-Pingala (Jupiter-Sun) operated from March 24, 1992 to May 24, 1992.

Jupiter is in RKA aspected by Mars, and is variously afflicted in the divisional charts. The role of the Sun has been already delineated.

During the second injury and treatment, it was the dasha of Bhramari-Bhramari (Mars-Mars) from May 24, 1992 to November 4, 1992, and Bhramari-Bhadrika (Mars-Mercury) from November 4, 1992 to May 24, 1993, respectively.

Mars is the 6th lord in the rashi chart, occupies the 6th house in the Navamsha, aspects the 4th lord, the 6th lord and the 6th house in the Drekkana, and aspects the 6th lord in the Dwadashamsha chart.

Mercury is the retrograde 4th lord under mixed malefic and benefic influences in the various charts.

4. TUBERCULOSIS

(from the *Jataka Tattva*)

1. Venus in association with the lagna lord in any of the Trika houses.
2. Mars in the 4th and Rahu in the 12th from the Karakamsha lagna.

   Note : 'Karaka' or the 'Atma Karaka' is a planet which has advanced the farthest in a sign. The sign occupied by the Atma Karaka in the Navamsha chart is called the Karakamsha lagna.
3. The Moon and the Sun involved in mutual exchange in the rashi or the Navamsha chart. The Moon and the Sun together in Karka or Simha also predispose the native to tuberculosis.
4. The Moon conjoined with Saturn and aspected by Mars.

   Note : In this case, the disease is contracted by association with a patient of tuberculosis.
5. The lagna aspected by Mars and Saturn.
6. Mercury in Karka.

   Note : All the above combinations are too generalised. They must only be applied with caution.

5. EPILEPSY

(from the *Jataka Tattva*)

1. Saturn and the Moon aspected by Mars.

   Note : The same combination has been mentioned under tuberculosis, vide supra.

2. The Moon and Rahu in the 8th house.
3. The 6th or the 8th house associated with Saturn and Mars.
4. The Sun, the Moon and Mars together in the lagna or the 8th house aspected by malefics.
5. Birth at the time of an eclipse, Jupiter in the lagna or a trine, Saturn and Mars in the 6th or the 8th house.
6. Rahu in the lagna and the Moon in the 6th house.

6. LEPROSY

(from the *Jataka Tattva*)

1. Mercury in Mesha, the Moon in the 10th house, and Saturn conjunct Mars in any house.
2. Saturn, Mars, the Moon and Venus in watery signs under affliction by malefics.

   Note : This combination leads to skin lesions that go on oozing.
3. The Moon aspected by Mars in the 4th from the Karakamsha lagna.

   Note : 'Karakamsha' has been explained earlier.
4. The Moon in the 4th from the Karakamsha lagna, aspected by Ketu.
5. The Moon in Mithuna, Karka or Meena Navamshas aspected by Mars or Saturn.
6. Vrisha, Karka, Vrishchika or Makara signs falling in the trines associated with or aspected by malefics.
7. The lagna lord, the Moon and Mercury falling in RKA.
8. Mars as the 6th lord in the lagna.
9. Saturn with the 6th lord in the lagna.
10. The Sun and the 6th lord in the lagna.
11. Mars in the lagna, the Sun in the 8th, and Saturn in the 4th house.
12. The Moon and Venus afflicted by malefics and located in a watery sign.

    Note : This leads to whitish patches on the skin.

13. The Moon in the 4th from Karakamsha lagna, and aspected by Venus.

    Note : This may produce the same results as the foregoing combination.

14. The Moon, Mars and Saturn together in Mesha or Vrisha.
15. The Moon in the lagna, the Sun in the 7th, and Saturn and Mars located in the 2nd or the 12th house.

The reader is forewarned here. The above combinations have been described under 'Kushtha Roga' which means leprosy when strictly translated. Many of these combinations, however, indicate nothing more than various skin afflictions and not necessarily leprosy in the strictest sense. A literal application of the classical dicta is always fraught with disastrous results. A very high degree of flexibility is required while actually applying these principles to individual horoscopes.

7. DENTAL DISEASE
(from the *Jataka Tattva*)

1. Mesha or Vrisha coinciding with the lagna or the 2nd house, and aspected by or associated with malefics.
2. Malefics in the 7th house unaspected by benefics.
3. Rahu posited in the 2nd from the 7th lord. This combination leads to prominent teeth.
4. The 2nd lord along with the 6th lord, associated with malefics.
5. Rahu in the lagna or the 5th house.

8. HYDROCOELE
(from the *Jataka Tattva*)

This is a disease wherein fluid collects in the scrotal sac, which enlarges as a consequence. It generally needs operative treatment.

1. Mars and Venus together in the 8th house.
2. Mars and Venus together in a sign owned by Mars (i.e., Mesha or Vrishchika).

3. The Moon and Venus in a sign owned by Mars, and aspected by Jupiter and Saturn.
4. Gulika placed in the Karakamsha lagna, aspected by Mercury alone.

9. HAEMORRHOIDS

This is known as 'piles' by the common man. It is said that a hundred percent people have piles; fifty percent develop problems and seek treatment. Any astrological combinations for such a disease might appear superfluous. However, haemorrhoids can sometimes cause a lot of trouble and need surgical treatment. The combinations from the *Jataka Tattva* are given below.

1. Saturn aspected by malefics.
2. Saturn in the lagna and Mars in the 7th house.
3. The Sun in the lagna, Mars in Vrishchika, and Saturn in the 7th house.
4. The lagna lord and Mars in the 7th house, and Saturn in the 12th house.
5. Saturn in the 12th aspected by Mars and the lagna lord.

10. SEXUAL INADEQUACY OR IMPOTENCE

(from the *Jatakalankara*)

1. Saturn and Venus together in the tenth house.
2. Saturn occupying the sixth or the twelfth house from Venus.
3. The Sun and the Moon in mutual aspect, while occupying odd signs.
4. Mercury and Saturn in mutual aspect from odd signs.
5. The Sun in an even sign in mutual aspect with Mars.
6. The Moon and the lagna in odd signs, both aspected by Mars from an even sign.
7. The Moon in an odd sign and Mercury in an even sign, both aspected by Mars.
8. The lagna, the Moon and Venus all occupying masculine (odd) signs.

Note : Some combinations, from the same source, for inability to sexually satisfy one's partner are as follows:

(i) Venus occupying the sign of a retrograde planet.

(ii) Lagna lord in the lagna and Venus in the seventh house.

(iii) Moon-Saturn conjunction in the fourth or the tenth from Mars.

11. MISCELLANEOUS DISORDERS

(One line combinations from the *Jataka Tattva*)

1. Jupiter, Mars and Saturn together in the 4th house produce heart disease.
2. Eleventh lord in the 6th house produces multiple ailments.
3. Saturn and Mars in the 6th house aspected by Rahu and the Sun lead to a chronic illness.
4. Rahu or Ketu in the 7th house, or Saturn in the 8th and the Moon in the lagna, lead to indigestion.
5. Jupiter and Rahu in the lagna produce dental disease.
6. Sixth lord in the 3rd house produces abdominal ailments.
7. Saturn in the 6th house afflicts the feet.
8. Rahu or Ketu in the 6th house causes disease of the teeth or lips.
9. The lagna lord located in a sign owned by Mars or Mercury, aspected by an inimical planet, leads to disease in the anal region.
10. Malefic association of the Moon in Karka or Vrishchika Navamsha leads to secret illness.

    Note : A secret illness may mean an illness that the native wants to conceal from others, or also a sexually transmitted disease.

11. Mars, Mercury and the lagna lord located together in Simha coinciding with the 4th or the 12th house produce disease in the anal and the perianal region.

12. A malefic in the 8th house produces a secret illness. Same results accrue from Jupiter located in the 12th house.
13. Mercury and the 6th lord together with Mars cause disease of the organ of generation.
14. Lord of the 8th located in the 8th house produces a disease-prone body.

In the above narration, we have mentioned combinations only for a limited number of ailments. There is a lot more, although generalised, information in the classical texts. It is, however, little use memorising that information without adequate research. The fact can, therefore, never be overemphasised even at the risk of repetition time and again, that only an extremely flexible, and not literal, application of these principles is called for. Only then can newer meanings be derived from the astrological dicta which embody abundant hidden information.

CHAPTER SIXTEEN

SUMMARY

यावत्स्वस्थमिदं शरीरमरुजं यावच्च दूरे जरा
यावच्चेन्द्रियशक्तिरप्रतिहता यावत्क्षयो नायुषः।
आत्मश्रेयसि तावदेव विदुषा कार्यः प्रयत्नो महान्
प्रोद्दीप्ते भवने च कूपखननं प्रत्युद्यमः कीदृशः।।

While the body is in health, free from illness, and old age away,
While the sense organs are sound and the life still remains,
The wise, for their good, must strive the hardest.
For what use is digging a well when the house is already afire?

—VAIRAGYASHATAKA

Chapter I provides an introduction to medical astrology. Both astrology and medicine are ancient disciplines and formed a way of life in India. The inseparable link between the two has been stressed. A dialogue between sage Pulastya and sage Narada, from the Vamana Purana, giving a description of various zodiacal signs representing different body parts, as also the physical appearance of these signs, has been reproduced. The relevance of medical astrology in the present times has been discussed. The role of astrologer versus the medical man, while dealing with disease, has also been explained. A figure representing the body parts, as related to various signs of the zodiac, has also been given, based on the description in the Vamana Purana.

Chapter II explains the various houses of the horoscope, signs of the zodiac and their characteristics, the horoscopic charts (the north Indian, the south Indian and the east Indian) and the nature of the various planets. Important aspects such as the nature of the planets, their lordships, exaltation and debilitation, Moola Trikona signs, natural relations, combustion and retrogression have been dealt with. The Nakshatras and their lords have been shown. The vargas as relevant to medical astrology have been discussed. Two important dasha systems, viz., the Vimshottari and the Yogini, have been briefly outlined. The relationship of various planets to the three basic elements of Ayurveda have also been hinted at.

Chapter III deals with the determination of benefic and malefic planets, yogakarakas as well as marakas, according to the well known principles of Parashara. A brief discussion about Gulika and Mandi has also been presented, along with the results of these malefics in different houses. Towards the end, such factors as the twenty-second Drekkana, the sixty-fourth Navamsha and the Sarpa Drekkanas have been briefly mentioned. Health and disease are determined on the basis of malefic and benefic planets only.

Chapter IV relates the various parts of the body to different houses in the horoscope and to various signs of the zodiac. The significations of different houses as appropriate to medical astrology have been outlined. A correlation between different parts of the body on the one hand and the Drekkana rising in the lagna on the other has been given according to the classical writers of astrology. In the end, various body parts, and the Nakshatras representing them have been presented according to the description of the 'Nakshatra Shareera' of lord Vishnu as given in the Vamana Purana. A figure based on this description is also presented.

Chapter V presents the significations of various planets as they pertain to medical astrology. These have been mainly taken from the Phaladeepika and the Prashna Marg. An understanding of these is important in order to determine the nature of illness.

Chapter VI deals with Balarishta. Detailed combinations for untimely death of children as well as diseases in childhood are given. Combinations indicating affliction to the mother as well as the father of the newborn have also been described. Methods of timing the occurrence of an adverse event have also been mentioned. The various principles have been elucidated by application to example horoscopes.

In **Chapter VII**, the various yogas causing cancellation of affliction to the newborn have been dealt with. No Balarishta can be said to be applicable to a chart unless the possible cancellation of the affliction has also been studied. These combinations, called as Arishta Bhanga, lead to qualitative improvement in a chart.

The occurrence of congenital illness in a native has been explained in **Chapter VIII**. Simple principles that govern health and disease, integrated with dasha scheme, have been applied to natives suffering from various congenital ailments. The importance of the MD, AD and PD operating at the time of birth has been stressed.

Chapter IX deals with principles that indicate sound and unsound health in a native. In an inherently healthy chart, minor fluctations in dasha scheme do not affect the health adversely. This may not be so in a chart which indicates an inherent weakness. The principles discussed here are extremely important for medical astrology.

Chapter X deals with the most important subject of the onset and outcome of disease. The astrologer is on a very superior ground by his ability to forecast the period of onset of an illness. Subtle astrological principles as applicable to medical astrology have been discussed in this chapter. Charts of twelve different natives, suffering from ailments of varying severity, have been analysed in detail in the light of the Vimshottari as well as the Yogini dasha. Toward the end of the chapter, a very sound method of determining the health of a native from the charts of her parents and siblings has been elucidated. These methods when carefully applied yield amazingly accurate results.

Chapter XI deals with mental illness. Classical combinations that produce mental disorders have been outlined. The astrological basis of mental illness, especially the role of the Moon, Mercury and Jupiter, has been highlighted. The various principles mentioned have been explained in relation to actual cases of mental illness.

Chapter XII deals with combinations leading to diseases of the eye. Various combinations selected from standard astrological texts, indicating poor vision, injury to the eye, blindness, and blindness in one eye, have been presented. The astrological principles underlying eye disease have been discussed and applied to example horoscopes.

Chapter XIII deals with the defects of hearing and speech. Classical principles producing ear disease and their underlying principles have been explained. The later part of this chapter deals with combinations for defective speech. Lastly, the research findings of Shunny Nigam in relation to children born deaf and dumb have been discussed, and illustrated by examples.

The very important subject of heart disease finds discussion in **Chapter XIV**. The underlying astrological principles for heart disease have been discussed in detail. Indications for curable and incurable forms of heart disease, congenital heart disease, and heart disease requiring medical or surgical treatment, have been highlighted and illustrated on actual horoscopes of patients of heart disease.

Chapter XV, labelled as *Miscellaneous Diseases*, deals with various medical ailments picked up at random. The medical conditions discussed here include diabetes, appendicitis, tuberculosis, leprosy, epilepsy, dental diseases, accident proneness, haemorrhoids, hydrocoele, abdominal ailments, impotence, etc. Many of the combinations described in this chapter are from the *Jataka Tattva*. While several of these combinations appear too generalised, they all embody important and subtle astrological principles.

INDEX